In Search of the Silent South

Contemporary American History Series

WILLIAM E. LEUCHTENBURG, GENERAL EDITOR

Contemporary American History Series

Lawrence S. Wittner, *Rebels against War: The American Peace Movement, 1941–1960*, 1969.

Davis R. B. Ross, *Preparing for Ulysses: Politics and Veterans during World War II*, 1969.

John Lewis Gaddis, *The United States and the Origins of the Cold War, 1941–1947*, 1972.

George C. Herring, Jr., *Aid to Russia, 1941–1946: Strategy, Diplomacy, the Origins of the Cold War*, 1973.

Alonzo L. Hamby, *Beyond the New Deal: Harry S. Truman and American Liberalism*, 1973.

Richard M. Fried, *Men against McCarthy*, 1976.

Steven F. Lawson, *Black Ballots: Voting Rights in the South, 1944–1969*, 1976.

Carl M. Brauer, *John F. Kennedy and the Second Reconstruction*, 1977.

Maeva Marcus, *Truman and the Steel Seizure Case: The Limits of Presidential Power*, 1977.

Morton Sosna, *In Search of the Silent South: Southern Liberals and the Race Issue*, 1977.

Southern Liberals and the Race Issue

In Search of the Silent South

Morton Sosna

1977

NEW YORK COLUMBIA UNIVERSITY PRESS

The Andrew W. Mellon Foundation, through a special grant, has assisted the Press in publishing this volume.

LIBRARY OF CONGRESS CATALOGING IN PUBLICATION DATA

Sosna, Morton.
In search of the silent South.
(Contemporary American history series)
Bibliography: p.
Includes index.
1. Liberalism—Southern States. 2. Southern States—Race relations. 3. Odum, Howard Washington, 1884–1954. 4. Dabney, Virginius, 1901–
5. Smith, Lillian Eugenia, 1897–1966. 6. Southern States—Biography. I. Title.
F215.S66 301.45'19'6073076 77-4965
ISBN 0-231-03843-7

COLUMBIA UNIVERSITY PRESS
NEW YORK GUILDFORD, SURREY
PRINTED IN THE UNITED STATES OF AMERICA

For Barbara

AND

In Memory of My Mother and Father

"It is the fate of the Southerner," wrote Ralph McGill, the late editor of the *Atlanta Constitution*, "to be involved in his region, always to feel himself held by it. He may never have believed the myths. The often cruel injustices of the rigid formula of race may have offended him and aroused him to open opposition. The cost of parochialism and injustice, not merely to the Negro, but to the material and spiritual welfare of his own people, may have long been on his conscience. But nonetheless, he is a part of what he has met, and been. And the past, in tales of his parents, his great-aunts and uncles, has been in his ears from birth." [1]

With these words McGill expressed the feelings not just of any Southerner but of a particular kind of Southerner. He spoke as a white racial liberal, a man who deeply loved his native region, who recognized its more glaring shortcomings, and who devoted much energy toward solving its problems. It can be said with a fair amount of certainty that the vast majority of white Southerners did not share McGill's concern. His life was spent in the Jim Crow era, a time when most Southern whites deemed legalized segregation and racial discrimination necessary for the maintenance of "white supremacy." Nor did McGill make any pretense at representing the feelings of black Southerners. The fate of the Southerner McGill described was the fate of the white liberal, a dissenting segment of the white South. His was a peculiar point of view, and one that helps to explain why so much of what has been written about the burdens, ironies, and tragic history of the South has been written by white Southern liberals.

These men and women, perceptive in their understanding of the region, have appeared to others as outcasts from it. Historically, they were the round pegs who did not fit the square holes of what white Southerners were thought to be—defenders of human slavery, secessionists, rebels, redeemers, maintainers of white supremacy, all of whom had conservative if not downright reactionary leanings. To be a white Southerner and a liberal was paradoxical, incongruous enough to attract immediate attention. Given the nature of Southern society in the nineteenth and twentieth centuries, it was hardly surprising when black Southerners became critics of it. But whites who did so seemed to belong to a separate species. Outside observers could not resist commenting on them, and by the 1930s the term "Southern liberal" came into its own. In his classic study of race relations in the United States, *An American Dilemma,* the Swedish social scientist Gunnar Myrdal said that "Southern liberalism is not liberalism as it is found elsewhere in America or in the world." The Southern liberals themselves were fascinating if somewhat quaint to Myrdal, who called them "beautiful and dignified." [2] Moreover, the puzzlement over Jimmy Carter, especially among Northern liberals and intellectuals, offers dramatic evidence that a Southern liberal is still considered something of an oddity.

Any treatment of so *sui generis* a phenomenon must begin with a definition. Though I realize that "liberal" can mean anything from John Locke's philosophical tenets to Franklin D. Roosevelt's New Deal programs, I am using the word despite its limitations. My test of the white Southern liberal lies in his stance on the race issue. I use the term broadly, classifying as "liberal" those white Southerners who perceived that there was a serious maladjustment of race relations in the South, who recognized that the existing system resulted in grave injustices for blacks, and who either actively endorsed or engaged in programs to aid Southern blacks in their fight against lynching, disfranchisement, segregation, and blatant discrimination in such areas as education, employment, and law enforcement. Though issues other than race could be used to determine one's disagreement with the Southern status quo during the Jim Crow era—advocacy of popular education, promotion of child labor reform, and support for labor unions, to name a few—the ultimate test of the white Southern liberal was his willingness or unwillingness to criticize racial mores. Accepting Ulrich B. Phillips's assertion that the desire to maintain white supremacy was the "central theme" of Southern history, I would further define white Southern liberals as critics who disapproved of the fact that this was a theme.[3] Also, however one chooses to define them, after 1920 whites in the South who sympathized with the plight of blacks became increasingly conscious of themselves as "Southern liberals."

Some may ask what moved a white Northerner like myself to choose such a subject. Actually my own non-Southern background led me to the study. Growing up in Chicago during the peak years of the civil rights movement, I first became conscious of the South through media coverage of that struggle. Needless to say, my impression of white Southerners was not flattering. I knew there must have been some who opposed the White Citizens Councils, the Klan, and the "massive resistance" politicians, but why did they seem so few and so ineffective? Many Northerners were asking the same question.

Later, as a graduate student searching for a dissertation topic, I decided upon a general study of white liberals. At the time, I was also an assistant to William C. Haygood, a native of Atlanta who was editor of the *Wisconsin Magazine of History*. He inquired whether I intended to include Southern liberals in my thesis. "Were there any?" I asked. He immediately referred me to a book written by his great-uncle, Atticus G. Haygood, and also spoke of acquaintances he had made during the 1940s when he was fellowship director for the Julius Rosenwald Fund. I soon discovered that white Southern liberals not only existed but merited serious attention.

Once some bona fide Southern liberals were identified, the outline of my study began to take shape. As befit a Northerner whose previous understanding of the South derived mainly from the region's starker events, I quickly adopted a "good guys" versus "bad guys" approach. Southern liberals, of whom I had known little, were to be the heroes of my tale and Southern racists, of whom I had been much conscious, its villains. All I had to do, I thought, was compare and contrast these two groups.

The more I pondered, however, the more my naiveté became clear. Southern liberals comprised an extremely diverse group whose views on the overriding race issue differed greatly. Furthermore, white Southern liberals of all persuasions exhibited attitudes, such as sensitivity over "outside interference" with the South's racial problems, that I had always associated with diehard Dixiecrats. Of such realizations easy theses are not made. If Southern liberals existed yet shared the basic beliefs of other white Southerners, what was the significance and meaning of white Southern liberalism?

I began by examining the racial outlook of George Washington Cable, the most outspoken white Southern critic of racial discrimination in the late nineteenth century. Cable was in many ways the intellectual father of the more recent Southern liberals. Publicly opposing Jim Crow just when the segregation movement was gaining momentum, Cable expressed ideas that reflected the quintessential outlook of the Southern liberal. Particularly important was his belief that the white South was not nearly as monolithic on race as it seemed. He used the term "Silent South" to characterize this less apparent but nevertheless significant element of Southern society. Cable's concept was echoed in one form or another by every Southern liberal who followed.

After briefly tracing the scattered actions of men like Cable, I shall turn to the efforts of Southern liberals to institutionalize their ideas. By 1920 Jim Crow in the South appeared permanent; any meaningful alteration of the existing pattern was unlikely. Yet, through such organizations as the Commission on Interracial Cooperation and the Association of Southern Women for the Prevention of Lynching, Southern liberals attempted to change white Southern perceptions of the region's racial practices.

How the Great Depression and the New Deal influenced Southern liberals will also be examined. The extraordinary circumstances of the 1930s gave rise to new hopes and sometimes revived long-forgotten ones. These will be discussed in context with the establishment in 1938 of the Southern Conference for Human Welfare, which represented the major effort of Southern liberals to link themselves with Roosevelt's New Deal.

The last section will deal with the influence of World War II and the immediate postwar years. I shall discuss how the war required Southern liberals increasingly to address themselves to the issue of segregation. An examination of the 1944 emergence of the Southern Regional Council and how that organization responded to a growing national consensus, which held that the South could not maintain its racial status quo for much longer, should be revealing. The study follows Southern liberals through the Supreme Court's momentous 1954 decision against school segregation.

Although Southern liberal organizations were important, they were not the whole story. White Southern liberals are not easily grouped together. Throughout this book, therefore, much attention will be focused on individuals. It should never be forgotten that white Southerners who became identified as racial liberals in the period between the 1920s and the 1940s grew up precisely when racism in the South was most bitter, violent, and blatant. To a large extent, Southern liberalism is a history of how these people each arrived at an island of tolerance in a sea of hate. This journey was a varied and sometimes moving experience. Some went further than others. Yet white Southern liberals of the Jim Crow generation had enough in common to give their story a meaningful collective dimension.

Numerous individuals will be considered, and extensive treatment will be given to three: Howard Odum, a sociologist at the University of North Carolina; Virginius Dabney, for many years the editor of the *Richmond Times-Dispatch*; and Lillian Smith, a white woman from Georgia who became a famous novelist and spokeswoman for racial justice.

The selection of these figures represents an effort to illuminate twentieth-century Southern liberalism by examining careers that reflected the respective influences of the Southern university, the Southern press, and the evangelical Southern conscience. Each of these played a vital role in giving Southern liberalism the mystique alluded to by Myrdal. Odum, Dabney, and Smith, moreover, illustrate the range of Southern liberal opinion.

It is hoped that this work will contribute to an emerging scholarship that will move beyond "good guys" versus "bad guys" in its treatment of our nation's racial experience. At a time when we see integration working more smoothly in many parts of the South than in the North and hear reports of blacks migrating back to the South, perhaps a study of Southern liberalism does have something to teach us, especially those of us who are not Southerners. The search for some nonracist basis of Southern life, though its object proved elusive, was not a fool's errand.

ACKNOWLEDGMENTS

When a project occupies nearly seven years, as this one has, an author builds up quite a list of friends and colleagues to whom he owes debts that can never fully be repaid. Limited space precludes my naming all such people individually, but I would like to mention some whose contribution to my effort has been particularly great.

My largest debt is to Barbara Moe Sosna, who has had to live with this study ever since we met in Louisiana during my first research trip to the South. I am certain that she did not know exactly what she was getting into (neither did I), but through it all her encouragement and good spirit have, to steal a phrase from William Faulkner, not only endured but prevailed.

A number of people at two institutions where I worked and studied for five years, the University of Wisconsin, Madison and the State Historical Society of Wisconsin, nurtured my interest in Southern history. Bill Haygood first suggested the subject of white Southern liberalism to me. John Cooper shared his wide-ranging knowledge of the field with me and suggested many fruitful lines of inquiry. E. David Cronon was an always encouraging thesis adviser. They, along with Paul Glad and Peter Kolchin, read the earliest versions of the manuscript. Michael Holmes, Donald Marks, and Clay McShane all shared their thoughts with me on my topic. Another venerable Madison institution, the "Old Red Gym," provided in its well-trod basketball court a needed source of refuge and solace.

Always I was received warmly and helpfully in my research travels. I am deeply grateful to the staffs at the Alderman Library, University of Virginia; Amistad Research Center, Dillard University; Franklin D. Roosevelt Library; Howard-Tilton Memorial Library, Tulane University; Library of Congress; and the Southern Historical Collection, University of North Carolina, Chapel Hill. Especially memorable are the extraordinary courtesies extended to me by Clifton H. Johnson of the Amistad Center and Carolyn A. Wallace of the

Southern Historical Collection. A number of individuals not only offered me hospitality but gave me the benefit of their own ideas about Southern history. These include Wayne Brazil, Elizabeth Jacoway, Philip Muller, Daniel Singal, and Joel Williamson. They did not always agree with my views, but conversations with them broadened the perspective from which I viewed Southern liberalism and helped sharpen my ideas. Dan Singal, in addition to arranging interviews and guiding me in using the Southern Tenant Farmers Union Papers, which he was helping to organize, subsequently read a draft of the manuscript and gave me a stimulating critique.

I am grateful to W. T. Couch, Mrs. George S. Mitchell, and H. L. Mitchell for permission to interview them as well as to Carl Braden, Jonathan Daniels, and Guy B. Johnson for allowing me to use their papers. I also appreciate being given permission to use the Hugo L. Black Papers. Virginius Dabney, the late Frank P. Graham, and Arthur Raper all granted interviews in addition to giving me access to their papers. In being helpful and encouraging, all whom I interviewed went well beyond what the situation warranted. They also allowed me to pursue any line of inquiry that I desired, even though in some instances they knew that my personal opinions and interpretations of events differed from theirs. I particularly cherish my interview with Frank Graham who, though ailing (he was to die a few months later), insisted that we talk despite the fact that I had come by only to obtain his signature on a document that would allow me to use his papers. We talked for two hours. As I know now, but was only vaguely aware at the time, it was an act totally in character.

A special thank you is due to Christine Moe, who freely offered her photographic talents to take the haunting picture of the Lee Statue in New Orleans that appears on the cover. This is the monument that in 1885 inspired George Washington Cable to write *The Silent South.*

A year at the Institute of Southern History at Johns Hopkins University during 1972–73 facilitated work on the project. David Herbert Donald, the institute's former director, read the dissertation version of the study and provided the kind of incisive criticisms for which he is justly famous. His thoughtful comments and judicious encouragement greatly aided the transformation of a thesis into a book. At the institute, I also had the advantage of meeting and exchanging ideas with other scholars of Southern and black history: Donald Avery, James Duffy, Anne Firor Scott, George Sinkler, and Norman Yetman. They each read portions of the manuscript and contributed suggestions, a number of which have been incorporated in this book.

Since that time, other scholars aided me in working out specific problems. These include Carl Degler, William Chafe, and Jacquelyn Dowd Hall. The late Letitia Woods Brown added new perspectives to my understanding of Lillian Smith.

I owe the National Endowment for the Humanities a very special twofold debt. First, as is the case with many works in the humanities, an NEH fellowship contributed tangibly to the publication of this volume by enabling me to spend a year at the Institute of Southern History. But in my instance there was also the intangible, yet ultimately more important, support given me by the staff of the Endowment's Fellowships Division. Its directors, James Blessing and Guinevere Griest, have encouraged me to see this project through to completion ever since I have been with the Endowment, even though it has sometimes caused inconveniences for our division and placed heavier burdens on my colleagues, particularly David Coder, Pete MacDonald, and Nancy Norman, with whom I have worked and who always bore such burdens gracefully. I also wish to thank James H. Jones and Ralph Janis, fellow American historians with whom I have worked at the Endowment; fortunately for this book, their judgments about history proved sounder than our combined thoughts as to how professional historians can best fit into the workings of the federal government. To those Endowment staff members who have by now come to indentify me with this project, I can only say that I will need to find some other excuse to break away occasionally from an office where a constantly heavy workload is cheerfully accepted as routine.

I also wish to express my deep appreciation to Columbia University Press for bearing with me. Bernard Gronert was always encouraging and, when entirely necessary, justifiably prodding. Karen Mitchell, who edited the final version of the manuscript, rescued me from numerous lapses and spared readers from unnecessary verbiage. Finally, my debt to William E. Leuchtenburg, the editor of the Contemporary American History Series, is immeasurable. Only those who have worked closely with him can fully appreciate his dedication to literary grace, rigorous scholarship, and informed historical judgment. Although we were sometimes in disagreement over matters of interpretation and emphasis, and will so remain, both I and the book have benefited greatly from his close attention to my efforts.

Needless to say, all responsibility for errors of fact or judgment is mine alone.

Alexandria, Virginia
March 1977

Morton Sosna

CONTENTS

The Southern liberal is aware of [the region's] past.
He works within its receding restrictions, if for
no other reason than there is as yet no other
way for him to work effectively. A suspect
among the defiant reactionaries at home,
who brand him a Communist, a "Nigger
lover" and Yankee tool, he is no
less for the militant, all-or-
nothing crusaders who wage
their war at a distance.

HODDING CARTER II

1949

The Silent South

Racial liberalism * in the South emerged during the late nineteenth and early twentieth centuries as a footnote to the declining status of Southern blacks. As had Southerners who were against slavery in the antebellum period, dissenters from the growing anti-Negro orthodoxy sensed their own isolation from the dominant mood of their region. Nevertheless, a few white Southerners expressed heretical ideas on the race issue. The most articulate among them was George Washington Cable, a fiction writer in post-Reconstruction New Orleans.

Cable was himself a native of the Crescent City. Born in 1844, he fled New Orleans after federal forces occupied the town during the Civil War. He enlisted in the Confederate Army at the age of nineteen and wound up as a clerk in a unit under the command of General Nathan Bedford Forrest. Cable served the Lost Cause dutifully, though by the end of the war he had come to question the wisdom of secession. After the conflict he returned to New Orleans and worked

* I have used the terms "racial liberals," "white liberals," "white Southern liberals," and "Southern liberals" interchangeably. Unless otherwise indicated, the word "liberal" always refers to white Southerners. See the preface for my definition of this tricky term.

as an accountant and newspaper reporter. He was fascinated by the city's varied past, particularly the cultural conflicts that arose when the descendants of its French and Spanish settlers had to adjust to American rule after 1803. In the early 1870s, Cable's stories about the Creoles of New Orleans appeared in such popular national magazines as *Harper's* and *Scribner's Monthly.* In 1879, they were published under the title *Old Creole Days;* within two years he had written *The Grandissimes* and *Madame Delphine,* novels that won both popular and critical acclaim. By 1885 George Washington Cable was ranked by his contemporaries alongside Mark Twain and William Dean Howells as one of the giants of American fiction.[1]

With his fame as a writer established, Cable turned his attention to the South's racial situation. His investigations into the operations of Southern courts and convict lease systems led him to condemn publicly the increasing discrimination, violence, and repression then being directed against the region's blacks. Moreover, he began to articulate a concept of white racial liberalism within the South.

In *The Silent South,* published in 1885, Cable explained that he was a white Southerner who was disturbed by the systematic reduction of blacks to an inferior status. Though he loved the South and embraced many of its traditions, the Louisiana novelist rejected the notion that proscriptions based on race were a necessary part of Southern life. He emphasized that a segment of white Southern society genuinely sought just treatment for blacks but pointed out that this element was usually drowned out by the more Negrophobic voices. Cable called the enlightened group a "Silent South." Though he could not have foreseen it at the time, Cable's attempt to identify racial unorthodoxy in the South would remain a working goal of white Southern liberals for the next eighty years.

The idea Cable presented was fairly simple. Speaking of the statue of Robert E. Lee that stood in New Orleans, he said that it symbolized "our whole South's better self; that finer part which the world not always sees; inaggressive but brave, calm, thoughtful, broadminded, dispassionate, sincere, and in the din of boisterous error round about it, all too mute." In other words, the social conscience of the South remained as silent as Lee's statue. Moreover, it was being overwhelmed by race-baiting politicians, Negrophobic journalists, and narrow-minded churchmen. The Silent South, according to Cable, needed a bit of prodding in order to speak out, and this was why he had undertaken a personal campaign on behalf of civil rights for Negroes. He wanted to keep open a question that was rapidly becoming closed and give a heretofore Silent South an opportunity to settle the race issue in a spirit of justice to both whites and blacks. Cable regarded himself as a harbinger of this Silent South whose voice would reveal a region "laying off its unsurrendered sword, leaving brawlers to their brawls, and moving out upon the plane of patient, friendly debate, seeking to destroy only error, and to establish only truth and equity and a calm faith . . . to solve the dark problems of the future."

Cable knew that the task was not easy. He realized that the Silent South as he saw it consisted of an educated, enlightened minority of white Southerners who in no way represented the region as a whole. These were either men of letters like himself or professional people, churchmen, and college teachers. Their influence would be qualitative rather than quantitative. But Cable held that if the "best people" spoke out against the increasing denial of the rights of citizenship to Southern blacks, fundamental beliefs could be changed.

An open forum on the race issue, according to Cable, was badly needed. Silence, which he saw as what most people wanted, would only put the problem in a state of "incubative retirement." The debate over the status of Southern Negroes had already caused one civil war and much bloodshed, and Cable wanted to make certain that it would not do so again. He characterized contemporary Southern treatment of Negroes as a "system of vicious evasions" and called for a "candid reconsideration" of racial practices. The current pattern, Cable insisted, was a "roosting curse" upon the entire South that greatly hindered development in the region. It would continue to be so until the "outraged intelligence of the South" stopped the wasting of black manpower in a caste structure that debased upright and intelligent Negroes solely for being black. Cable thought it a mistake to equate the relative absence of criticism over developing racial patterns with total acceptance of them. There were thousands of white Southerners, he maintained, "who see the wrong and folly of these things, silently blush for them, and withhold their open protests only because their belief is unfortunately stronger in the futility of their counsel than in the power of a just cause." [2]

Cable had made most of these points earlier in "The Freedman's Case in Equity," an address delivered before the American Social Science Association in February 1884 and published by *Century Magazine* in January of the following year.[3] The reaction of the white South to Cable's views had been predictable. The Southern press had accused Cable of being a traitor to his section, of desiring to please his Northern readers and to publicize his speaking tours, of expounding ideas that would lead to intermarriage, racial warfare, and the ruin of the South. Henry Grady, the leading propagandist for sectional reconciliation under the banner of a "New South," said that Cable's sentimental admiration for the idealized quadroons of his writings had developed into a "confirmed negromania." [4]

In *The Silent South* Cable tempered his arguments, hoping to allay white criticisms. He carefully distinguished between civil and social rights and insisted that, even if the two races were not equal, the whites' fear of "social intermingling" could not be used to deny blacks their fundamental legal privileges. He said, "We must find that boundary line between social relations and civil rights, from which the one has no warrant ever to push the other." He thought surely that the "best intelligence" of the white South recognized the folly of defining the Negro's status solely on the basis of race without taking into account ability, education, or behavior. Blacks, according to Cable, needed the freedom "to earn the indiscriminative and unchallenged *civil—not social*—rights of gentility by the simple act of being genteel."

Despite this cautious dissection of the problem, Cable continued to be attacked. Robert L. Dabney of Virginia, a vehement defender of the Old South who had served as Stonewall Jackson's chief of staff, was his most vicious critic. Cable, in Dabney's view, was being paid to tell Northerners what they wanted to hear about the benighted South. Charles Gayarré, a widely read historian from New Orleans, also ridiculed his fellow writer. Gayarré found it impossible to understand how Cable could ignore the fact that "the existence in the same country of two races, as different as day and night in their physical and spiritual endowments and incapable of fusing into a homogeneous whole, is the most dreadfull calamity that ever could befall a community." Cable did not take such vilification lightly. In 1886 he left the South and moved to Northampton, Massachusetts.[5]

From Massachusetts, Cable organized an Open Letter Club so that he and those white Southerners who shared similar viewpoints—the hitherto Silent South—could express their thoughts in universities, newspapers, magazines, and public lectures in the South. He wrote to a number of Southern acquaintances whom he considered to have enlightened opinions on the race issue to ask for their help and also for the names of other potential members of the club.

One of the men Cable contacted, Robert T. Hill, a native Southerner who in 1886 worked for the U.S. Geological Survey in Washington, warned him of the difficulty of locating racial liberals. Hill, himself sympathetic to the aims of an Open Letter Club, found it painful to confess that, despite his extensive Southern contacts, he could not recall the name of anyone unprejudiced enough to face the issue squarely. Hill, though, kept his eyes open. When he finally was able to come up with a name for Cable a short time later, he was exuberant. "Often I beat the bushes and get no game," he wrote, "but today I found one more true Southerner—one of the silent ones." By 1888, Hill, now at the University of Texas, had become discouraged with the prospect of solving the race problem through reaching the sensitivities of concerned whites, but he vowed to continue trying. A few months later he told Cable that he was on the defensive. Said Hill: "If I open my mouth it means decapitation, and the warning axe hangs ready. I am doing some good but must not be too hasty." In December 1889 Hill informed Cable's secretary, Adelene Moffatt, that he no longer had either the strength or desire to agitate about the Negro question any further at the University of Texas. Though he still sympathized with Cable's plans, Hill emphasized that the white South stood firmly against opening the race issue. Hill's connection with Cable's symposium endangered his job at Texas, and he told Moffatt that Southern liberals had best be careful.[6]

Other members of the Open Letter Club also concluded that they could not press the race issue as hard as they had originally hoped. Julius D. Dreher, the president of Roanoke College in Salem, Virginia, informed Cable that some of the college's "best friends" had "advised" him not to discuss the Negro question in any political context, and thus he could no longer speak his own mind. Similarly, Professor William M. Baskerville of Vanderbilt University, an enthusiastic supporter of the club in 1888, told Cable three years later that it was no longer wise to dwell on the race issue. Baskerville had found his connection with Cable particularly embarrassing following Cable's November 1889 visit to Nashville, during which the Louisiana novelist had lunched with James C. Napier, one of the city's leading black citizens. Local newspapers looked upon the meeting as proof of Cable's belief in social equality between the races. "Yes you did raise Cain!" Baskerville wrote Cable after the incident, "and for several days I had to take the brunt of the attack." Baskerville thought that by raising the specter of "social equality," Cable had played into the hands of enemies.[7]

By 1891 the Open Letter Club had passed from the scene and with it Cable's hopes that a Silent South could be stirred to action. Cable himself turned his attention to other matters and spent his remaining years without engaging in racial or sectional controversy. He died in 1925 at the age of eighty-one, his racial crusade of the 1880s long forgotten.[8]

It would be easy to dismiss George Washington Cable as a heretic who had little impact on his native region. Even in his own New Orleans, where urban and Catholic influences gave blacks more opportunities than in other parts of the South, their status continued to decline. But as one who eloquently voiced the credo of the modern Southern liberal, Cable cannot be ignored.

Cable very early sketched out the basic tenets of Southern liberal thought. He emphasized his own Southernness and first-hand expertise on the racial problem, and he argued that white Southerners themselves would have to arrive at some solution. Cable referred to Reconstruction as a "dreadful episode" and dismissed the notion that the federal government could coerce the South into providing equitable treatment for blacks. By insisting that significant material progress in the South was impossible as long as the mass of Southern blacks continued to live amid poverty and blatant discrimination, Cable appealed to white self-interest. He also tried to convince Southerners that segregation was more a problem than a solution.

Cable also stirred black leaders who hoped to gain support for their own aims. Booker T. Washington greatly admired him and believed that there were many whites who felt as he did but who lacked the moral courage to express their sentiments. W. E. B. Du Bois, then a young instructor at Fisk University in Nashville, applauded Cable's refusal to apologize for having dinner with Napier. "In the midst of so much confusion and misapprehension," he said, "it is doubly welcome to the young Negro who is building a nation." And a black man who left the South to live in Wisconsin wrote that Cable had "raised a hope in our bosoms that our old neighbors and friends are at last allowing their own hearts to speak for us, and that we will soon see the dawn of a brighter day for our country and our children." [9]

Though Cable was the most outspoken Southern liberal of his time, there were others who actively sought better treatment for blacks. Atticus G. Haygood, the president of Emory College and later the bishop of the Southern Methodist Episcopal Church, wrote an appeal in 1881, *Our Brother in Black*, that called upon white Southerners to support education for blacks. Haygood deplored the intimidation, violence, and discrimination directed against Negroes as "un-Christian." His admission that Southern whites had not always acted wisely in racial matters brought Haygood to the attention of Northern philanthropists, and from 1884 to 1891 he served as the first head of the Slater Fund, which helped support Negro schools in the South. Haygood, unlike Cable, did not attack segregation, but he did argue that the debate over social equality was irrelevant. He also insisted that Negroes should have the right to vote and was an active member of Cable's short-lived Open Letter Club.[10]

Haygood's message that white Southerners would have to reconcile themselves to blacks as free men and fellow citizens, however bland by today's standards, provoked a great deal of hostility in the 1880s. Many (in all likelihood almost all) white Southerners had concluded that black people lacked the potential to become independent members of the community. Southern Negroes, they contended, had degenerated morally and physically since their emancipation from slavery, and hence the maintenance of white supremacy required even more extreme measures.[11] In such a climate it was not surprising that in 1882 the black newspaper editor Timothy Thomas Fortune, despite his denunciation of Southern whites, regarded Haygood as "a man of the largest culture, Christian intelligence and progressive ideas." [12] Indeed, Haygood's major legacy to future racial liberals in the South was his insistence that the basic tenets of Christianity demanded modification of existing patterns of race relations.

In contrast to Haygood's emphasis on the religious duty of Southern whites to help their black Christian "brothers," a Virginia businessman, Lewis H. Blair, stressed that white self-interest made it imperative for blacks to receive all the rights of citizenship. Cable had touched upon this theme, but his arguments were primarily moral. Blair, however, made his case strictly on a cost-accounting basis. In his 1889 *Prosperity of the South Dependent upon the Elevation of the Negro,* Blair contended that the South would not overcome disease, poverty, and ignorance until measures were taken to upgrade the status of black men. "Like a malignant cancer which poisons the whole system," he wrote, "this degradation seems to intensify all the other drawbacks under which we labor." As Blair saw him, the Southern Negro was an "extremely defective tool"; he lived in poverty and ignorance and was so shackled by caste that he could hardly be blamed for not having any self-respect or a desire to uplift himself. Blair wanted black people to have adequate education, equal protection before the law, and free access to public accommodations, not because this would be right but because it would be profitable. "Just as we would urge the South to improve its animals, tools, and methods of planting," said Blair, "so we urge the elevation of the negro, because the better men and citizens they are, the more we, the whites, can in the end make out of them." Blair freely acknowledged that he based his "exhortation to elevation" upon dollars and cents. Later racial liberals would also employ the self-interest theme, though not with the vehemence of Blair, whose later conversion to unqualified racism suggests that his economic plea was not merely tactical. [13]

The appeals of Cable, Haygood, and Blair were the first stirrings of white disenchantment with a Jim Crow South. But the influence of these men was slight: the noose of racial orthodoxy tightened. Though the spirit they represented never disappeared entirely, these early racial liberals were voices in the wilderness. Their ideas, however, would surface again.*

In contrast to these middle- and upper-class liberals, who spoke as gentlemen and Christians for the benefit of others of their kind, the "third party" struggles of the 1880s and 1890s added a new dimension to Southern liberalism: class alliances across racial lines. Though the extent to which white Independents, Readjusters, and Populists sought justice for Negroes has been hotly debated by historians, one point is clear. An appeal, however fleeting, was made for the poorer whites and blacks to lay aside traditional animosities and together work for their mutual economic benefit. In 1892 Tom Watson of Georgia, who in later years would come to symbolize white Southern Negrophobia, declared that "the accident of color can make no difference in the interest of farmers, croppers, and laborers." Watson, then running for reelection to Congress on a Populist ticket, urged white Democrats and black Republicans to support his candidacy. "You are kept apart that you may be separately fleeced of your earnings," he told them.[14] A vital element that Cable had not included, a plea to lower-class whites, was added to Southern liberalism.

The Populists, however, like the more genteel Southern liberals, did not make much headway. Defeated repeatedly by white Democrats who raised the specter of "Negro domination," the Populists achieved success only when they managed to out-niggerbait their foes. In the end the Populists and the Democrats healed their differences largely at the expense of blacks, whose status, as a result of the disfranchisement and strict legal segregation that followed the Populist struggles, came to be even more precarious. By 1909 Tom Watson was trumpeting "the superiority of the Aryan" and character-

* Several historians have pointed out that Cable, Haygood, and Blair, though liberal compared with the majority of white Southerners, nevertheless held racist assumptions that prevented their viewing blacks as true equals. This is the main argument in a chapter on Cable in Lawrence J. Friedman, *The White Savage: Racial Fantasies in the Postbellum South* (Englewood Cliffs, N.J., 1970), pp. 99–117, and is also stressed by George M. Frederickson in *The Black Image in the White Mind: The Debate on Afro-American Character and Destiny, 1817–1914* (New York, 1971), pp. 198–227. However, it is misleading to characterize these men primarily as racists, since they—particularly Cable—did put forth arguments that shattered the assumptions of a Jim Crow South.

izing the Negro as a "hideous, ominous, national menace." [15] Compared to him and those like him, the inheritors of the less flamboyant tradition of white dissent, even when they were not as outspoken as a Cable, a Haygood, or a Blair, could justifiably lay claim to being Southern liberals.

Still, though the Populists failed to build a biracial alliance, the idea that poorer Southern whites and blacks could form an effective coalition did not die. Future Southern liberals, most notably those who would be influenced by the impact of the Great Depression and the New Deal, would pick up the theme, cleanse it of its racism, and present it as an alternative to a Jim Crow South. C. Vann Woodward, the biographer of Tom Watson, would expand the idea of Populism's lost innocence and provide a source of inspiration to liberals against the belief that white supremacy was the South's unshakable destiny.*

* C. Vann Woodward, *Tom Watson: Agrarian Rebel* (New York, 1938), pp. 219–23. While having a great impact on Southern liberals, Woodward's interpretation that white Southern Populists were sympathetic, if only briefly, to the cause of Negro rights has stimulated one of the larger controversies in American historiography. Some scholars have strongly challenged the idea that Tom Watson—and by implication Southern Populists generally—ever represented a significant hope for blacks. They insist that Watson was anti-Negro prior to becoming a Populist, that he told black audiences one thing and white audiences another during his 1892 congressional campaign, and that his venomous Negrophobia after 1898 is really not all that ironic. (Charles Crowe, "Tom Watson, Populists, and Blacks Reconsidered," *Journal of Negro History*, 55 [April 1970], 99–116; Friedman, *The White Savage*, pp. 77–98; Robert Saunders, "Southern Populists and the Negro 1893–1895," *Journal of Negro History*, 54 [July 1969], 240–61.) On the other hand, Lawrence C. Goodwyn came out mostly on the side of Woodward in a fine article that shows the complexity of trying to prove whether the Populists were or were not racial liberals. ("Populist Dreams and Negro Rights: East Texas as a Case Study," *American Historical Review*, 76 December 1971, 1435–56.) Goodwyn further clarifies his own views in *Democratic Promise: The Populist Movement in America* (New York, 1976) pp. 276–306. An excellent discussion of the entire problem, which puts the overtures to blacks by the Populists and other Southern independent groups of the late nineteenth century in perspective, is in Carl N. Degler, *The Other South: Southern Dissenters in the Nineteenth Century* (New York, 1974), pp. 264–371. For the importance of Woodward to Southern liberal thought see Michael O'Brien, "C. Vann Woodward and the Burden of Southern Liberalism," *American Historical Review*, 76 (June 1973), 589–604 and Morton Sosna, "The South Old and New: A Review Essay," *Wisconsin Magazine of History*, 55 (Spring 1972), 231–35.

Though the historical accuracy of Woodward's interpretation of Southern history

But for Southern liberals in the early twentieth century, Populism's lesson was less encouraging. They concluded that by appealing for Negro votes, the Populists had opened up a Pandora's box. The fruitless debates over "Negro domination" reminded them of the xenophobic white reaction to radical Reconstruction, which was now viewed as the prime example of a wrong-headed approach to Southern racial problems. Furthermore, not only had Populism been crushed, but some old Populists seemed to have adopted the worst prejudices of their white supremacist opponents while adding a flair for political showmanship that boded ill for the liberals' appeal to the finer instincts of white Southerners. The Dixie Demagogue had arrived.

The years between 1890 and 1920 were in many ways the grimmest that blacks had faced since the end of slavery. Violence, disfranchisement, and tightening segregation characterized Southern race relations, and, in addition to Tom Watson, the era was the heyday of such Negro-baiting politicians as James K. Vardaman, the "White Chief" of Mississippi, "Pitchfork" Ben Tillman and Cole Blease of South Carolina, Hoke Smith of Georgia, Jeff Davis of Arkansas, and Tom Heflin of Alabama. These factors posed immense problems for the minority of Southern whites who recognized racial injustice. Among some there was grave doubt as to the wisdom of raising the race issue at all.

Walter Hines Page, a native of North Carolina, exhibited extreme uneasiness. Journalist, publisher of such popular magazines as *Forum* and *World's Work*, and a well-known commentator on the South who later served as Woodrow Wilson's ambassador to Britain, Page

---

is still being debated, there is little doubt about his own commitment as a Southern liberal. For example, in writing to a fellow Southern liberal about his *Origins of the New South 1877–1913* (Baton Rouge, 1951) he noted: "What was perhaps most gratifying about your reaction was that you felt behind my savage exposures an underlying pity and sympathy. That was what I was most concerned about—that the compassion that motivated me would be smothered in the irony with which I wrote. It was, after all, such a beastly, sordid, unheroic period. . . . And my sympathies were obviously not with the people who ran things, and about whom I wrote most, but about the people who were run, who were managed and maneuvered and pushed around." (Woodward to Virginia Durr, June 8, 1952, Box 8 in the Hugo L. Black Papers, Library of Congress.)

confided in 1899 that he had not been able to forget the race problem in twenty years of thinking; the pathos of it was eternal. In 1907, in a series of frank letters to his wife, he revealed his acute awareness of the horrors that confronted black people in the lower South. Yet in 1911, in advising Edwin Mims of Vanderbilt University on how to write about the South, Page warned his professorial friend against dwelling on the race question, told him readers were bored to death with the subject, and suggested that Mims scrupulously avoid stirring up unnecessary controversies. Page's thoughts on the Fifteenth Amendment further attest to the persistent vacillation of his racial outlook. In 1900, when repeal of the Fifteenth Amendment was a live issue in Southern politics, Page believed that the amendment's adoption had been a grave mistake but that its repeal would be an even graver one. Page was regarded by many in the North as well as in the South as one of the leading Southern liberals of his generation. His discomfort with the race question, though, cast a shadow on his otherwise optimistic picture of a region that was becoming more enlightened. For blacks, the words of Walter Hines Page had a hollow ring.[16]

An even more pointed denial of the existence of a Silent South that would deal intelligently with race came from Carl Holliday, a professor of English at Southwestern Presbyterian University in Memphis. In 1909 Holliday had forty-eight of his students, all of whom were white—and supposedly enlightened—Southerners, prepare themes on the future of the Negro in the South. On the basis of the sentiments expressed in their papers, Holliday viewed as a myth any notion that the racial outlook of young Southerners was becoming more Christianized. He predicted that the black man would continue to be "restrained, hampered, brow-beaten, [and] discouraged within the next quarter of a century as never before in all his bitter years of existence on this continent." [17]

These years of increasing color consciousness put Southern liberals on the defensive. Caution in the matter appeared more necessary than before. Edgar Gardner Murphy, an Alabama Episcopal clergyman who wrote extensively about race relations in the South, warned the New York philanthropist Robert C. Ogden against any action on behalf of Negroes that could be played up by the demagogues. "For these men to openly attack you would not only be unpleasant," he said, "but would 'drive to cover' men on whom we—and the negro—*must* depend for fairness and patriotism." Such an admission did not sit well with Murphy, who added, "I feel 'like a dog' to have to say these things, but I know our people." Murphy's fellow Alabamian, William Garrott Brown, a frequent critic of the South, referred to the racial bigotry of Vardaman—who once said that a Negro had "no more conception of the importance of the elective franchise than the chimpanzee had of understanding the nebular hypothesis"—and pessimistically reported that not much could be done about it because too many whites shared Vardaman's views.

When another philanthropist, George Foster Peabody, urged bolder action in the area of Negro education before a meeting of the Southern Education Board, University of Virginia president Edwin A. Alderman compared the race issue to a "sore tooth"—the more one thought about it the more it hurt. Alderman said that racial liberals wanted to influence public sentiment and stop being silent, but warned that they should proceed prudently and "not so spectacularly as to set back the movement." [18]

Despite private forebodings about their own work, Southern liberals adopted a more optimistic tone in public. Murphy, for example, denied that racial demagogues adequately reflected Southern opinion. "Damaging as is our more violent leadership," he said, "it is not so general or so representative as has often been assumed." During the first decade of the twentieth century, Walter Hines Page constantly assured his readers that the "true" South deplored the Tillmans and Vardamans. For Page this "real" South was made up of enlightened businessmen, teachers, and politicians who opposed racism, demagoguery, and intolerance. Despite his private statements to the effect that most Southern whites hated Negroes and that the black man's condition would worsen, Page's published writing emphasized that white Southerners were basically innocent victims of evil ideas who bore no real malice against blacks. [19]

As the pressure for racial orthodoxy grew, even slight departures brought personal trauma to white Southerners who questioned the system. In 1902 Andrew Sledd, a Methodist minister from an old Virginia family and a Latin professor at Emory College (then located in Oxford, Georgia), wrote in the *Atlantic Monthly* that Southern whites had deprived Negroes of their fundamental rights. Vehement reaction to the article forced Sledd to resign from Emory a year later. In 1903 John Spencer Bassett, a history professor at Trinity College (now Duke University) in Durham, North Carolina, wrote a mildly critical article of white supremacy in which he referred to Booker T. Washington as "all in all the greatest man, save General Lee, born in the South in a hundred years." Bassett came very close to losing his job, and even his defenders made it clear that the issue was one of academic freedom rather than a sharing of Basset's views. In 1912, when Joel E. Spingarn of the National Association for the Advancement of Colored People (NAACP) met John D. Hammond, the president of Paine College in Augusta, Georgia—one of the few educational institutions for Negroes owned and operated by Southern whites—Hammond's wife warned Spingarn of the confidential nature of the meeting and told him that in public she spoke "differently" on the race issue. The Hammonds' silence, however, did not sufficiently protect them; community pressure ultimately forced them to leave Paine College.[20]

Between 1890 and 1910 Cable's worst fears were realized. The vast majority of white Southerners considered the status of black people a closed question; those with reservations conducted their activities so as not to threaten prevailing practices. The popular clamor for strict legal segregation presented a particularly thorny problem and circumscribed the actions of white liberals.

A case in point was Edgar Gardner Murphy's organization in 1900 of the Southern Society for the Promotion of the Study of Race Conditions and Problems in the South. Murphy induced about two dozen prominent citizens of Montgomery, Alabama to support a meeting in the city. Originally he had intended to invite a few blacks, but after realizing that some whites would object, he thought better of the idea. The participants, all white, included politicians, newspapermen, professors, businessmen, and churchmen. The conference caused relatively little controversy and was primarily a debate between those who, like Murphy, thought that Southern whites should improve conditions among the black population of the region and those who believed that such action was a waste of time. Little came from the venture. The society published its Montgomery proceedings, but Murphy dropped plans for a second conference in 1901 when no Southern city offered to host the organization.[21]

Yet even during these trying times, scattered white Southerners continued to voice liberal sentiments. Vicious mob violence directed at Negroes during a race riot in Atlanta in 1906 shocked a few and convinced them that the white supremacy movement had gone too far. John E. White, a Baptist minister in the city, noted discouragingly that but for "a prompt Gatling gun and a troop of forty soldiers, the largest Negro institution in Atlanta [a crowded church] would have been burned to the ground." He attributed such senseless violence to the failure of the best white people of the South to formulate a program for the betterment of race relations. White maintained that scattered discussions among isolated individuals were not a substitute for such an effort, spoke of "Anglo-Saxon obligation and opportunity" in the South, and blamed the depravities of lower-class whites on the "inaction they see in the ranks above them." White also emphasized the existence of a more liberal South. "I believe there is under the froth of individual opinion," he said, "a common sense and a common will that can be ascertained and pronounced. I believe that there is in a land and among a people as responsive as ours to the standards of the Christian Gospel, a conscience to support a program of basic righteousness."

Another commentator in the aftermath of the Atlanta riot was John C. Kilgo, the president of Trinity College and later the head of the Southern Methodist Episcopal Church. Kilgo reiterated the racial liberal's familiar refrain that the Tillmans, the Vardamans, and the vigilantes did not represent the true feelings of the South and expressed disgust with the efforts of some Southerners to create "fictitious strife" between the races. He wanted enlightened white Southerners to demand the kind of leadership that would allow them to get rid of the demagogues and begin to secure material, educational, and religious advancement for all Southern people. "I have unlimited belief in the integrity of the silent South," Kilgo concluded. "My only complaint is that it has been too long silent. The hour has struck when it should speak, when it should rise in its patriotic might and play a part in all the affairs of society."[22]

The Atlanta riot also convinced some Southern liberals that bridges were needed between blacks and whites in order to avert future violence. A group of prominent white citizens in Atlanta invited Booker T. Washington to the city for a meeting on the theory that communication between the "better element" of both races could avoid trouble. Soon afterwards, a temporary "interracial" committee was formed. A feeling began to emerge among the liberals that if they made clear that they accepted segregation and did not favor "social equality," measures could be taken to aid blacks and stem the tide of violence. Such a posture, they believed, would enable them to combat some of the excesses that the white supremacist movement had produced: lynching, the movement to segregate blacks in rural communities, and a campaign to base state educational allocations for black schools solely on tax dollars collected from blacks themselves.[23] Though such sentiment was certainly a dilution of the demands that Cable had made in the 1880s, advocates looked upon it as a breakthrough in this bleak period.

In the years before the First World War, W. D. Weatherford, a Vanderbilt-trained leader of the Southern YMCA movement, emerged as spokesman for such a policy. Combining interest in the latest scientific theories of race and facts about Southern Negroes with a missionary zeal to help uplift blacks, Weatherford's work prompted Oswald Garrison Villard, grandson of the abolitionist William Lloyd Garrison and one of the founders of the NAACP, to refer to him as a hopeful sign of changing attitudes among white Southerners. In *Negro Life in the South* in 1910 and *Present Forces for Negro Progress* in 1912, Weatherford outlined his thinking. Southern college men, he recommended, should study the race question and acquaint themselves with the tremendous problems that faced black people in the South. He emphasized that the destiny of each race was "inextricably intertwined" with that of the other. He called upon Southern whites to meet blacks who were not in servile occupations and admonished them to help stamp out such evils as lynching. While alluding to some significant black accomplishments since slavery, Weatherford stressed that the mass of blacks still suffered from ignorance, immorality, and disease, and that they required the help and understanding of whites to upgrade themselves and the South.

He was also careful to point out that the "sane" members of both races did not believe in "promiscuous mingling." [24]

Weatherford and others, particularly James E. McCullach, a Methodist minister from Virginia, also trained at Vanderbilt, succeeded in organizing the Southern Sociological Congress, which met in Nashville for three days in May 1912. More than seven hundred delegates attended the convention and discussed a number of Southern social problems. The Congress set forth a program with some specific demands: abolition of the convict lease system, extension of juvenile courts, abolition of child labor, suppression of prostitution, compulsory school attendance laws, and proper care for the insane, crippled, and blind. But on the race question the congress remained more vague. It called for dealing with the problem "in a spirit of helpfulness to the Negro, and of equal justice to both races." Between 1913 and 1919 subsequent congresses stressed similar objectives. [25]

Shortly after the Nashville meeting, James Hardy Dillard, a Virginian who headed the Phelps-Stokes Fund, organized the University Commission on Southern Race Questions as a working group of the Southern Sociological Congress. Dillard believed that state universities in the South had an obligation to provide leadership in racial matters. Eleven representatives from Southern universities made up the organization, which was chaired by Charles H. Brough, a professor at the University of Arkansas who in 1916 would become the state's governor. [26]

Though neither the Sociological Congress nor the University Race Commission was a militant organization, blacks obtained some nominal recognition. At the 1913 Atlanta convention of the Southern Sociological Congress, about ninety blacks attended sessions. Not formally members of the organization, they nevertheless came to the meetings as "responsible citizens." This prompted one black Atlantan to praise the Congress for demonstrating "the possibility of young white men of the new order sympathizing in and appreciating the hopes and aspirations of the Negro today."

Heartening to blacks, too, was the new groups' emphasis on curbing racial violence. In 1915 the Sociological Congress, meeting in Houston, called for a "new chivalry" in the South that would concern itself with public health rather than the protection of white women, and by 1916 Dillard and Weatherford were spearheading one of the first organized efforts in the South to combat lynching. Yet the Northern journalist Ray Stannard Baker surely exaggerated when he observed that the congress represented a "new departure in the Southern attitude toward the Negro." [27]

The statements of members of the University Commission and the Sociological Congress indicated how much even Southern liberals compromised with the pervasive racism of the times. Chairman Brough, in describing the work of the commission, referred to Reconstruction as a "reign of ignorance, mongrelism, and depravity" that had done irreparable harm to race relations. Brough characterized segregation laws as "wise," though he admitted that discrimination often made these unfair to blacks. (He also termed the then-popular movement to allocate funds to black schools on the basis of the proportion of the taxes paid by blacks "dangerous and insidious.") Another commission member, W. O. Scroggs of the University of Louisiana, blamed much of the unequal treatment of blacks on unreasoning racial demagogues who first denied them the opportunity to vote and then allocated to them inferior public accommodations, subquality services, and unfair shares of public school funds. But Scroggs carefully pointed out that he in no way meant to criticize social segregation, which he looked upon as a "basic fact" of race relations. James Hardy Dillard said white Southerners wisely realized that Reconstruction idealists, such as Thaddeus Stevens and Charles Sumner, had erred in moving too swiftly for Negro rights, and optimistically believed that Southern whites were prepared to alter affections, prejudices, and relationships that grew out of the slavery era if they were allowed to do it slowly. Weatherford, while calling for the enlistment of Southern welfare agencies to improve living conditions of blacks, also acknowledged the necessity of segregation. "My only fear for white supremacy," said Mrs. Lily H. Hammond, who sponsored housing to benefit urban Negroes, "is that we should prove unworthy of it." A pervasive acceptance of segregation had come to characterize Southern liberals and would hang over them like an albatross for many years.[28]

During the first decade of the twentieth century there solidified a "separate-but-equal" brand of racial liberalism that emphasized the "equal" rather than the "separate." In contrast to the blatant Negrophobes whom they continually denounced, white liberals, as "decent" Southerners, argued that they best understood Southern race relations. They believed that, with segregation conceded, positive steps could be taken to improve the status of blacks and thereby raise living standards throughout the South. Though patronizing, they departed from traditional paternalism in that they believed blacks should become self-reliant citizens. Success depended on their ability to locate an increasingly vocal white liberal sentiment within the South. They continually pointed out that Northern criticism of Southern racial practices only played into the hands of their own and the Negro's worst enemies—the demagogues who whipped up racial fears by crying that outsiders who did not understand blacks would endanger white supremacy. Anyone who demanded too rapid a change in Southern racial patterns or who argued for federal assistance to Southern blacks would only repeat the horrible mistakes of Reconstruction. By 1914 Southern liberals were no longer as isolated as Cable had been, but they posed no threat to prevailing racial practices.

CHAPTER TWO

The Commission on Interracial Cooperation

Although their actual achievements at this point were small, Southern liberals at least took heart that the racial situation appeared to be stabilizing rather than deteriorating further. Before America's entry into the First World War, some even sensed that perhaps the worst years were behind them, and that they represented a feasible alternative. "As a Southern man trained in a Southern University living daily in the midst of these vexatious [race] problems," Weatherford wrote in 1913, "I feel decidedly that the outlook is brighter than it has ever been in our history." [1]

Such optimism had an impact on a young Methodist minister in Nashville, Will W. Alexander. Born and raised on a farm in Missouri and ordained in 1901 while still a youth of seventeen, Alexander went on to receive a divinity degree in 1912 from Vanderbilt, where he came in contact with people such as Weatherford. While in Nashville, Alexander, who had grown up in a community that had no Negroes, acquired firsthand experience with racial discrimination by police and local courts and used his influence to prevent black children from being thrown in jail. He became convinced that poverty and racism were the twin evils of the South and regretted that his church did not do more to alleviate these problems. When the United States entered the war in 1917, he resigned from the ministry and worked with Southern YMCA groups in conjunction with the War Department to maintain as much racial harmony in the South as possible. The enthusiasm of Southern Negroes for the war moved Alexander, who felt the experience of mobilization would inaugurate a new, more positive era in race relations.

Possessed of such hope, Alexander was shocked by the unprecedented wave of racial violence that swept the South and the nation in 1919. Rumors spread that returning black soldiers would not be content with their former status in Southern society and that blacks were purchasing all available arms in preparation for a coming race war. In 1919 the lynching of blacks, which had declined somewhat in the prewar years, rose sharply and the Ku Klux Klan began a grisly resurgence. In this climate of fear and hate, Alexander traveled through the South to avert bloodshed where racial violence appeared imminent. When he asked one elderly white minister whether there was any local trouble with Negroes, the man answered, "No we had to kill a few of them, but we didn't have any trouble with them." [2]

To defuse the situation, Alexander, still working for the War Department, attempted to bring together white and black representatives who would be influential enough among their respective peoples to quell rumors and avert violence. He organized interracial committees similar to the one that had been set up in Atlanta following the 1906 race riot. Alexander soon became convinced that such temporary agencies merited a more formal organization. John H. Egan, president of the American Cast Iron Pipe Company in Atlanta, agreed to provide some of the necessary funds. Alexander also sold the idea to the War Work Council of the YMCA, which furnished him with $75,000 for the project that soon became known as the Commission on Interracial Cooperation. Northern philanthropic associations—particularly the new Julius Rosenwald Fund, whose wealthy Chicago founder was concerned with the welfare of American Negroes—also showed interest and lent additional financial support. The Interracial Commission had the backing, too, of such prewar Southern liberals as Weatherford and Dillard. Twenty-five years later Gunnar Myrdal would characterize the commission as "*the* organization of Southern liberalism in its activity on the Negro issue." [3]

The commission's interracialism was not meant to challenge segregation. Yet the idea of a Southern organization in which blacks would be members and be allowed to voice complaints was new; in 1900 Murphy had deemed it unwise to include Booker T. Washington in his Southern Race Conference, and neither the Southern Sociological Congress nor the University Race Commission had allowed black members. Whether they intended to or not, Southern liberals had made a dent in Jim Crow.

Ironically, commission supporters pointed out that segregation itself demanded such an organization. The commission would provide a necessary link between otherwise segregated whites and blacks in the South. Samuel Chiles Mitchell of the University of South Carolina referred to the "genius" of the plan and said it met "a vital need in a bi-racial community in order to secure counsel on all matters touching the common good." Though the prevention of violence remained a prime objective, supporters of the Interracial Commission argued that promotion of "better understanding" between the races was also vital. They repeatedly emphasized the interdependence between people who lived, as one white liberal put it, "side by side, yet apart." Weatherford organized a white study group that met during the summers at Blue Ridge, North Carolina, and one for blacks was established at Gammon Theological Seminary in Atlanta. Occasionally there was an exchange of students. In short, the Interracial Commission presented itself as an organization of Southerners who were dealing with a Southern problem. More interracial in name than in fact, the commission was nevertheless an unprecedented expression of white racial liberalism in the South. [4]

As an organization, the Commission on Interracial Cooperation was amorphous. It began and remained more or less an expression of sentiment rather than an official group with carefully defined policies. The commission united roughly seven thousand individuals who differed markedly in the extent of their racial liberalism and who frequently made conflicting public statements on particular issues, largely because its structure was minimal. Its board of directors, led by Chairman Alexander, was located in Atlanta, and it established committees in each of thirteen Southern states with the hope of branching out to the county level. But there was no precise relationship between the regional body in Atlanta and the local groups. The loose connection, it was claimed, would give local bodies the greatest degree of flexibility; but in fact, outside Virginia, North Carolina, and Georgia, local action was infrequent. "Never, during its twenty-five years of existence, did it become a clearly delineated setup," a student of the commission has noted. "It is to be doubted whether for any given month or year anyone involved with it at the time, or anyone now, could give a perfectly true picture of the actual organization in its entirety." [5]

Though Southern churches endorsed racially discriminatory policies, religious sentiment—both organized and individual—greatly influenced the activities of the commission. Alexander's own interest in racial matters stemmed largely from religious convictions. In his mind, no white Christian could condone the blatant discrimination directed against "the colored brother in our midst." An early commission declaration of principle of a few hundred words mentioned "Christ" or "Christian" ten times, and one of the commission's Blue Ridge conferences stated as a "profound conviction that the real responsibility for the solution of interracial problems in the South rests directly upon the hearts and consciences of the Christian forces of our land." Many of the commission's members were in fact church leaders or educators at church-related schools: Theodore D. Bratton, the Episcopal Bishop of Mississippi; William Louis Poteat, a leading Baptist theologian and the president of Wake Forest College; Robert E. Blackwell, the president of the Methodist Episcopal Randolph-Macon College in Virginia. In 1920 they stated that, above all, Southern race relations required the "influence of the Christian religion." [6]

Alexander sought to give the commission's avowed Christian sentiments some practical outlet, and thus carefully nurtured cooperation between church leaders and university people who were interested in social service work. Southern sociologists such as Howard W. Odum, Thomas J. Woofter, Jr., and Arthur F. Raper joined the Interracial Commission and supplied myriad facts to support its moral arguments. [7]

Pragmatic interracial activities were necessarily cautious. During the summer of 1920, white liberals went into North Carolina black communities to seek out "key men" and establish rapport with them. Blacks were asked what most offended them, and their usual first reply was being called "Uncle" or "John" rather than "Mister." Whites then arranged private meetings with some of the blacks who voiced other complaints: unnecessary Jim Crow signs in a park, delays in mail service, inadequate school terms for black children, unrepaired water mains in the black section of town. The whites responded by agreeing to correct these grievances and also to maintain communication with the blacks upon any news of possible mob violence. In no way did either the whites or the blacks associated with the commission fundamentally challenge segregation. But in the 1920s, with the Ku Klux Klan far more potent in the South than was the Commission on Interracial Cooperation, people greeted such meetings as these in North Carolina as giant steps forward in race relations.[8]

Commission members sensed their isolation, yet remained optimistic. In 1925 Thomas Woofter, the organization's research director, published *The Basis of Racial Adjustment*, a book used as a text for commission-sponsored college courses on race relations. He thought that the white Southern liberal stood apart from three classes of people who made race relations difficult. First, there were Northerners who felt that all white Southerners hated, lynched, and discriminated against blacks—an opinion that Woofter insisted was belied by the very existence of the Interracial Commission. Second, there were white Southerners who blamed Yankees for interfering in Southern race relations and who made a fetish out of constantly emphasizing their superiority to all Negroes as a race. Third, there were militant blacks who, according to Woofter, hated and mistrusted all whites. Woofter, however, felt gratified that the relative influence of these classes was declining compared to "the growing power of cooperative groups which are successfully at work." Though many Southern whites claimed to know the Negro, he added that only a very few of them had any accurate grasp of conditions among Southern blacks and the complexity of the racial situation.

Woofter's major point was that agitation—be it pro- or anti-Negro—inevitably impeded progress. He went so far as to suggest that unfortunate incidents should be consciously ignored by the press and overlooked by sensible men of both races. A skillful use of common sense, Woofter hinted, could turn bitterness and prejudice into cooperation and mutual respect. He related the story of a newspaper editor who overlooked the opposition of white farmers to holding a meeting with blacks. The man instead printed that everyone favored an interracial meeting with a farm demonstrator, and as a result the session was held to the satisfaction of both whites and blacks, including the whites who had originally opposed the idea. The whites came away realizing that progress for them as well as for black Southerners necessitated interracial cooperation, and that this did not imperil the social segregation of the races. Woofter pointed out that blacks voiced complaints about segregation only because highly prejudiced whites often administered it brutally and used it as a means to degrade and exploit them, not from any desire to mix socially with whites. Though admitting that some forms of segregation were cruel and useless, Woofter believed that, on the whole, separate-but-equal was just and wise.[9]

Woofter's insistence upon segregation was fully consistent with a racially liberal view in the South of the 1920s. The historian Clement Eaton, a native of North Carolina and a student at Chapel Hill during the 1920s, later noted that he and his classmates—"we the young liberals!"—had felt no more guilt over segregation than antebellum slaveholders had over the nature of slavery.[10] During the twenties, segregation was more solidly entrenched than ever before or since; it already had a tradition going back at least thirty years, and no significant protest against its continued existence had appeared. Even the NAACP during these years concentrated its efforts on alleviating more blatant examples of intolerance such as lynching.

Will Alexander brought a good deal of fire upon himself and the Interracial Commission by merely suggesting disenchantment with segregation. When asked his opinion of it during a 1926 interdenominational youth conference in Birmingham, Alexander replied that he could not defend segregation laws, since he thought they worked an injustice upon blacks, but that whether to repeal them was quite a different matter on which one man's opinion was as good as another's. Alexander's utterance was misinterpreted as a call for the abandonment of segregation and led a number of commission members to restate their commitment to the principle of racial separation. The Birmingham ministers who sponsored the conference immeditely drafted a statement maintaining that, though they believed in "fair, brotherly, and Christ-like treatment of all people and races," Alexander's remarks made him an unsuitable representative for their group. The incident served as a warning to Southern liberals. Whatever their feelings about segregation, almost all of them believed that to be identified as antisegregationists would negate any positive influence they might have.[11]

Alexander, as his comment in Birmingham revealed, was not a hard-line segregationist but was unwilling to take up a fight before the time seemed ready. His own great-uncle, he often pointed out to associates, had been lynched in Texas just before the Civil War because of his outspoken abolitionist views. Alexander emphasized that in order to be effective, a campaigner for racial justice could not remain too far ahead of the thinking of the man on the street. "America is an aggregate of Gopher Prairies large and small," he said in 1922, "and the idea of better race relations must be made to take root in the hard soil of their Main Streets." Alexander saw himself as part of a group of white Southerners who, though relatively few in number, were "the leaven which, if kept alive and working, will permeate the mass of white and Negro citizens with a new race attitude." He once defined the Interracial Commission as a "usable piece of community machinery" that had special value for whites as well as for blacks. Like most Southern liberals, Alexander believed that the whites paid the ultimate price for racial intolerance—continued poverty and government by demagogues.[12]

As an agency, the commission embodied Cable's idea that the key to racial liberalism lay in organizing the better element of whites into some purposeful group. The commission's founders assumed that if such people could be sold on the virtues of improving the status of Negroes, more enlightened attitudes would eventually drift down to a larger body of white Southerners. But the first task was to win leaders. The membership of the Interracial Commission was representative of the growing white middle class of the South. Those who worked with the commission, usually Methodists, most often came from the university, the press, and the church. Overwhelmingly they were men of the urban rather than the rural South. Some businessmen could be found to support the commission's aims, but the organization included few, if any, representatives from among the white landowners of the black belt. When members of this latter group expressed concern for the problems of blacks, they generally did so from within the paternalistic tradition of helping "their niggers" in times of trouble, a tradition commission supporters fought against. For Southern liberals saw helping the Negro to help himself as a departure from rather than a contribution to paternalism.

George Fort Milton, an editor for the *Chattanooga News*, exemplified the typical outlook of the white Southern liberals who worked with the Interracial Commission. Milton wanted racial patterns in the South to change, but above all he desired to avoid controversy so that "the dislocation of readjustment can be kept from being too wrenching, too savage, too hurtful to large sections or groups of our society." Milton thought that the South was, in some respects, changing for the better. For example, in 1933 he said that whites were becoming much more amenable toward allowing qualified Negroes to vote. Yet, instead of working for black enfranchisement, Milton preferred to speak in generalities. Southern Negroes, he said, needed "just treatment and fair dealing." In discussing slavery, Milton reminded Northern audiences that there had been "two slaveries," commercial and patriarchal. Abolitionists and Free Soilers had only recognized the former; they had refused to admit that deeply affectionate and complex relations had often developed between masters and slaves. On the other hand, the defenders of slavery had frequently ignored the peculiar institution's darker side. Milton accepted the thesis holding that, if not for the extremists on both sides of the Mason-Dixon Line, the Civil War could have been avoided. For Milton, this was a tragedy. Had there been no war, he argued, "slavery would have soon died of its own economic immutability and . . . the relations between the white and Negro races would have been substantially better than they were in the 'Eighties or 'Nineties, and perhaps today." Milton, like other liberals, believed that white Southern hostility to blacks and Northerners was a consequence of "the stupidities and evils of Reconstruction." Particularly pernicious in his eyes were the Radical Republicans who undermined President Andrew Johnson's farsighted policy of "evolutionary readjustment" of race relations. Radical Reconstruction was destructive, and the biggest losers of all, according to Milton, were the freedmen.[13]

Alexander carefully tried to bring his organization to the attention of influential whites like Milton in the South's towns and cities. To head off racial violence in a community, he would, for example, get a white insurance broker and lawyer to exert pressure upon a sheriff to prevent a lynch mob from taking action. A newspaper editor who was friendly to the commission and who received its literature and press notices about the bad effects of racial violence could also be helpful in this regard. To increase the effectiveness of such processes, the commission's Atlanta office assembled files with the names of people reputed to be sympathetic to the aims of the organization. Alexander himself kept confidential notes on the extent to which certain individuals could be expected to support the commission's activities. In doing all this, he became a vital source of information about the South. Adept at obtaining money from Northern philanthropical foundations to finance his own organization, "Dr. Will," as he came to be called, could also obtain fellowships and grants from groups like the Rosenwald Fund for those who he believed possessed the talent and desire to make the South more tolerant.

Alexander kept the Interracial Commission broad enough to gain support from those whose liberalism was not as advanced as his own. One such man was M. Ashby Jones, an Atlanta Baptist minister. Jones joined the commission in 1919 because he felt "a high and holy responsibility for the future of the weaker race." He maintained that the refusal of the "better class" of white Southerners to treat the Negro as a Christian brother resulted in the dehumanization of blacks by lower-class whites who thus felt justified in committing acts of barbarism. Though Jones acknowledged that white Southerners needed to accept nonservile blacks, however, he characterized antebellum slavery as "the most benevolent that has ever been known" and painted the usual seamy picture of Reconstruction. Jones did argue that scientific evidence for Negro inferiority was flimsy and injurious to a people he preferred to call "disadvantaged," and he emphasized that such ideas, by giving whites a false sense of superiority, harmed them even more than blacks. However, since race consciousness did exist, the "integrity" (i.e., segregation) of each race had to be strictly maintained, he said. Uncertainty over this point during the Reconstruction era, Jones insisted, had caused great damage and led to deteriorating race relations that groups such as the Interracial Commission were only beginning to overcome. Given these views, it was hardly surprising that one white participant at a commission meeting at Tuskegee College that featured a speech by Jones observed that the predominantly black audience "didn't appreciate all the goodness in his attitude toward the problem." [14]

Alexander's desire to work with men like Jones did not prevent him from infusing the commission with younger, more liberal members. In 1926 Alexander visited the University of North Carolina and recruited Arthur F. Raper, a native of Winston-Salem and one of Howard Odum's most promising sociology students, to succeed Woofter as the organization's research director. Unlike Jones, Raper never thought that segregation was good or that it would last indefinitely. Alexander promised to get Raper away from the "brick buildings" of Chapel Hill and send him out to do research in local communities. While with the commission, Raper produced such seminal works as *The Tragedy of Lynching* in 1933 and three years later *Preface to Peasantry*, an account of the severe problems of white and black sharecroppers in two rural Georgia counties. Raper was among the first of "Alexander's boys"—young white Southerners who achieved prominence through their association with the Interracial Commission and Dr. Will.[15]

Alexander's loose confederation of liberals also included Southern white women. Before World War I women's church groups in the South had taken up causes of social betterment, but, except for helping individual Negroes, they had scrupulously avoided racial issues. In the spring of 1920, Alexander appeared before a meeting of the Woman's Council of the Southern Methodist Episcopal Church and told them that the war and its aftermath required them to rethink their programs relating to blacks. The Woman's Council appointed a committee headed by Mrs. Luke Johnson, the wife of a Georgia minister, to arrange a meeting with black church women. In October 1920 the interracial meeting took place in Memphis. Alexander was one of only four men present. As Mrs. Johnson was speaking, the black women filed in en masse. Everyone waited with bated breath to see what would happen. The white women proceeded to stand as a group as the Negro women started singing "Blessed Be the Tie That Binds," and emotions were so intense that during the singing many of the ladies cried openly. Soon after this meeting the Interracial Commission created a special women's division headed by Mrs. Johnson.

In 1924 Mrs. Johnson was replaced by a forty-year-old widow from Texas, Mrs. Jessie Daniel Ames. A veteran of the women's suffrage movement in Texas, Mrs. Ames was a woman of indomitable personality who remained with the commission for the next twenty years. She had an almost messianic sense of the unique role women could play in dealing with racial iniquities in the South and was frequently at odds with male co-workers who she felt stifled her own efforts. "I found that a woman can be borne down . . . with the making of gingham dresses and darning stockings in her few leisure hours," she once informed Mrs. Johnson, "instead of keeping fit in order to be able to go before the people in a none-too-popular cause and convert them to her belief." She thought Alexander a fine man but unsatisfying. "I am never sure that he has spoken freely when he talks to me. I am left with a general idea that he didn't go as far as he might have, if I were a man." [16]

This diverse group of people was held together by the same factor that had prompted Alexander to form the commission, abhorrence of racial bloodshed, and despite its activities in other areas during the 1920s and 1930s, the commission continued to perceive the prevention of mob violence as its primary task. The lynching of Negroes disturbed white liberals more than any other aspect of Southern race relations, and the need to stamp out the practice was one issue upon which all of them were in agreement. If Southern liberals wanted to make their presence known, lynching was the most logical target.

When the lynching of blacks had become widespread during the 1890s, some white liberals at first were not prepared. Atticus Haygood, for example, admitted that lynchings were barbarous, but apologetically said they resulted from black sexual assaults upon white women. Though he did not directly condone mob justice,

Haygood argued that the torture suffered by a ruined woman was greater than that of a burning black man. However, the continuation and increasingly brutal nature of lynching—bodies were often mutilated—ultimately led racial liberals to condemn it under any circumstances. In 1902 John C. Kilgo maintained that even rape did not justify mob violence and that the real cause of lynching was the whipping up of Southern racial sensitivities by demagogic politicians and newspaper editors.

At the same time they denounced lynching, white Southern liberals, unlike blacks and Northern liberals, opposed national action to deal with the problem. Kilgo, for instance, cautioned against Northern sympathy for black victims, arguing that it intensified an already charged atmosphere and lessened chances for cooler thought. Southern liberals thought that a federal antilynching law would repeat the Reconstruction futility of outside interference. When in 1929 the NAACP's Walter White wrote his lynching exposé, *Rope and Faggot*, to demonstrate the necessity of such legislation, they reacted coolly both to the book and the idea. Only white Southerners themselves, the liberals emphasized, could end lynching.[17]

To accomplish this, Southern liberals sought to convince fellow whites that lynching hurt them more than blacks. "The wrong that it does to the wretched victims," the Southern University Race Commission reported in 1916, "is almost as nothing compared to the injury it does to the lynchers themselves, to the community, and to society at large." Southern liberals also portrayed lynching as a stain upon the honor of the South. In 1919 an antilynching resolution of the Georgia Federation of Women's Clubs declared that "the fair name of our State" had been greatly damaged by recent lynchings, and the *Birmingham Age-Herald* described mob violence as a "corroding ulcer." Racial liberals argued, moreover, that failure to end the infamous practice would bring further grief to Southern whites. The *Atlanta Constitution* noted that unless the lynchings were stopped the federal government would eventually step in.[18]

The Interracial Commission attempted to give such sentiment some effective direction. Alexander believed that, though many white Southerners deplored mob violence, the majority still tolerated it, and that the commission should undertake its antilynching activities in a manner least likely to offend white sensibilities. Woofter, in his 1925 textbook, called lynching "the most spectacular and intensified" form of racial injustice. But he also characterized it as primarily a menace to white civilization and referred to the Dyer antilynching bills introduced in the Congress in 1922 and 1924 as "partisan and sectional" and thus foolhardy measures. In 1928 the commission, appealing to Southern churches with missions overseas, circulated a press release stating that lynching discredited American professions of Christianity abroad and that even heathen areas had no customs that paralleled its barbarities.[19]

In 1930 the frequency of lynching once again rose. South Carolina's Cole Blease said during his gubernatorial campaign that year that whenever the United States Constitution stood between himself and defending the virtue of white Southern womanhood, "to hell with the Constitution." In July the Interracial Commission moved more aggressively against mob violence and the spirit Blease represented by creating the Southern Commission for the Study of Lynching.

The Lynching Commission was composed of a blue-ribbon group of representatives from Southern newspapers, churches, and universities, chaired by George Fort Milton. Three Negroes, John Hope of Morehouse College, Robert R. Moton of Tuskegee, and Charles S. Johnson of Fisk, were also members. The Lynching Commission decided to undertake a detailed study of every lynching that occurred in the South for the year 1930. They chose Arthur Raper to conduct extensive investigations among whites in Southern communities where lynchings had occurred; and Walter Chivers, a sociology student at Atlanta University, did the same among blacks.[20]

The commission's findings resulted in the 1933 publication of Raper's *The Tragedy of Lynching*. The Interracial Commission distributed copies to almost every Southern newspaper and church. The book, published by the University of North Carolina Press, presented overwhelming documentation of something many people already knew: Southern blacks were almost always lynched for reasons other than assaults upon white women. Raper gave vivid accounts of the torture, mutilation, and burning of black lynch victims. "One is forced to the conviction," he wrote, "that their [the lynchers'] deeper motivation is a desire not for the just punishment of the accused so much as for an opportunity to participate in protected brutalities." Raper found that in every community where a lynching had occurred whites from all walks of life—professional people as well as lower classes—openly justified what had been done. In one case he found a county judge who called those who removed an accused black murderer from jail and hanged him an "orderly" mob of "high class" people. Raper presented every conceivable argument against lynching—ethical, economic, practical, and political. Walter White, a tireless campaigner against lynching who was often at odds with Southern liberals, congratulated Raper and said the book would do "a tremendous amount of good . . . because it was the New South itself speaking." [21]

The Tragedy of Lynching attracted wide attention in the South, almost all of it favorable so far as the commission could tell. Its findings, which few contested, did not come as a shock to white Southerners, and the book's detailed facts were difficult to dispute. The general receptiveness to *The Tragedy of Lynching* convinced Raper that there was sufficient antilynching sentiment in every Southern community to warrant a federal antilynching law, which would give witnesses to mob violence an opportunity to testify in a courtroom. His support for a federal law put him at odds with other members of the commission, particularly Jessie Daniel Ames.[22]

In November 1930 Mrs. Ames, who believed that women should spearhead the Southern antilynching movement, had organized in Atlanta an antilynching conference of twenty-six Southern white women to protest the idea that protection of their womanhood justified mob violence. The group expressed their complete dissatisfaction with the "crown of chivalry which has been pressed like a crown of thorns on our heads." They resolved that lynching did not serve as a deterrent to black sexual crimes and was instead a "menace to public safety" and "triumph of anarchy" that greatly brutalized the community in which it occurred, including women and children, who frequently witnessed these orgies. Lynching, they concluded, only brought contempt upon the South and discredited the Christian religion and the United States around the world.

The meeting, which had Will Alexander's approval, resulted in the formation of the Association of Southern Women for the Prevention of Lynching (ASWPL). Mrs. Ames herself later admitted that the association was never really an organization in any commonly understood meaning of the term. Its members did not pay dues, they held few meetings, and most of their work was done informally. The Interracial Commission totally financed the group's activities. The ASWPL hoped that the utterly respectable nature of its membership could bring pressure upon local police and political officials to see that no lynchings occurred in the members' communities. It had long been a tenet of racial liberals that if the "best people" only spoke out on the matter, lynchings could be averted. "I feel that the greatest help that could be done for lynching," said Willie Snow Ethridge, one of the ASWPL's founders, "would be for us who are intelligent to bring pressure to bear and let mobs know that when they do lynch we are going to do all in our power to bring them to justice." According to Mrs. Ethridge, the daughters of the South were going to "make war upon barbarism that has flourished in their name." [23]

Liberals failed to eliminate lynching from the South, but they contributed toward its steady diminution. Lynching did in fact decline markedly during the 1930s. Although it is difficult to make a direct correlation, the removal of vestiges of respectability from the practice by the ASWPL and the Southern Commission for the Study of Lynching undoubtedly aided the reduction.* Most white Southerners who knew of the groups' existence endorsed their findings, which received extensive and favorable coverage in Southern newspapers. In 1931, to be sure, Mrs. J. E. Andrews of Georgia did organize a Woman's National Association for the Protection of the White Race.

* Jacquelyn Dowd Hall, "Revolt against Chivalry: Jessie Daniel Ames and the Women's Campaign against Lynching," (Paper presented at annual meeting of the Southern Historical Association, Dallas, 1974). As Hall notes, the sociologist John Shelton Reed in "An Evaluation of an Anti-Lynching Organization," *Social Problems*, 16 (Fall 1968), 172–82 and "A Note on the Control of Lynching," *Graduate Sociology Society Journal*, Columbia University, 6 (September 1966), 6–11, offers evidence that the ASWPL had measurable success in preventing lynchings. Reed, classifying all Southern counties where lynchings occurred between 1919 and 1941 on the basis of the amount of "treatment" they received from Ames's group, found that lynching declined most dramatically after 1930 in those counties where the ASWPL had been most active.

TABLE

Persons Lynched in the United States, by Race: 1882–1956

YEAR	TOTAL	WHITE	NEGRO	YEAR	TOTAL	WHITE	NEGRO
1882	113	64	49	1920	61	8	53
1883	130	77	53	1921	64	5	59
1884	211	160	51	1922	57	6	51
1885	184	110	74	1923	33	4	29
1886	138	64	74	1924	16	—	16
1887	120	50	70	1925	17	—	17
1888	137	68	69	1926	30	7	23
1889	170	76	94	1927	16	—	16
1890	96	11	85	1928	11	1	10
1891	184	71	113	1929	10	3	7
1892	230	69	161	1930	21	1	20
1893	152	34	118	1931	13	1	12
1894	192	58	134	1932	8	2	6
1895	179	66	113	1933	28	4	24
1896	123	45	78	1934	15	—	15
1897	158	35	123	1935	20	2	18
1898	120	19	101	1936	8	—	8
1899	106	21	85	1937	8	—	8
1900	115	9	106	1938	6	—	6
1901	130	25	105	1939	3	1	2
1902	92	7	85	1940	5	1	4
1903	99	15	84	1941	4	—	4
1904	83	7	76	1942	6	—	6
1905	62	5	57	1943	3	—	3
1906	65	3	62	1944	2	—	2
1907	60	2	58	1945	1	—	1
1908	97	8	89	1946	6	—	6
1909	82	13	69	1947	1	—	1
1910	76	9	67	1948	2	1	1
1911	67	7	60	1949	3	—	3
1912	63	2	61	1950	2	1	1
1913	52	1	51	1951	1	—	1
1914	55	4	51	1952	—	—	—
1915	69	13	56	1953	—	—	—
1916	54	4	50	1954	—	—	—
1917	38	2	36	1955	3	—	3
1918	64	4	60	1956	—	—	—
1919	83	7	76				

SOURCE: U.S. Bureau of the Census, *Historical Statistics of the United States, Colonial Times to 1957* (Washington, 1960).

She told a North Carolina ASWPL member that "an organization of white mothers had arisen to defend our girls, both against negro men and you" and informed George Fort Milton that his commission was an unholy alliance between the Atlanta wing of Tammany liquor interests and the "National Association for the Advancement of negroes," which was dedicated to the ruination of the white race. But such expressions were few. Even Southern congressmen, though they filibustered against federal antilynching bills, no longer defended mob action. Instead, they argued that whites were dealing satisfactorily with the situation and that antilynching legislation was therefore unnecessary. Senator Tom Connally of Texas, the leader of the successful Southern effort to prevent enactment of the federal law, pointed out in 1940 that only two Negro lynchings had occurred in the previous year.[24]

Yet lynching remained frequent enough to provoke continued demands for a federal law against it, particularly from the NAACP. By 1935 many members of the Interracial Commission had come to agree with Raper that federal legislation was the next logical step toward the ultimate extinction of such barbarism. Mrs. Ames, however, remained adamantly opposed to any federal intrusion, even going so far as to provide Senator Connally with information he could use in leading the 1939 fight against the Gavagan antilynching bill. Jessie Ames, fearful her own efforts would be overshadowed and still insistent that her women's group was the most effective means of combating racial violence, confided that her position was "far from popular with the Commission."[25]

Because Southern liberals demanded prompt trials for accused Negro rapists as a safeguard against lynching, the infamous Scottsboro case in 1931 caught them off guard. For Alabama had convicted nine black youths in kangaroo-court proceedings that amounted to a legal lynching. "It is a problem that never confronted us before and it is hard to get the proper perspective," one unnerved ASWPL member wrote Jessie Ames. "Just as we adjust our thinking and act upon one line of cooperation and justice, something new comes up to confront us." Mrs. Ames herself realized that at Scottsboro a lynching was averted only "at the expense of the integrity of the law."[26]

Outspokenness over Scottsboro, however, required a degree of militancy that the liberals associated with the Interracial Commission lacked. They showed no great initial inclination to take over the defense of the nine youths, and when the International Labor Defense League finally hired the New York attorney Samuel S. Liebowitz to handle the case, they argued that outside interference only jeopardized the boys' chance for a fair trial. Will Alexander, clearly disturbed by the controversy surrounding the case, instructed the secretary for the commission's Atlanta office to conduct an investigation into the backgrounds of Victoria Price and Ruby Bates, the two white women whom the blacks allegedly had raped. A detective agency in Huntsville confirmed the fact that they were prostitutes, but the commission failed to publicize this finding, and white Southerners continued to assert that such allegations were only the lies of non-Southern agitators who wanted to defame the women's characters. Though the Interracial Commission observed the case closely, Alexander carefully avoided public statements that would identify his group with either Liebowitz or the Labor Defense League. It is true that matters were greatly complicated by the Communists, who tried to reap propaganda out of the case; nevertheless, the Scottsboro affair revealed the weakness of racial liberalism in the South. When the NAACP tried to get the Interracial Commission to join it in wresting the case from Communist control and defending the Scottsboro boys, the commission rebuffed its efforts.[27]

The commission's trepidations in dealing with the Scottsboro affair increased already existing black disenchantment with the organization. In 1926 W. E. B. Du Bois had criticized the Interracial Commission for its failure to work with younger, more militant Negro leaders. Northern blacks frequently argued that the white racial liberals who ran the commission deliberately misled Southern blacks to keep them in a subordinate position. In truth, blacks had very little voice in the organization, and their main function was to lend an aura of black support for the commission's activities. As of 1934 there was only one paid Negro in the organization, and no Negroes worked in the commission's Atlanta office. Moreover, the whites who determined the commission's policies decried any signs of black militancy, which they thought would only worsen race relations. Indeed the liberals' interest in justice for Negroes was motivated in part by the desire to avert indigenous black protest.[28]

The shortcomings of the Commission on Interracial Cooperation were numerous. In attempting to soften and humanize segregation as it was practiced in the South during the 1920s and 1930s, the commission in effect sanctioned the idea of the Southern Negro as a second-class citizen. All the good will and sensitivity to the problems of blacks shared by white Southern liberals did not obviate this fact. When in time the caste structure of the South came under direct attack by blacks and Northern whites, Alexander's organization would begin to look more like an obstacle than a stimulus to progress. Furthermore, segregation was such a dominant fact of Southern life during these years that the interracialism of the commission was necessarily forced and artificial. William O. Brown, a white Southerner who taught sociology at the University of Cincinnati, noted in 1933 that sessions between "mutually ghettoized" Southern whites and blacks had a "farcical" aspect about them.[29] Finally, the commission too frequently substituted expressions of optimism for genuine achievements.

Inevitable conflict arose between white liberals associated with the commission and those demanding bolder actions to deal with racial problems in the South. When in 1933 Louis R. Reynolds of the North Carolina Interracial Commission heard that a Negro in Greensboro was organizing a civil liberties defense council, he strongly doubted the value of such an organization. "I think we might as well get prepared to find all kinds of radicalism at work even in the remote places," he told a fellow commission member, "and perhaps some of our so-called sane leaders, giving ear to its teachings." Another North Carolina commission member, N. C. Newbold, characterized Negroes who wanted to undertake legal action against discriminatory treatment by Southern school systems as "a few irresponsible individuals who apparently would be willing to scrap much of the good that has been done in order it seems to get themselves further into the limelight." [30]

By the mid-1930s the commission had lost much of its earlier vitality. It continued to agitate for better treatment of Negroes within the confines of a Jim Crow system at a time when more and more people—especially blacks themselves—were beginning to question the discriminatory nature of segregation itself. The NAACP's early suits in the area of discrimination in Southern education did not augur well for the commission. In the spring of 1935, Will Alexander left Atlanta for Washington to work under Rexford Tugwell in the Resettlement Administration. Though Alexander retained the directorship of the commission, the actual running of the organization fell into the hands of less dynamic subordinates. A white Southern organization to fight lynching and promote less discriminatory treatment for Southern blacks may have seemed novel in 1919, but in the South of the depression years it was beginning to appear excessively patronizing, a bit stale, and too much a part of the racial status quo.

As a result of the Commission on Interracial Cooperation, Southern liberals had been induced to speak out more forcefully than they had in the past. Whether they any longer spoke loud enough or to the point, however, remained an open question.

Still, it was through this commission that modern Southern liberalism came of age. When George Washington Cable had dissented from the anti-Negro racial practices of the 1880s, his striking lack of success in opening up intelligent debate, combined with the denunciations that he received from his fellow white Southerners, led ultimately to his decision to leave the region permanently. The Southern Populists' occasional flirtations with enlightened policies toward blacks had also failed to promote racial liberalism. The legacy of the Populists, despite the initial appeals of some of their white leaders for cooperation between poor Southern whites and blacks, was in the end counterproductive—a bitter heritage of racism and demagoguery. The Interracial Commission, on the other hand, not only managed to flourish in the South, but with the leadership of Will Alexander it moved, at times hesitatingly and always under great constraints, toward spreading the realization among a significant minority of Southern whites that racial inequities were the South's gravest problem. Although the commission did not have clearly defined policies—too many of its members made different, often mutually exclusive, pronouncements—the members all agreed that Southern blacks were being treated badly and unfairly, and that to perpetuate this treatment for the sake of "white supremacy" was wrong. Moreover, some whites in every part of the South (more, to be sure, in Atlanta and Chapel Hill than in Mississippi, but nonetheless even in Mississippi) were influenced by and supportive of the commission's approach.

But Southern liberalism paid a price for the accomplishments of the Commission on Interracial Cooperation. When Cable had called upon a Silent South to promote racial justice, he had spoken out against the intimidation, disfranchisement, and segregation of blacks. His successors, however, dropped their opposition to segregation and disfranchisement and limited their disapproval largely to intimidation, the most extreme example of which was, of course, lynching. For some this retreat was mainly tactical. Will Alexander adopted a moderate stance because he thought the commission could do more to help Southern blacks in this way than it could by challenging Jim Crow head-on. But for many Southern liberals, such as M. Ashby Jones, the reluctance to criticize segregation and disfranchisement represented a basic commitment, however softly voiced, to these policies. Those who carried forward Cable's plea kept the issue of racial justice alive, but because it was difficult to distinguish between the tactical and ideological adherents of separate-but-equal within their own ranks, Southern liberals would have great difficulty in dealing with a race issue that, by the 1930s, was becoming considerably more complex.

As entrenched as racial discrimination in the South seemed, changes were in the air. To a large extent, the maintenance of a Jim Crow South depended on the acquiescence of Northerners to the assumptions of blatant racists. This was becoming much less certain in the era of the Interracial Commission than it had been during the late nineteenth and early twentieth centuries. The concept of innate Negro inferiority, which had been advanced by scholars and commentators disillusioned by Reconstruction, was being attacked by social scientists such as Franz Boaz and John Dollard. Increasingly, their views were prevailing. Moreover, black migration from the rural South to both Northern and Southern cities was greatly expanding the influence that a previously powerless minority group could bring to bear on its own situation. In 1930 the NAACP aided in defeating the nomination of the North Carolina Judge John J. Parker to the Supreme Court because of his racial views. This portended developments that Southern liberals would not have predicted: the growing influence of black protest, a political alliance between organized labor and blacks, the growing importance of the black vote, the movement of blacks into the Democratic party, and the willingness of Northern Democrats to abandon their Southern colleagues on race-related issues. Together, these factors would greatly reduce the complacency of Southern liberals and force some to make difficult, wrenching decisions.[31]

A man whose career demonstrates the kind of painful transitions that many Southern liberals would have to make was the University of North Carolina sociologist Howard W. Odum.

The Silent South of Howard Odum

Howard Odum, who during a long academic career would write some twenty books and over two hundred articles on his native region, to a large extent considered himself the archetypal white Southerner of his generation. He was born in 1884 on a farm near Bethlehem, Georgia, and grew up in an era when memories of the Civil War and Reconstruction were still vividly ingrained in the lives of people he knew.[1] His family owned its own farm and was neither poor nor well off. His maternal grandfather had been a plantation-holding slaveowner, while his paternal one was a small yeoman farmer who had owned his own land but no slaves. Both had supported the Confederacy. For Odum, they and their progeny represented the backbone of the white South and epitomized "Southern" racial, religious, and social attitudes.[2]

Odum's early education was the product of hard work, borrowed money, and rural teaching, and was grounded mainly in the classics. In 1897, in order to send their children to the staunchly Southern Methodist Emory Academy and College, his parents moved to Oxford, Georgia. Odum received his A.B. from Emory in 1904 and then taught at a rural school in Toccopola, Mississippi. Toccopola was only twenty-one miles from Oxford, the location of the University of Mississippi, and Odum frequently commuted to "Ole Miss," teaching as a fellow, studying, collecting local folklore, and observing and recording facts about Negro life in the area. In 1906 he earned his M.A. in classics there.

At Ole Miss, Odum came under the influence of Thomas Pearce Bailey, a native of South Carolina who was professor of psychology and education. Bailey had recently received his Ph.D. in psychology from Clark University in Worcester, Massachusetts, where he had worked under the pioneering American psychologist G. Stanley Hall. At Mississippi Bailey established a seminar to study the race question in the empirical spirit of his mentor at Clark. Bailey as a boy had "red shirted" for Wade Hampton to help the Confederate war hero run the carpetbaggers out of South Carolina, and as a scholar he was steeped in social science literature that purportedly "proved" that blacks were congenitally inferior to whites. Thus he held racial views that were entirely conventional in turn-of-the-century Mississippi. Nevertheless, Bailey believed that the South's racial situation required further impartial inquiry. "It is science and science alone," he passionately insisted, "star eyed science, spiritually intellectual science—it is the Twentieth Century's greatest power, the scientific research of today, that can prepare us for the . . . solution of this [race] problem." [3]

Bailey passed on his enthusiasm for scientific racial studies to young Odum who, under the professor's influence, changed his interest from the classics to the social sciences. Bailey encouraged Odum to gather data about blacks and work toward an eventual doctoral degree. Armed with a collection of Negro folk songs and studies of Negro town life, Odum completed two Ph.D.'s: one with Hall at Clark in 1909 in folklore and a second in 1910 in sociology with Franklin H. Giddings at Columbia.

Both of Odum's dissertations were soon published and quickly established him as an authority in his field. His Clark study of Negro folk songs appeared as scholarly articles in 1909 and 1911 and revealed that Odum possessed, in addition to devotion to the social sciences, an almost mystical belief in the virtues of "the people." Indeed, beneath the outward image of tough-minded empiricist lurked a romantic. Resulting tensions made Odum a prolific but often confusing writer, who at times gave the impression that even the indeterminate could be scientifically ascertained: "To know the soul of a people and to find the source from which flows the expression of folk-thought is to comprehend in a large measure the capabilities of that people." Odum meticulously studied a black folk music tradition replete with stories about vagabonds, gigolos, infidelity, gambling, jealousy, and assorted everyday wants and emotions. Reflecting the racial attitudes then still prevalent in scholarly as well as in common thought, he concluded that black folk music, while unique and beautiful in its own way, nevertheless offered empirical evidence that Negroes as a race were mentally and morally inferior to whites.

> It will thus be seen that the songs of the most characteristic type are far from elegant. Nor are they dignified in theme or expression. They will appear to the cultured reader a bit repulsive, to say the least. They go beyond the interesting point to the trite and repulsive themes. Nor can a great many of the common songs that are too inelegant to include be given at all. But these are folk songs current among the Negroes, and as such are powerful comment upon the special characteristics of the group.

Even what he described as the "doleful and gruesome" verses of early blues songs only convinced him of the "wantonness and simplicity" of blacks.[4]

Odum's Columbia dissertation, published in 1910 as *Social and Mental Traits of the Negro,* offered a massively detailed but grim portrayal of Southern Negro life. The aim of the study was to understand the "real" Negro, which for the scientifically minded Odum meant an objective treatment. (He often used the word "organic" interchangeably with "objective.") Odum scrupulously investigated black Southern churches, fraternal organizations, health conditions, schools, criminal offenses, and attitudes toward labor, morals, and family life. He did this because in his mind any ultimate solution of the Southern race question required adaptation to known conditions. Emotional responses, be they pro- or anti-Negro, would not help the situation, for they had failed to do so in the past. Whites had to be fully aware of blacks' experiences, capacities, and current status before they could undertake any particular racial policies. Odum's own early research led him to the conclusion that blacks differed fundamentally from whites. "Little need be said concerning social and political equality," insisted Odum. "There is no absolute race equality in any sense of the word. The races have different abilities and potentialities. Those who would assist the Negro should remember this and not exact too much of him, either in demanding his results or offering him the completed ideals of the whites." [5] Odum was to revise these opinions when anthropological and psychological findings after the First World War contradicted his early studies, and in 1936 he would refuse to allow his publisher to reprint *Social and Mental Traits.* [6]

After spending the next two years in Philadelphia, where he studied the status of blacks in public schools for the city's Bureau of Municipal Research, Odum returned to the South in 1912. He first went to the University of Georgia and from there to Emory to be professor of sociology and dean of liberal arts. While at Emory, Odum aided the school's move from Oxford to Atlanta and its transition to university status. In 1920, his professional credentials thoroughly established, Odum moved on to the University of North Carolina at Chapel Hill, where he was to stay for the next thirty-four years. The Georgia-born scholar was instrumental in transforming North Carolina from a relatively undistinguished Southern state university into the foremost educational institution in the South.

Odum spent his first few years at Chapel Hill organizing a department of sociology, initiating and editing the *Journal of Social Forces*, and establishing the school's soon-to-be-renowned Institute for Research in Social Science. Odum fit in well with North Carolina's dedication to the "Wisconsin idea" that the prime function of a state university was to be of service to the people of the state. He hoped that the *Journal of Social Forces*, first published in 1922, would serve as a link between the university and a larger community. *Social Forces* carried news items and service information as well as academic articles, which was unusual for a scholarly publication. Odum wished the magazine to contribute toward making democracy work more effectively in the "unequal places," those parts of the South where poverty and caste were still prevalent. In accordance with his scientific outlook, he wanted its contribution to be "definite," "concrete," "substantial," and "clear-thinking," in line with "reality." "What is needed . . . is not simply subjective theorizing," said Odum, "but essential facts and broad bases upon which objective programs may be based." He spoke of the "great danger" of "self-appointed intellectuals" or "pure experimentalists" who possessed the ability to discover facts but who lacked either the inclination or the competence to devise programs. Odum warned of the "provincial autocracy" of learned individuals who could not apply their ideas to the world, and he hoped to avoid their errors.[7]

Odum recognized that the race issue was the most difficult question that *Social Forces* would face. But the new journal would not ignore it; even in this touchy area Odum hoped to make substantial contributions. *Social Forces* reflected its founder's belief that racial problems could be dealt with dispassionately. Reason would prevail once people recognized that the relationship between Southern whites and blacks was a complex yet discernible phenomenon that needed scientific solutions. To Odum the Ku Klux Klan was not so much an evil group as one of "unscientific and . . . unthinking agitators." A trained sociologist, he thought, surely had better insights than the Klan.[8]

Odum's perception of the South focused on the white middle class. This was the group from which he had come and on which he believed the success or failure of the region depended. Such people, according to Odum, were the product of a painful history, and their attitudes toward blacks, if not justifiable, were at least explainable. These whites were the majority, and the status of Southern blacks could change only with their approval. Odum believed this approval could be obtained. He insisted that white Southerners had a tremendous capacity for goodness, but that they were the victims of circumstances that led them to perpetrate numerous evils. Odum's dictum was that white Southerners were the best people in the world who often did the world's worst things.

During the 1920s, many assailed these white Southerners for their racial intolerance, religious bigotry, and general ignorance. The South was frequently portrayed as a land of cultural stagnation. H. L. Mencken, America's foremost social commentator of the time, referred to the region as the "Sahara of the Bozart." *

* Mencken's "Sahara of the Bozart" essay (playing on the words "beaux arts") had a great impact on Southern writers and intellectuals after it appeared in his *Preju-*

Such attacks made Odum uneasy. "The North's attitude toward the South and its wild opinions and judgments about us sometimes provoke me," he admitted in 1926, "and I can sympathize with those who feel that propaganda on the South is one of the chief indoor sports of unstable folk in other climes." Odum was aware that more than enough barbarities took place to lend credence to the South's critics, but this "Southerner of Southerners," as he frequently called himself, believed that outsiders also needed enlightenment, particularly Mr. Mencken.[9]

Mencken was an irrepressible critic of the South whose "caustic ebullience," as one historian described his prose, could lead him to castigate the barbarity of white lynchers and stupidity of black "coons" in the same sentence. He was at his best (or worst) during the 1925 Scopes trial in Dayton, Tennessee, when he characterized local whites who opposed the teaching of evolution in public schools as "morons," "hillbillies," and "peasants" and referred to the "degraded nonsense which country preachers are ramming and hammering into yokel skulls." In 1923 Mencken praised Odum for his objectivity in dealing with the subject of race relations and suggested that the main problem in the South was the rising power of "low grade" Caucasians who were rapidly blighting the region. He wanted the degeneracy of such people exposed so that Southerners could reinvigorate their cultural life and come to grips with pressing problems.[10]

Odum shared Mencken's goal, but not his analysis of the South, and he did not blame the South's ills on the poor whites. Speaking of his native Georgia, Odum said that the two dominant personalities who had done more harm to the state in recent years than all other forces combined—the political demagogue Tom Watson and the ec-

dices: Second Series (New York, 1920). It outraged some, but stimulated others. Odum himself was among a small circle of Southerners who exchanged detailed thoughts with Mencken about the region's virtues and vices. Others included the newspapermen W. J. Cash of the *Charlotte Observer* and Gerald W. Johnson of the *Greensboro Daily News*. Johnson eventually joined Mencken as an editor for the *Baltimore Sun* and Cash's speculations, heavily laced with ideas developed in correspondence with Mencken, were published in his now classic *The Mind of the South* (New York, 1941). Mencken's gibes, in short, prompted serious intellectual efforts on the part of liberal white Southerners. See Joseph L. Morrison, *W. J. Cash: Southern Prophet* (New York, 1967).

clesiastic reactionary Warren A. Candler—both came from a relatively high social class. "I can cite to you many of the reactionary leaders," Odum informed Mencken, "and you will find them ranking among those of the older lineage. Some of their very unsocial, reactionary, and exclusive principles have led to at least a part of the mob reaction that has followed the war." Odum later explained to Josephus Daniels, the former Secretary of the Navy and editor of the *Raleigh News and Observer*, that many middle- and lower-class whites—he cited the example of his own family—refused to be swept into the Klan or other organized expressions of political and religious intolerance. Though Odum found that the current tide pushed other, equally sincere men into such movements, he refused to censure them for their bigoted actions. "It has been largely a matter of wrong leadership and a lack of chance to free expression and worship," he concluded. For Odum, intolerance and an attraction to demagogues were not a natural inclination of the mass of Southern white people but "simply a stage in the undeveloped technique of democracy and social development." The anti-South hyperbole resulting from the Scopes trial deeply perturbed him. He found the satire and jests of the critics superficial, an evasion of their responsibility to come up with suggestions to avoid similar fiascos. Odum spoke disgustedly of a "learned ignorati" who dismissed Southerners for having an inferior mentality. This was self-defeating. The proper role of intellectuals, he contended, was to close rather than widen the gulf between educated and common people.[11]

Odum outlined his developing ideas in an introduction to a 1925 volume that he had edited on social thought in the South.[12] He began by asking why the South no longer produced such leaders as Washington, Jefferson, Jackson, Lee, and Wilson. Odum rejected the notion that the region did not have the potential for positive leadership and said that the South needed more of the "spirit of the university," which he defined as the free pursuit of knowledge and ideals. A lack of open-mindedness had brought about the "querulous" and "pessimistic" South of the 1920s.

In his assessment, Odum explained contemporary difficulties much as Cable had in the 1880s. Racial sensitivity was still the overriding factor. White Southerners of the current generation, however, were afraid not of "Negro domination" but of themselves. They feared truth "because of what the folks will say," and they were also afraid to face what they regarded as unwarranted criticism by Northerners. In addition, most Southerners usually esteemed those whom Odum called "the demagogues and dogmatics in politics and religion." As long as these attitudes prevailed, the South stagnated; the promise of a just and prosperous region remained unfulfilled.[13]

Odum's major contribution toward realizing the Southern promise was as a scholar and university teacher. He strove to liberate racial studies from the biases of the past, insisting that new research in the field had to be truly scientific.[14] In 1925 and 1926, in collaboration with Guy B. Johnson, a fellow sociologist at the University of North Carolina, Odum wrote two books on black folk music that were relatively free of the Anglo-Saxon moralizing that had characterized his earlier treatments.[15] The books coincided with a rising, if not faddish, white interest in Negro folk culture that prompted Odum to undertake one of his more ambitious projects.

What he had in mind was a semifictional account of Southern Negro life based upon his authoritative knowledge of black folklore. At first glance, it seems illogical for such a hard-nosed empiricist to want to write a novel, especially when the writer was given to prose so turgid—"Odumesque" his own students called it—as to be almost incomprehensible. Yet, however difficult it would have been for him to admit it, much of Odum's writing on the South was impressionistic, even sentimental. The poetic appeal of the farm and the black belt was as important to his work as the scholarly influence of the classroom and the library. Typically, Odum used science to justify his fusion of art and sociology; he claimed that together they could provide a "portraiture" of life more realistic than that offered by either discipline alone.[16]

In 1927 Odum began *Rainbow Round My Shoulder,* the first novel of a trilogy dealing with the wanderings of a "Black Ulysses." [17] The work was based upon the experiences of an itinerant black construction worker whom the author had once overheard and whom he later befriended. At times, Odum descended into a literary vogue of the twenties that led white writers to portray blacks as romantic yet shiftless darkies. But on the whole, his black character was more than a stereotype. Left-wing Gordon, the one-armed hero of the books, was a product of a particular time and place. He was a likeable rogue whose humanity, manliness, and sense of humor offset numerous personality flaws. Odum explained the conditions that had produced this Black Ulysses in language showing that he no longer accepted a racial explanation for black behavior:

> Town and village homes of the Southern Negro. Parents and children in the hard way of life. Children disciplined, consciously and unconsciously in the strenuous give and take of the Southern order. Survival values of hard work, required deference and obedience, unheeded admonitions, irregularity of food, sleep, work, play and school. A people peculiarly separate from the white folk at home and school and church. Strikingly close to the white man and keen observers of his life, manners and morals at his work and play. At once servants and critics, imitators and molders of the white man's destiny. Paradox of light-hearted, jovial good nature and humor, with silent, morose, ill-natured and sullen tempers and moods. A dispensation of hard work and economy of the world's goods alongside shiftlessness and undisciplined wastefulness in the chief modes of life. Broken homes and family disorganization, open strife and struggle, wasted energies and resources in men, women and children. Nature folk in an uneven struggle for survival and development. Black Ulysses himself, the child, an every-day example of millions of his kinsfolk at the turn of the twentieth century and after.[18]

Odum constantly reminded *Rainbow's* publisher, Bobbs-Merrill, that the book had to be authentic as well as lively and interesting; only the moral sensibilities of the day prevented him from using the profanity of Black Ulysses' real-life prototype or dealing more explicitly with his sexual feelings. Though Odum did not hesitate to portray his hero's weaknesses, some of which conformed to racial stereotypes, his devotion to accuracy led him to reject some of the traditional ways in which blacks were usually represented in literature. For example, Odum expressed displeasure with the original illustrations for *Rainbow*. He instructed artists to "soften down the details of mouth and facial expression" so that blacks were not illustrated as "minstrel types," a detail which, if not corrected, Odum believed could mar the whole intent of the book. In the preparation of the subsequent volumes of the trilogy, he would again admonish artists to portray Negroes with dignity. Odum spared no effort to make *Rainbow* as authentic as possible, once traveling to Atlanta to contact "the one person in the South perhaps best equipped to give me a complete and vivid description of the really artistic Negro crap game." He himself said of the completed work: "The story shows up the black man in pretty realistic form and sometimes seems a little hard on him, but the story is first and last an exact picture and as such must stand. It is a sort of untouched photograph, nevertheless presented with the idea that the Negro after all is a human being, with a sort of timeless and spaceless folk urge. . . . We have refused to sentimentalize the Negro, on the one hand, or to ignore his finer points of humor, pathos, and poignancy." *Rainbow Round My Shoulder,* though condescending, nevertheless represented an advance over *Social and Mental Traits of the Negro.*[19]

Odum's racial outlook made him a close associate of members of the Commission on Interracial Cooperation, including Will Alexander. Though he did not formally become a member of the commission until 1927, Odum worked closely with the group from the time he came to the University of North Carolina. With the Interracial Commission's aid, he helped coordinate the sociology departments of Southern universities in the teaching of undergraduate courses on race relations. In addition, Odum's Institute for Research in Social Science cooperated with the commission in a number of specific racial studies. Odum's own temperament blended in well with the generally pragmatic viewpoint of Alexander's group, and as an academic leader he used his influence to drum up support for the activities of the Interracial Commission's North Carolina committee.

Odum expressed many of the attitudes peculiar to Southern liberals. He showed a marked disdain for any cooperation with Walter White or the NAACP, an organization he regarded as a well-meaning but unscientific agitation agency that did more harm than good. Moreover, Odum thought that the South was not ready for militant action over social issues. During 1928 and 1929 a series of events convinced him that sectionalism had risen to a dangerous level. There was great southern hostility to the presidential nomination of the wet, Catholic governor of New York, Alfred E. Smith; violence generated by a textile workers' strike in Gastonia, North Carolina demonstrated the South's opposition to organized labor; and a meeting between Mrs. Herbert Hoover and the wife of Illinois Republican Representative Oscar De Priest, the first black to win election to Congress since Reconstruction, resulted in a white Southern outcry against "social equality." Odum saw Southern liberals being squeezed by radicals on both sides, and he drew parallels between current emotions and those described by Claude Bowers in his saga of post–Civil War America, *The Tragic Era*. "It is after all a near serious and tragic era," said Odum in 1929, "in which the militant elements of Christianity," who were busy criticizing the South, "and the dogmatic fundamentalists," who were busy defending it, together might "obscure the real spirit of Christianity." When in the wake of the Gastonia violence the University of North Carolina came under attack for its failure to mediate the strike and prevent bloodshed, Odum demanded that Northern spokesmen clean their own houses first. The University of North Carolina, Odum explained to the sociologist William F. Ogburn, was no more to blame for Gastonia than the University of Chicago was responsible for the rantings of Mayor William H. "Big Bill" Thompson and the city's gang warfare.[20]

Odum's sensitivity to outside criticism of the South reflected his own mixed emotions regarding the behavior of white Southerners. He loved them and certainly considered himself one of them, but in his own writings he increasingly denounced their racial prejudices and intolerance toward anyone who even remotely threatened traditional values. In 1931 Odum became depressed over the difficulties involved in trying to make North Carolina a great university and at the same time not lose contact with the people of the state. He spoke of his own mother and father as "typical of the best of the common people," but added that one could not expect them to have ideas about how a university should be run. Odum acknowledged his growing awareness that perhaps, after all, the expert and the common folk could not act as one. "Love the people, yes, but don't let them misrule by ruling in a technological situation," he said. "Worship them, yes, but don't let them rule or ruin. Slave for them, yes, but do it by standing by their interest and not their mob psychology."[21] Odum was cautious about pushing white middle-class Southerners too hard, yet he pinned his hopes for change on these very same people, whom he idealized, often excessively. This caused him frustration and accounted for his often hazy stands on racial issues.

Odum usually attributed the discriminatory actions of white Southerners to "folkways" that had evolved over centuries. Though he did not go so far as to say that such habits would take as long to change, he adamantly insisted that they could not be restructured overnight, save at great cost. This was, for example, his reaction to W. E. B. Du Bois's *Black Reconstruction*, a book highly critical of post–Civil War Southern whites for their failure to extend full democracy to blacks.[22]

In some areas, however, he fully recognized that white Southern folkways had to be altered immediately. Odum, who served on the Southern Commission for the Study of Lynching, could explain how the practice of mob justice toward blacks took root in the South. But lynching had to be eradicated, even if it meant enacting laws that conflicted with established customs. In a 1931 article for the *Nation*, Odum denounced the practice as totally unjustified.

> Lynching attains none of the ends for which it has been defended. It proves no superiority. It glorifies no issues. It brings no happiness. It adds nothing to the richness of human living or the development of social personality. It accentuates devastating fear. It sets the folkways over against the stateways in lawless revolt. It cheapens human life and lessens respect for human liberty and personality. It defeats the ends of justice. It violates all the better traditions of Southern honor and ideals. It sets the strong brutally over the weak. It negates the South's charm for excellence and genius in the science of politics. Its cost is frightful in money and in men. It drains off energies and resources. It blackens the reputation of every State. It cripples a race and handicaps a region. It intensifies social animosities, isolates a section, sets people against people, and retards a wholesome integration of national culture.[23]

In 1930 Odum published *An American Epoch*, a highly personalized account of Southern history since the Civil War generation based upon the experiences of members of his own family. Indeed, his principal characters, "Old Major" and "Uncle John," were patterned after his grandfathers. Aside from his then still unwritten

Southern Regions of the United States, it probably stands out as his best and most enduring single work. In it Odum aimed to do for the whole South what he had set out to do with Negroes in the Black Ulysses novels—combine art with social science to offer the firmest possible understanding of the subject. In 1929 he told W. J. Cash, a North Carolina newspaperman who was then working on *The Mind of the South*, that he planned to have the book "largely in episodes and pictures with very little of the philosophical appraisals except by indirection and portraiture." [24]

Though Odum saw that the South was making progress in abandoning some of the old sectional ideals, *American Epoch* described a region still shackled by color consciousness. The race issue, he noted, crept into other problems and held the South in "mental and spiritual bondage." To be sure, the frequency of lynching had been reduced, and white Southerners now generally recognized the validity of the black man's claim to an education and economic opportunities. Yet widespread resistance still existed toward any substantial upgrading of Southern Negroes. White chauvinism, the experience of Reconstruction, and the usual unwillingness to face the problem, Odum pointed out, prevented Southern blacks from becoming productive citizens. But injustice to blacks was only half the South's racial tragedy; whites, too, paid for their racism. Odum spoke of the "bare-faced reality that nowhere, perhaps, was there a white person who had an untrammeled freedom to develop, free from racial prejudice or imposed conditioning." Yet he saw a paradox: blind racial prejudice existed side by side with love and respect for individual blacks. It would be the task of white Southern liberals, Odum insisted, to reduce the one and facilitate the other through a process of adjustment that had to be gradual:

> The appeal of many liberal Southerners was that they be not asked to accomplish the impossible, or that they be urged with undue pressure to hasten issues which in another generation would probably not exist. They wanted to meet whatever issues came in the day's work but they regretted the tendency to search out issues of conflict in which to test the strength, will, and endurance of those who were to carry the load. It was, they thought, expecting too much of humans to turn back the hands of time, to violate the laws of science, or to turn against family

and friends on issues that if not forced to the test, would gradually adjust themselves.

American Epoch once again expressed Odum's ambivalence over the nature of any liberal South. At one point he argued that vehement white supremacists reflected genuine sentiments among the people; at another he claimed that the Southern people were better than their demagogic leaders who "exerted a dominance entirely out of proportion to the esteem in which they were held." Despite the inconsistencies, however, the book generally affirmed the existence of a submerged, more just, more genuine, potentially more liberal South than was portrayed in most discussions.

For Odum, the "middling" white folk of his own family background made up this South. "Much of the glory that was the South and of the grandeur that was *not* was found in the experiences of the millions of middle-folk not commonly recorded in the annals," he wrote. "Indeed the culture of the Old South and of the new was found exclusively neither in the romanticism of its aristocratic gentry nor in the tragedy and comedy of the much described poor whites, but in the living drama of its common folks." If there was a Southern spirit that was hopeful rather than destructive, it was carried by such people. If there was a Southern promise to fulfill, they would be the ones to fulfill it. Along with blacks, this middle group of Southern whites provided the main cultural component of the modern South. But the folk spirit of Southern Negroes—represented by Black Ulysses—was still shiftless and unpredictable, in Odum's view, compared with the yeoman virtues of his own Silent South.[25]

Odum's conception of this Silent South was the key to his developing ideology of "regionalism," a word that during the 1930s and 1940s would be practically synonymous with his name.* Regionalism became the widely accepted Southern liberal alternative to the steadfast, sometimes Negrophobic agrarianism of a heretic faction of white liberals, the Vanderbilt "fugitives," who in 1930 offered their anti-in-

* This is not to say that the regionalist outlook identified with Chapel Hill was solely the work of Odum. Others, particularly Rupert B. Vance, contributed a great deal. See Vance, *Human Factors in Cotton Culture: A Study in the Social Geography of the American South* (Chapel Hill, 1929) and *Human Geography of the South* (Chapel Hill, 1932).

dustrial views in *I'll Take My Stand.** Like the agrarians, who defended their beloved Dixieland to the point of making its vices appear as virtues, Odum acknowledged the peculiarities of the South, and indeed of all regions of the United States. In contrast to the Vanderbilt group, however, Odum denied that all Southern peculiarities were good. Racism, intellectual intolerance, and fear of outside criticism, he wrote, were as Southern as magnolia blossoms yet highly malignant; they were the main components of "sectionalism," the struggle for supremacy between rival areas, which had manifested itself in slavery, civil war, violent resistance to Reconstruction, the Ku Klux Klan, lynching, and racial discrimination. Regionalism, on the other hand, would be an antidote to sectionalism.

The regionalists, led by Odum, saw the United States as being naturally divided into six distinct regions. Kentucky plus the former Confederate states with the exception of Texas composed the "Southeast." (The others were the Northeast, the Middle States, the Northwest, the Far West, and the Southwest, which included Texas.) The regionalists' principal argument was that resource planning could advance the nation's welfare provided the differences between the six regions were taken into account. In their view, the whole would, and should, be greater than the sum of its parts. To ignore that there were parts, however, would create "dead levels of uniformity" and destroy the cultural and physical diversities that added richness to American life. Thus regionalism must be a reference point for all social research and planning. Odum proposed a national planning agency that would adopt the regionalist approach while recognizing that the Southeast needed the most attention.[26]

In 1936 Odum published *Southern Regions of the United States*, which quickly became the regionalist bible. Over six hundred pages

* Twelve Southerners, *I'll Take My Stand: The South and the Agrarian Tradition* (New York, 1930). Agrarianism derived many of its values from the classical liberalism of John Locke and John Stuart Mill, but the views of the agrarians (who were led by John Crowe Ransom, Donald Davidson, Allen Tate, and John Donald Wade) differed so greatly from those of most Southern liberals as to what constituted a proper basis for progress in the South that they belong in a different category. The implications of *I'll Take My Stand*, if not outright racist, were at least hardline white supremacist (though some of the agrarians—particularly Robert Penn Warren and H. C. Nixon—later changed their views about blacks).

of maps, charts, tables, and text written in "Odumesque," the book nevertheless enjoyed such a wide popularity that, according to the historian George Tindall, an entire generation of college students became more or less familiar with Odum's ideas.[27] Odum maintained that there was not one but many Souths—a black belt South, a piedmont South, a river delta South, a mountainous South, and a South of forests and piney woods. Together, they made up an area of vast resources and tremendous potential, but one that lagged behind other regions in providing a decent standard of living for the majority of its people. The major theme of *Southern Regions* was that, as a result of sectionalism, the South was wasting its land and its people. Indeed, the words "lag" and "waste" stood out conspicuously. In almost any socioeconomic condition that could be measured—everything from per capita income to the number of families per radio—the Southeast was at or near the bottom.

When Odum spoke of "regional development" for the South, he meant that his beloved white middle-folk, most of whom lived outside the black belt, needed an opportunity to fulfill their potential. In the past they had been unable to do so. For too long the South had been dominated by the powerful whites of the black belt who exercised disproportionate influence. Odum reasoned that since black-belt whites were the most color conscious, their economic and political predominance retarded progress throughout the region. Positive changes could occur, he argued, only after the less racist whites in other segments of the South became more assertive. These up until now inarticulate people constituted a Silent South.

> Among the important neglected factors in the interpretation of the agrarian South is that of the large number of upper middle class, non-slaveholding white folks who constituted the backbone of reconstruction and recovery. Their contributions were definitive in the regional culture. It was upon their sturdy character and persistent work that the "New South" was largely built. . . . This group stands out in contrast to the "planter class" to which so much attention has been given, who numbered in the Southern states less than 200,000 as compared with no less than a million and a half of those farm folk corresponding to the upper farmer class in the earlier East and Middle West. This group, however, constricted round about by the Negro and tenant, on

the one hand, and artificial patterns on the other, has not been normally articulate. Yet in all the averages and distributions of deficiencies and lags this group still constitutes the norm around which judgments should be made and plans developed.[28]

Odum and his colleagues at Chapel Hill thought that through regionalism the South could retain much of its uniqueness yet become an integrated part of the nation.

By the 1930s, Odum had gained a deserved reputation as one of the South's leading liberals. Indeed, the North Carolina sociologist had made a significant contribution to Southern liberal thought. Prior to Odum, Southern liberals had not tried to systematize their ideas. There were a number of recurrent themes—the South is better than it seems, the "true" Southerners are not always heard, and specific evils can be alleviated, to name a few—but no single person had previously tried to weave the strands of Southern liberalism into an organized concept.

Throughout his life Odum held fast to his early faith in the ability to deal scientifically with the South's racial situation. During the racial controversies of the 1930s, and 1940s, Odum would continually reaffirm the credo he learned from Bailey, Hall, and Giddings that it was the moral duty of the social scientist to provide analysis and realistic recommendations for the country's most pressing problems. He always insisted that the academic sociologist could not afford to theorize merely for the sake of theory. For Odum, a conscientious social thinker had to have an impact on the world in which he lived.

Odum's attempt, through regionalism, to make racial liberalism palatable (in theory, at least) to the majority of white Southerners was particularly important. The Interracial Commission was an elite group of Southern intellectuals, professionals, and religiously oriented people, and in all likelihood most of its members believed that any liberal South necessarily had to exclude the white masses. Odum, while he supported the activities of the Interracial Commission and was himself a member, was nevertheless saying that racial liberalism could ultimately find a much broader base of white endorsement.

In the end, though, Odum failed. Despite his insistence that scholars like himself should lead the way, there was too much ambivalence in Odum's own suggestions for change in Southern racial patterns. He was too attached to the white "forgotten men" who, though perhaps less color conscious than the black-belt whites, were by his own admission potential rather than actual liberals; he never could convincingly demonstrate how helping them would improve the status of blacks. Moreover, the degree to which such people could accept Negroes as fellow citizens represented, for Odum, the limits of white racial liberalism in the South. This fuzziness on his part would become even greater when first the New Deal and then World War II would make the Jim Crow South appear, especially to blacks and Northern liberals but even to some Southern liberals, more and more a relic that had to be changed. Odum would increasingly plead for time so that the South could heal old wounds and work out its own solutions. Others were demanding more immediate action.

Southern Liberals and the New Deal

The Great Depression gave Southern liberals a new sense of urgency about their region's problems. The South had not participated fully in the prosperity of the 1920s, and the poorest people, white and black, experienced more misery than Americans in other sections. For many, the only alternative was migration to the West and North. As bad times became worse, the South's image took on new shapes more grotesque than the ones they replaced. During the 1920s the Klan and the Scopes trial had symbolized the region's cultural backwardness. In the next decade, economic rather than cultural poverty would attract the most notice. The image of the depression-ridden South was evoked by photographs of weary tenants and sharecroppers trying to eke out a living on lands devasted by single-crop farming. "The South has been taking a beating for a long time," said Georgia-born writer Erskine Caldwell in an introduction to one such pictorial collection, "and the pain and indignity of it is beginning to tell." Caldwell's own *Tobacco Road*, enormously popular in the North, did much to convey the horror of this poverty to outsiders.[1]

In Franklin D. Roosevelt, the country had a president who realized that the South was in deep trouble. While FDR was still recovering from the effects of polio, George Foster Peabody, a native of Georgia who had become a New York banker and philanthropist, invited Roosevelt to visit his estate at Warm Springs and bathe in its soothing waters. The therapeutic effect of the "miracle of warm water" so encouraged Roosevelt that in 1926 he purchased the resort from Peabody. From Warm Springs, which he visited regularly and where he was to die, FDR acquired first-hand knowledge of the South's distress. "For better and for worse," Frank Freidel has pointed out, "the destinies of Franklin D. Roosevelt and the South were inextricably intermingled." Whatever the New Deal would turn out to be, it was headed by a man who had an awareness of Southern problems.[2]

Though Southern liberals were pleased to have Roosevelt in the White House, their major concern was the impact of New Deal policies on their region. Would new relief programs be adequate? What would be done to aid agriculture, the prosperity of which was essential to the well-being of Southerners? Would Southern labor unions, traditionally held at bay by the connivance of local management and state officials, finally be allowed to organize? Could the problems resulting from tenancy and sharecropping be alleviated? And, finally, how would the New Deal affect race relations?

To those seeking change in the South, it soon became apparent that the New Deal offered hope. Although FDR worked with old-line Southern politicos in Congress to forge his legislative programs, from the beginning of his first administration he caught the imagination of more liberal Southerners who were interested in regional reforms. Nowhere was this more apparent than in the attitude of Southern liberals to the Tennessee Valley Authority (TVA). Proposed by Roosevelt in April 1933, the TVA immediately struck in them a responsive chord.

Particularly enthusiastic was George Fort Milton, the Chattanooga newspaper editor who had served as the head of the Southern Committee for the Study of Lynching. Milton had long favored a public takeover of the Muscle Shoals complex along the Tennessee River, which the army had originally begun in 1917 to power a nitrate plant needed for munitions. Milton was interested in seeing the development of the Tennessee River, which would have far-reaching effects on the lives of the white and black people, most of them desperately poor, who lived in its valley. He was elated to find Roosevelt sympathetic, and after a meeting with FDR, Milton reported that the president was "concerned that the region should become a great laboratory for testing as to optimum living conditions, socially as well as economically." Noting that the Tennessee Valley contained the scenes of both the Scopes and the Scottsboro trials, Milton said that a new order was needed "if our next generation is to be happy in the new American Ruhr." Once Congress enacted TVA, Milton's visions were almost limitless. He informed Howard Odum:

> We have Negro slums and some white slums here in Chattanooga, in both of which the people are living poverty-stricken lives, socially as well as financially, and we are very much impressed with the benefits which would come from transplanting these people to new colonies, perhaps three or four miles from the city, establishing each family in a nice little cottage with a half acre or an acre of ground along with it. If this man could be close enough to the city to walk to his factory in the morning, when he got back home in the afternoon he could do farmwork. It would of course be a very much healthier condition of living for both his family and for himself.

Odum initially shared Milton's enthusiasm for the TVA. In June 1933, he, Milton, and Thomas J. Woofter, another sociologist and fellow member of the Interracial Commission, petitioned Arthur E. Morgan, the newly appointed chairman of the TVA, to consider the research on the Tennessee watershed that had been under way since 1931 as part of Odum's larger study of Southern regions. They pointed out that in the last decade Southern universities had engaged in cooperative research on ways to utilize land, identify submarginal areas, and investigate geography, agriculture, industry, commerce, education, and public welfare. "There are plenty of hectic times ahead," Odum reminded Milton shortly afterward, "and our function is to carry on in this work in a steady, substantial, and independent way." Ironically, Odum would come to believe that the TVA never properly took advantage of his regional studies, and this would later contribute to a break between him and the New Dealers. But he was an exception.[3]

On the whole Southern liberals adopted a positive attitude toward the New Deal. That some agencies themselves practiced segregation (such as the TVA, which eventually built the model community of Norris, Tennessee and then limited the new town's occupants to whites) did not greatly disturb them. For Southern liberals, such an attitude was, after all, consistent with the outlook that the Interracial Commission had nurtured: help blacks but do not directly challenge Jim Crow. This the New Deal appeared to be doing.

A symbiotic relationship developed between Southern liberals and the New Deal that gave the former a new vigor and the latter, especially in its racial policies, a distinctly Southern liberal flavor. On both state and national levels, Southern New Dealers would often demonstrate a willingness to question some of the South's most cherished myths, including racial ones. In identifying themselves with the goals of the Roosevelt Administration, they saw the New Deal coinciding with the interests of Southern blacks. At the same time, like President Roosevelt himself, they never conceived of the New Deal as a head-on assault against white supremacy. Most now thought the major burdens facing blacks were economic, and while they included Southern blacks in their reform aims, their primary goal was always the alleviation of misery in the South. Whenever possible, they deemphasized the race issue to win broad support for needed programs. This would make them, more than white Northern liberals or blacks, the natural allies of FDR in the New Deal's general approach, which consisted of gaining the allegiance of the increasingly important black vote without losing the support of the Southern wing of the Democratic party. Indeed, for the most part it would be white Southern liberals who would direct the Roosevelt Administration's efforts to help blacks. Not surprisingly, the agencies most sensitive to Negro aspirations—the Farm Security Administration, the National Youth Administration, the Fair Employment Practices Committee, the Works Progress Administration, and the Public Works Administration—would either be headed by white Southern liberals or strongly influenced by their presence in high positions.

Will Alexander in many ways was typical. The Interracial Commission's director saw FDR as a harbinger and believed that the New Deal would change the South for the better. "There was something unusual about him [Roosevelt]," he recalled later. "I had a hunch that Washington was going to become the center of the country." At first Alexander was content to stay in Atlanta and do what he could to help get New Deal relief to blacks. He also made the Department of Agriculture aware of how hard the depression had hit Southern tenants and sharecroppers. Utilizing his foundation connections, Dr. Will undertook an investigation of conditions in the cotton belt and discovered that the situation was even worse than he had thought. He published a brief study early in 1935 on the collapse of the tenant system that attracted wide attention for its criticism of the policies of the Agricultural Adjustment Administration (AAA). Shortly thereafter, the head of the new Resettlement Administration, Rexford G. Tugwell, appointed Alexander as his assistant. Alexander took over the organization after Tugwell resigned and from there went on to direct the Farm Security Administration (FSA). He wanted to help blacks as well as whites, but as a New Dealer he avoided confrontations over race. Recalling the attitude of the FSA, he said: "In the South we accepted the fact that Negroes usually lived in their own communities, and so we provided projects for them—Negro projects." A more glaring instance of discrimination, perhaps, was the failure of the FSA's purchase program to reach black tenants. Since Negroes were usually too poor credit risks to qualify for consideration, they did not greatly benefit from the FSA's most important activity: low-interest loans to enable tenant farmers to purchase their own land.[4]

It would be unfair, however, to characterize Alexander's running of the FSA as insensitive to blacks. He had come to Washington primarily because he believed that he could do more from there to improve Southern race relations and aid poor farmers, many of whom were black, than he could by remaining in Atlanta. Under Alexander's leadership, the FSA was in fact less racially discriminatory than the Subsistence Homestead Corporation or the Resettlement Administration, the New Deal's earlier attempts to alleviate rural poverty. Although locally FSA programs were administered by committees of white farmers, Alexander appointed vigorous race-relations advisers, and the FSA employed a larger percentage of black supervisors than any other New Deal agency. Moreover, though FSA projects involving Southern blacks were almost invariably segregated, the percentage of blacks affected by such projects corresponded favorably with the percentage of black farm operators. By 1940, the 1,400 black families who were living on FSA homesteads comprised 25 percent of all such families, and over half of those on FSA rental cooperatives were black. Testimony of the agency's importance to Southern blacks was once provided by a young black pupil in a backcountry Arkansas school. When his teacher asked him to name the President of the United States, the student replied: "Miss Myrtle, I don't know who the President is, but Mr. Hanna is our Farm Security supervisor."

Though they fell short of attacking Jim Crow, the FSA's attempts to help blacks nonetheless aroused anxieties in the South. In 1937, for example, the agency purchased land near Orangeburg, South Carolina for subdivision into family farms for Negroes. The area was to be quietly segregated, and precautions were taken to isolate the project from the surrounding white farms. Still, the local whites were not satisfied. The FSA had to mollify them with such assurances as the maintenance of a "protecting belt along the highway across from land tenanted by white families on which no Negro families would live." Will Alexander harbored no illusions about fighting segregation, but to have to place the FSA on record so blatantly in defense of it was a bitter pill for him to swallow.[5]

More encouraging to him was his success in moving other Southern liberals into the Roosevelt Administration. In 1933, while still in Atlanta, he succeeded in getting one of his younger staff members on the Interracial Commission, Clark Howell Foreman, appointed as a special adviser on Negro matters for Secretary of the Interior Harold Ickes, who had been chairman of the Chicago NAACP. Born in Atlanta in 1902, Foreman came from a distinguished Georgia family and was the grandson of the owner of the *Atlanta Constitution*. After graduating from the University of Georgia in 1921, Foreman went on to study at Harvard and the London School of Economics. A lynching he witnessed while a student at Georgia had made him acutely aware of Southern racial problems, and in 1923 he returned to Atlanta to work with the Interracial Commission. Under Ickes, the young Georgian tried to reduce racial discrimination within New Deal agencies, particularly in the National Recovery Administration

(NRA), and ultimately concluded that the situation called for the appointment of blacks to high administrative positions, a view most whites did not share in 1933. A Harvard-educated Negro economist, Robert C. Weaver, was recruited by Foreman and eventually replaced him as Ickes's adviser on racial affairs when Foreman moved elsewhere in the government.[6]

Another young Southern liberal whom Alexander brought to Washington was George S. Mitchell. As the son of Samuel Chiles Mitchell, one of the original supporters of the Interracial Commission, George Mitchell had arrived at his racial liberalism naturally. He was educated at the University of Richmond, Johns Hopkins, and Oxford (while a Rhodes scholar), and then went on to earn a Ph.D. from Columbia in economics. He taught at Columbia from 1929 to 1935 before serving with Alexander in the Resettlement and Farm Security administrations. Together with the black sociologist Horace Cayton, in 1939 he would publish *Black Workers and the New Unions*, an important study of the movement of blacks into the labor movement that had been financed by the Interracial Commission, and in 1944 he would become Southern regional director of the political action committee of the Congress of Industrial Organizations. After World War II, Mitchell would direct the Interracial Commission's successor, the Southern Regional Council, which under his leadership finally would take a strong stand against segregation.[7]

Foreman and Mitchell were typical of a new breed that came to the fore during the Roosevelt years: dedicated Southern liberals who in their own states would never have achieved the prominence they found in New Deal administrative positions. In this period, Washington became a congenial center for white Southern liberals, one which allowed them to bypass the closed political systems that they found back home. Moreover, white liberals who left the Southern states became less apologetic about race relations than those who remained. For some Southern liberals, involvement with the New Deal was a liberating experience that strengthened their commitment to racial justice.

The precise relationship between the New Deal and Southern liberals was complex, but one factor stands out. The more white Southerners were attracted to the New Deal, the more liberal they tended to become on the race issue. In general, New Dealers at the national level believed that the powers of government should be expanded in order to promote the general welfare, with special attention given to those citizens who were worst off. A logical extension of this philosophy was support for federal efforts to assist Southern blacks. Although Southern liberals traditionally had been wary of federal intervention in racial matters—memories of Reconstruction lingered—those who became committed New Dealers were an exception. The career of Aubrey Williams, a conspicuous figure in New Deal relief agencies, offers a case in point.

Though he spent much of his adult life outside the South, Williams had deep Southern roots. He was born in 1890 in Springville, Alabama and grew up in nearby Birmingham, where his father ran a blacksmith shop. Williams's grandparents had come to Alabama from Virginia and North Carolina during the first quarter of the nineteenth century. Cotton was king, and the families prospered through their ownership of land and slaves. When the Civil War began, both of Williams's grandfathers freed their slaves and joined the Confederate army. They survived the war but lost everything. Aubrey's father, who had a genteel upbringing, moved to Birmingham and became a blacksmith. As a wagon and carriage builder, he won awards in Paris and St. Louis, but he managed only a meager living for his family.

Work and religion shaped Aubrey Williams's early life. He worked in Birmingham department stores for twelve consecutive years, beginning as a cashboy when he was nine. By the time he was twenty-one, Williams had had only one full year of formal education. For the most part, his schooling was a sporadic mixture of night courses and tutoring. Williams's mother was very religious; she saw that her son's main diversions consisted of church and Sunday school. While in his teens, Aubrey came under the influence of an itinerant preacher who taught him that God meant every man to help those less fortunate than himself.

Williams lived in the Avondale district outside Birmingham, where he saw New South poverty at its worst—the hard lives of the "lint-heads" who worked in the textile mills. With his evangelist friend, Williams would spend Sundays in the mill workers' community. There they read the Scriptures and played baseball with factory workers and their families. In effect, the two men created a crude neighborhood settlement house. Williams also carried on unaided, spending some Sundays with black convict laborers from the nearby coal mines.

In 1911, Williams decided to advance his formal education. He began by preparing for the ministry at Maryville College, a Presbyterian school in Tennessee. By taking odd jobs he managed to stay in school for five years. He studied sociology and political economy under Arthur Calhoun, a liberal thinker whose unconventional outlook later caused him to leave the college. Exposure to such as Calhoun only whetted Williams's appetite for education. He managed to save enough money to enter the University of Cincinnati in 1916. A year later, shortly before the United States entered World War I, Williams went to Paris as a student representative of the YMCA. Restlessness led him to join the French Foreign Legion, but he soon got out in order to serve with the American Expeditionary Force. Wounded in action, Williams remained in France after the armistice and used his disability pay to attend the University of Bordeaux. In 1919, he returned to the United States and reentered the University of Cincinnati, where at the age of thirty he earned a bachelor's degree in social work.

While attending the university, Williams became pastor of a Lutheran church in Kentucky across the river from Cincinnati. He built up a loyal congregation, but some of his social welfare ideas shocked the church fathers, who forced him to leave. Williams's next job was as a recreation director in Cincinnati. In 1922 he received an offer to become head of the Wisconsin Conference of Social Work. Williams accepted and embarked on a public career that carried him to the highest levels of the Roosevelt Administration.[8]

The Wisconsin Conference, located in Madison with access to both the University of Wisconsin and the state government, perfectly suited a zealous young social worker like Williams. Its function was the study and promotion of social legislation. Its spiritual founder, the noted labor economist John R. Commons, had championed the idea of a social service state. He drafted legislation that made Wisconsin a laboratory in such areas as industrial regulation, workmen's compensation, and unemployment insurance. Commons remained close to the Wisconsin Conference during Williams's directorship, and his ideas strongly influenced the transplanted Southerner. Williams spent ten satisfying years in Madison gaining a national reputation as an effective proponent of public welfare programs.[9]

In 1932, Frank Bane, the executive director of the American Public Welfare Association, asked Williams to join his agency. Bane was having difficulty getting state governors to accept relief loans from the Reconstruction Finance Corporation (RFC), the Hoover Administration's answer to the economic crisis. Williams's first assignment was North Dakota, and he showed adeptness in convincing recalcitrant local politicians who found federal relief a violation of their devotion to self-reliance that they had better face up to the realities of the depression. This led to a similar foray into Mississippi.

Williams's work had taken him away from the South, and when he visited Mississippi in October 1932, he found conditions "sad and desperate." Food riots had occurred in Cleveland, McComb, and other towns; grocery stores had been broken into and plantation commissaries raided. With a million dollars in RFC money, Williams wanted to inaugurate work relief by giving people small sums to plant gardens, which would feed them. Not surprisingly, he ran into opposition from landowners who did not want their black sharecroppers raising vegetables rather than cotton. But the situation was so severe that in the end even the planters of the Mississippi Delta finally agreed to support work relief. Williams at times resorted to subterfuge to get white Mississippians to go along with his plans. By arguing that only a Negro could get the truth out of other Negroes, for example, he got the mayor of Jackson to hire black caseworkers for black relief applicants. In less than two months, Williams personally organized relief in eighty-two counties, hired and directed personnel, and established procedures for the country's first statewide work relief program.

In May 1933, after similar efforts in Alabama and Texas, Williams was called to Washington by Harry Hopkins, the director of Roosevelt's Federal Emergency Relief Administration (FERA). Williams's experience with work relief impressed Hopkins, who intended to undertake a major federal effort to create jobs for the unemployed. He made Williams relief director under FERA for the Southwestern District—Oklahoma, Texas, Arkansas, Louisiana, Mississippi, and Alabama.

Williams's background, education, and social work experience made him ideal for the job. When he joined FERA, controversy raged over whether Congress's $500 million relief appropriation should be channeled through private charity organizations, as was currently being done, or whether it would be more appropriate for the government to administer the money. When Hopkins put this question to Williams, the latter unhesitatingly answered that only the government could insure that those most in need of help would get it. This was the answer Hopkins wanted, and he made Williams his chief assistant. Together they began planning for the Civil Works Administration (CWA), the first federally run work relief program.

Williams played a crucial role in the New Deal, but his zeal to promote social justice quickly made him a target of conservatives. Shortly after joining FERA, Williams criticized the administration of relief in Arkansas. In Little Rock he spoke out in support of striking cotton pickers, quoting Thomas Jefferson to justify their protest. This prompted Senator Joseph Robinson to request that Williams be fired. Although Hopkins persuaded Roosevelt that the incident should be overlooked, Williams had displayed a penchant for making enemies that ultimately would force him out of the government.[10]

Under Hopkins, Williams became a major public advocate of New Deal relief policies, which he defended in speeches, articles, and on radio. As deputy administrator of the CWA and then the Works Progress Administration (WPA), Williams oversaw the spending of billions of dollars and helped put large numbers of men and women to work. Moreover, he believed that the government's responsibility extended beyond the current crisis, and he called for the continuation and extension of relief measures even when the economic situation improved. To both friends and foes of the New Deal, Williams represented the new kind of public servant that Roosevelt had brought to Washington. The anti-Roosevelt *Memphis Commercial Appeal* once described him as "a do-gooder among do-gooders . . . in the galaxy of bleeding-hearts produced by the Rexford Guy Tugwell school of screwball social planners and uplifters."[11]

Williams's outlook remained that of a Southern Populist. During the depression, many Southern liberals, recalling Tom Watson's old argument, believed that "the interests" fostered racial prejudice in order to exploit poor whites and blacks.* Williams belonged to this school. Often he blamed social injustice on such entities as "arrogant aggregates of concentrated economic power" and "monopolistic fascism." "Those who in the eighteenth century believed in the divine right of kings," he said in 1937, "now believe in the untrammeled freedom of the corporate executive." He thought that if entrenched privilege could be made accountable to a watchdog government, the American people would benefit. Williams romanticized the common man and had few qualms about his inherent decency. Needless to say, Williams, whom even Eleanor Roosevelt characterized as an "idealist," was precisely the kind of Southern liberal who would not have achieved prominence were it not for the New Deal.[12]

When an executive order created the National Youth Administration (NYA) in June 1935, Williams was appointed head of the new agency, which offered part-time employment on useful projects to young people who would not otherwise have been able to continue their education. As with the WPA, the government contracted all work directly. The NYA, like most New Deal agencies, had a clause in its authorization prohibiting the denial of benefits to persons on account of race, creed, and color. But where others ignored this requirement, Williams succeeded in making the NYA responsive to black as well as white youths. He established a Division of Negro Affairs and to head it brought in Mary McLeod Bethune, a black Florida educator.

Under Williams and Bethune, the NYA achieved a well-deserved reputation as the most racially enlightened agency in the government. It directly aided approximately 300,000 black youth while forbidding either racial or geographical discrimination. Indeed, because it was Williams's policy to distribute NYA funds to black students on the basis of the total black population of each state rather than the total student population, of which blacks were only a very small percentage, black students actually received a disproportionally high

* The appearance in 1938 of C. Vann Woodward's biography of Tom Watson had a great impact on Southern liberals. It gave a new respectability to the Populists, especially their unsuccessful efforts to form a biracial political coalition, and convinced many white liberals that an alliance between poor whites and blacks was both possible and desirable.

share of the agency's money. Moreover, they were paid exactly the same wage rates as whites, and half the blacks employed worked at professional or semiprofessional jobs that were related to their future occupational interests. Williams repeatedly issued directives to his white state administrators (one of whom was a young Texan named Lyndon Baines Johnson) admonishing them to treat Negroes fairly. But he went beyond this. To make certain that blacks received NYA benefits, Williams hired black state supervisors of Negro affairs. They helped the NYA avoid such controversies as the Civilian Conservation Corps had faced when it gave blacks less than equal treatment in segregated camps and the Tennessee Valley Authority had started when it established all-white towns and allowed preferential treatment for white workers on TVA projects. Williams, who remained with NYA until 1943, when Congress refused to renew its appropriations, was continually praised by blacks for his running of the agency.[13]

Along with Will Alexander and Harold Ickes, Williams also influenced Eleanor Roosevelt's interest in racial matters. When she came to Washington in 1933, Mrs. Roosevelt had little conception of the immense problems that blacks faced. Her impulse was to help people; but to avoid appearing patronizing, she needed the counsel of those more sensitive to black aspirations. If not for them, it is unlikely that Mrs. Roosevelt would have become a symbolic figure whom blacks greatly admired. Williams developed great respect for her over the years as her grasp of social problems grew. "You have meant so much to so many of us," he told her in 1940, "that we adore you and set our compasses by what you do and what we think you would do in situations in which we find ourselves." [14]

Despite efforts by men like Alexander and Williams, the administration of New Deal programs often resulted in severe inequities for Southern blacks. Prejudiced whites frequently denied blacks relief money or kept them off the roles altogether. The Agricultural Adjustment Act (AAA) called for acreage reduction, which had the effect of forcing many of the South's poorest tenants and sharecroppers, white and black, to leave the land.* In addition, these landless agricultural

* Though there is ample evidence that both the NRA and the AAA were racially discriminatory, it is not altogether clear that the AAA itself caused blacks to leave the land. For example, as Harvard Sitkoff has pointed out, the decline in the number of

workers had no mechanism to insure that they would receive the share of parity payments due them under the AAA, and what they got depended on the fairness of their landlords—a system that made abuse inevitable. Rather than pay blacks wages guaranteed by the codes of the National Industrial Recovery Act, Southern employers fired them and hired whites, who were now glad to get any type of job even if it meant doing "nigger work." So widespread was this practice that blacks sarcastically referred to the NRA as the "Negro Removal Act." The NAACP, while continuing to fight against traditional forms of racial discrimination, often called attention to the inconsistencies between the New Deal's egalitarian rhetoric and actual practices.[15]

FDR received strong Southern backing for his early legislative programs, but the majority of white Southerners who supported the New Deal did so only as a last resort to deal with severe distress. A student of New Deal agencies in Georgia found that most whites in that state accepted federal intervention reluctantly, fearing that such action would help blacks more than was minimally necessary and thus endanger white supremacy. Even those who genuinely wanted to help Negroes were reluctant to test community sensitivities. Such people, generally strong supporters of the New Deal, thought that too pro-Negro a stance could jeopardize any good they might accomplish. Thus in Georgia even relatively liberal New Deal officials capitulated to pervasive racism. Gay Shepperson, the head of the state's FERA, consistently aroused the ire of Governor Eugene Talmadge because of her liberal racial outlook. Still, Georgia's black press frequently attacked her for ignoring the needs of blacks.[16]

Negro farmers was considerably less during the 1930s than it had been during the 1920s ("The Emergence of Civil Rights as a National Issue in the New Deal Era," unpublished Ph.D. dissertation, Columbia University, 1975). Nonetheless, black migration from the rural South continued, and the AAA, even if it only contributed to a well-established trend, was a factor. This was particularly true in areas, such as the Mississippi Delta, where acreage reduction in cotton was the most severe. See Charles S. Johnson, et al., *The Collapse of Cotton Tenacy: A Summary of Field Studies and Statistical Surveys 1933–1935* (Chapel Hill, 1935); Howard Kester, *Revolt among the Sharecroppers* (New York, 1936); Gunnar Myrdal, *An American Dilemma: The Negro Problem and Modern Democracy* (New York, 1944), vol. 1, pp. 251–78; David Conrad, *The Forgotten Farmers: The Story of the Sharecroppers in the New Deal* (Urbana, Ill., 1965).

Southern liberals found that the New Deal was a problem as well as a solution. In October 1934 Will Alexander, shortly before joining the New Deal, wrote of how he had hoped Southern Negroes would receive a fairer share of federal funds than they usually got from their states. His optimism, however, had been premature: "The facts are that the people in Washington feel that the South is just so sensitive that they must not say anything about these matters at all. Consequently, these injustices . . . are wholesale, and Washington accepts them as inevitable and necessary." Since the New Deal purported to help those hardest hit by the depression, Alexander feared that if the degree of discrimination became generally known, it would discredit FDR's entire program. This prospect did not sit well with Dr. Will, whose own compromises with racism while head of the FSA underscored the intensity of the problem.[17]

Despite discrimination, the New Deal did set in motion forces that had an unsettling effect upon traditional Southern racial practices. This was particularly true in the case of white Southern liberals engaged in labor union activities in both agriculture and industry. As in other sections of the nation, Southern unionists were encouraged first by Section 7a of the National Industrial Recovery Act and later by the Wagner Act, both of which guaranteed workers the right to form unions. The consequent growth of organized labor brought a new element into the picture of Southern liberalism.

Racism and the willingness of employers to hire Negroes as strikebreakers traditionally had stifled the growth of labor unions in the South. White unionists, prejudiced and fearful that interracial cooperation spelled doom for their movement, as it had for the Southern Populists in the 1890s, adopted racial exclusionary clauses in their charters. Unions affiliated with the American Federation of Labor (AFL), as well as the railroad brotherhoods, were notorious for this practice. Blacks reciprocated by showing distrust and hostility toward organized labor. Frequently, they needed little encouragement to work as scabs for employers whom they regarded as more responsive to their own needs than were labor people. In the coal industry, the effectiveness of the United Mine Workers (UMW) diminished in direct proportion to the number of blacks in a particular area. Thus the UMW was stronger in Illinois, Indiana, Ohio, and Pennsylvania than in West Virginia and Alabama, where the available supply of black labor was greater. For blacks, more opportunities existed in nonunion coalfields. In a study undertaken a few years prior to the New Deal, Sterling D. Spero and Abram L. Harris concluded:

> By tradition and nurture, Negro leaders are pro-employer in sympathy and outlook. In nearly every important controversy between organized labor and capital in which Negro labor has been involved, the Negro leader has sided with capital. He has approved and often encouraged the use of Negro labor for breaking strikes. He defends his position with the argument that the exclusion of the Negro worker from many trade unions forces him to accept strike breaking as his weapon against the unions and as the only means of obtaining employment in many industries.[18]

It was no wonder that the South, which as late as 1920 still contained 85 percent of the nation's black population, was historically the region where labor unions met with least success.

Unsuccessful attempts to organize industrial workers in the Birmingham, Alabama area typified the failure of the labor movement in the South prior to the New Deal. Until 1933 miners and metalworkers in the New South's largest industrial center had lived without trade unions, despite many strikes and much violence. The UMW had been trying since 1893 to organize the Alabama coalfields, the majority of whose workers were black. This in itself was a great obstacle to white union leaders, but even when blacks could be persuaded—or threatened—into joining, the mine operators broke the union by bringing in Negro convict labor or by recruiting blacks from the cotton plantations. In 1908 the union had attempted to erect tents for white and black strikers who had been evicted from company houses. The governor of the state ruled that this constituted a dangerous interracial mobilization. State militia cut down the tents, and the two-month old strike was called off. Similarly bitter strikes failed in 1920 and 1927.

The UMW, though more favorably disposed toward Negroes than most AFL unions, offered them only a limited voice in group activities and assigned them to segregated locals. The racial antipathies of whites and the companies' professions of paternalism toward Negroes combined to prevent the UMW from forming a strong union in the

Birmingham area. "It is doubtful," Spero and Harris predicted in 1931, "the union will ever re-appear in Alabama within a generation." [19]

Though the history of the labor movement in the South is one of failure, even before the New Deal there were scattered instances of whites and blacks cooperating toward common economic goals. In the case of the Populists, and in independent state movements such as the Readjusters in Virginia during the 1880s, economic alliances evolved into open political coalitions only to be crushed by enemies who exploited the race issue. Some Southern unions, though never politically significant, carried on the spirit of the Populists and the Readjusters. Whites in these unions practiced a peculiar brotherhood with black workers that was based on economic necessity rather than ideological commitment to racial justice. An effective labor movement in the South depended on some degree of cooperation between whites and blacks, and to secure black support white unionists often found it necessary to deviate from the path of orthodoxy.*

* One such union was the Brotherhood of Timber Workers. Organized in 1910 by Southern whites in the lumbermill country of western Louisiana and eastern Texas, the union wanted to improve the squalid conditions prevalent in company towns. White unionists recognized that, without the cooperation of blacks, their efforts were bound to fail; the risk of nigger-baiting from their bosses was preferable to the companies' hiring Negro scabs to break a lily-white union. The isolation of the lumber towns worked to the union's advantage, for strict segregation was difficult to maintain in remote areas of the South where whites and blacks not only worked side by side, but shared the same saloons and brothels. Nevertheless, racism was a reality that union organizers did not ignore. The original constitution of the timber workers provided separate lodges for Negro members and control of all dues by whites. Blacks protested, and under pressure from the IWW, with whom the timber workers affiliated in 1912, the union rescinded these restrictions. At its peak the union organized 35,000 workers, about half of whom were Negroes, and forced the curtailment of such obnoxious practices as payment in script good only at the company store. By 1913, however, a campaign of terror, blacklisting, and concessions to nonunion employees enabled the lumber men to break the union. Even though blacks belonged to the brotherhood, the lumber barons added to its racial tensions by bringing black belt Negroes and Mexicans into the pine country as scabs.

The timber workers did demonstrate that organized labor could make dents in Southern racism; the experience of working in an interracial union was likely to make erstwhile foes respect one another. "There were white *men*, there are Negro *men*, and Mexican *men*, but no 'niggers,' 'greasers,' or 'white trash,' " exclaimed one white organizer. "All *men* are on the side of the union, and all greasers, niggers and

Encouraged by New Deal legislation, in 1935 the AFL's Committee for Industrial Organization, led by UMW president John L. Lewis, broke with the parent organization over the issue of industrial versus craft unionism. The new CIO undertook massive organizing drives in the steel, automotive, and textile industries. Lewis's major concern was the recruitment of as many workers as possible into CIO unions, and he was willing to allow Communists, Socialists, and other radicals to work with him toward this end. In the South, the CIO openly supported interracial unionism and turned what had been a novelty into a common phenomenon in the region's urban centers, which earned the organization the eternal enmity of diehard white supremacists.

Southern liberals who in the past had seen organized labor as a compounder rather than a cure of racial problems generally applauded the efforts of the CIO. Some, such as Katherine Du Pre Lumpkin of Georgia and Lucy Randolph Mason of Virginia, became executives in Southern offices of the new union. Miss Mason, a descendant of two of Virgina's oldest families, did important public relations work for the CIO throughout the Southeast. She was in close touch with other Southern liberals, keeping them informed of the CIO's goals, and also maintained contact with a wide array of Southern civic leaders in her role as a "roving ambassador" for the unions. "Madam, I don't know what the CIO pays you," exclaimed one antiunion Southerner after hearing of her lineage, "but I am sure you are worth it." Miss Lumpkin also came from an established Southern family whose ancestors had been planters and slaveowners. In her 1947 autobiography, she poignantly revealed her transformation from a woman with traditional Southern racial attitudes into a dedicated white liberal. Before joining the CIO, both women had been active in the YWCA, where they had been exposed to the influence of W. D. Weatherford and Will Alexander.[20]

The attitude of Southern liberal unionists on race closely paral-

white trash are on the side of the lumber trust." James R. Green, "The Brotherhood of Timber Workers 1910–1913: A Radical Response to Industrial Capitalism in the Southern U.S.A.," *Past and Present* 60 (August 1973), 161–200. Also see Carl N. Degler, *The Other South: Southern Dissenters in the Nineteenth Centry* (New York, 1974), pp. 230–371.

leled the thinking of the New Dealers. Though white liberals like Mason and Lumpkin took pride in the interracialism of the new CIO unions, their goal was to organize unions rather than tear down white supremacy. They knew that most whites participated in interracial unions only out of economic necessity. Southern opponents of the CIO argued that the organization practiced social equality and threatened Jim Crow; the prounionists maintained that mixed unions could lead to better race relations within the confines of existing laws. Seeing any cooperation between white and black Southern workers as a step in the right direction, liberals countenanced policies that in effect made white and black union members brothers but not equals.

The racial practices of the new unions resembled those of the Interracial Commission. In 1935 George Mitchell visited a number of mixed union meetings in the Birmingham area. What he witnessed convinced him that whites participated in such meetings primarily because the survival of the union depended on it. The two races sat apart from each other. On the rostrum, the black representative was usually a preacher who led the meeting in prayer. Negroes, when making a point to the whites, frequently spoke with deference and addressed them as either "Brother" or "Mister." Whites called Negroes by their first names or referred to them as "Brother," but almost never "Mister." The fewer Negroes there were in a particular local, the more Jim Crow prevailed. Yet Mitchell was struck by the fraternal spirit that permeated the gatherings. "The interesting thing about such meetings," he reported, "is the balance they strike between adherence to and departure from traditional Southern ways." A strange compromise had been effected.[21]

The depression and New Deal made interracial unionization a possibility even in the South's most economically backward and racially sensitive area—the Mississippi Delta. Although New Deal price supports and acreage reduction helped the owners of cotton plantations, the effect of the AAA on tenants and sharecroppers—who in the 1930s comprised 80 percent of the Delta's farmers—was disastrous. Beginning with the initial reductions of cropland in 1933, much of this labor force became expendable. Many whose existence even in the best of times was marginal had no alternative but to move elsewhere, and those who managed to stay found living conditions even more wretched than before. But few would have predicted that their discontent would lead to an interracial union.

Prior to 1934, periodic attempts to unionize landless Southern agricultural workers, for the most part undertaken by American Communists, had failed.[22] But in July of that year, in a brotherhood of desperation, twenty-seven white and black sharecroppers met in Tyronza, Arkansas, a town in the Delta located about thirty-five miles north of Memphis. They discussed how to obtain AAA benefits and other mutual problems. The group elected a white sharecropper chairman and a black minister vice-chairman. A holiness preacher was appointed chaplain. A few of the whites at the meeting had been Klan members, and they suggested the formation of a secret fraternal order but were overruled by those who thought it would be better to have an open union. This decision gave birth to the Southern Tenant Farmers Union (STFU).[23]

For help in organizing, the farmers turned to H. L. Mitchell, a one-time sharecropper who was now operating a small dry-cleaning business in Tyronza, and Clay East, the owner of a local filling station. Mitchell and East, both white, were known throughout the area as "square shooters." They were also followers of Norman Thomas's American Socialist Party, and Mitchell had once even arranged for Thomas to speak in Tyronza. Mitchell became secretary of the STFU and East its president. They were assisted by E. B. McKinney, a charismatic black preacher from nearby Marked Tree. Two other whites, J. R. Butler, an ex-schoolteacher, and Ward H. Rogers, a young Methodist minister who had been preaching in the Ozarks, joined the STFU as organizers. "Unionism" quickly developed into a new gospel in impoverished eastern Arkansas. Every day Mitchell and East's battered old car could be seen going to some outlying church loaded with sharecroppers ready to organize a new local.[24] Delta planters soon took note of the new union, which by the summer of 1935 had 15,000 members, and fought it with all the violence and intimidation that they could muster, which was considerable.*

By any measure, the growth of a Socialist-led union of white and

* The planters banned union meetings, forced evictions, hired vigilantes, burned churches, and attempted assassinations. See Jerold S. Auerbach, *Labor and Liberty: The La Follette Committee and the New Deal* (Indianapolis, 1966), pp. 35–44.

black tenants in the Delta was remarkable. Moreover, the STFU was a spontaneous movement. Common economic grievances rather than socialist ideology or racial liberalism held its white and black members together. Farmers were not in attendance when Norman Thomas spoke in a Tyronza high school auditorium in the spring of 1934. Instead, they were holding secret meetings behind barn doors, deciding how to prevent a notorious landlord from evicting them. The idea to form one union for both whites and blacks did not come from H. L. Mitchell, who was already a dedicated racial liberal, but from Arkansas sharecroppers like Burt Williams, a burly white man who said that though his "pappy" had ridden for the original Ku Klux Klan to drive Republican officeholders out of Crittenden County, times had changed and an effective union needed the cooperation of blacks. Although they may have sat separately from whites at union meetings, blacks like Ike Shaw readily agreed. Shaw had been involved in the Phillips County movement in which black Arkansas sharecroppers' trying to obtain a better deal from their landlords so aroused white hostility that their leaders were systematically searched out and shot in what euphemistically became known as the Elaine "race riot" of 1919. For Negroes, the presence of whites in the union lessened the chance that violence would again be directed at them so indiscriminately.

The union's interracial character may have prevented the wholesale slaughter of Delta blacks, but it certainly did not prevent planters from seeking to suppress the STFU. After the union had filed suit against a landlord to prevent the eviction of tenants, a Poinsett County school official discovered Ward Rogers teaching a racially mixed group of sharecroppers how to read, write, and—most important—count. When the intruder objected and told Rogers to do his teaching elsewhere, the young preacher responded that he could not be ordered about and that, if he wished, he could lead a lynch mob against any plantation owner in Poinsett County. STFU members cheered, but Rogers was later arrested and sent to prison.

Rogers's remarks also led to a reign of terror against the union. The body of a union organizer was found in the Coldwater River south of Memphis, and in Wynne a mob killed a prounion minister. The lawyer who defended Rogers and E. B. McKinney, the highest-ranking black in the union, both had their homes riddled with gunfire. Mitchell happened to be with McKinney that night and narrowly missed death. Norman Thomas, who took an increasing interest in the STFU, returned to Arkansas in 1935. While delivering a speech at Birdsong in Crittenden County, he was pulled off the platform and escorted to the Memphis Bridge. For their own safety, union leaders moved their headquarters from Tyronza to Memphis.

Despite the intimidation, the union managed to recruit new members and by 1938 reached a peak membership of about 31,000. National magazines dramatized the tenant farmers' attempts to organize, and a "March of Time" newsreel showed millions of Americans brutal instances of flogging and peonage in the Delta. But, aside from publicizing social injustice, the STFU did not make much headway in its battle with the planters. Arkansas courts dismissed the union's lawsuit to gain AAA benefits for tenants, and Secretary of Agriculture Henry Wallace did not intervene on the STFU's behalf despite a visit to Washington by Mitchell, East, and McKinney.[25]

In an effort to help the struggling tenant farmers, in 1935 Norman Thomas sent one of his associates, Howard Kester, into Arkansas to direct relief efforts and act as an adviser to the union. A Presbyterian clergyman as well as a Socialist, Kester exemplified the religious influence that motivated so many Southern liberals.

Howard Kester grew up in a middle-class Virginia household where much emphasis was placed on sin and salvation. He took his Christian teaching seriously, and the stories of neighborhood lynchings that he heard as a small boy deeply upset him. Kester could not understand how Negroes, who had always treated him graciously, suddenly became the objects of mob violence. "The horror of it gripped me," he recalled years later. While he was a student at Princeton during the 1920s, Kester's outspoken defense of Negro rights made him a pariah among his Southern classmates, who once threw him in a water fountain for his views. Such experiences did not stop the young man from applying New Testament teachings to Southern social problems, especially race relations. Kester practiced what he preached, and during the early thirties worked as a lynching investigator for the NAACP. The association honored him with a luncheon in New York in 1934, which had to be held in secrecy so as not to reveal the identity of this useful white Southerner. Once he joined the Tenant Farmers Union, Kester became the most persistent white voice for total racial egalitarianism in all STFU activities.

For Kester, the race question was primarily one of Christian ethics, and during the depression, he envisioned the South dealing with its problems through a radical religious fundamentalism. In 1936, he and a few like-minded whites founded the Fellowship of Southern Churchmen. The group dedicated itself to the "healing" of the South. It practiced "prophetic evangelism" and advocated a direct approach to people by way of tent and open-air meetings. The South had seen many tent meetings, but few had ever advocated the objectives of a Howard Kester. Mitchell, who became his close friend, once admitted that Kester would have made a great Klan organizer.[26]

Even with Kester, however, the STFU was not an idyllic racial democracy. Whites thought that blacks too often put their racial interests above those of the union. Blacks, on the other hand, believed the STFU gave them only a secondary role in union affairs. E. B. McKinney charged the white union leadership with placing matters affecting Negroes low on the agenda; J. R. Butler replied, "You are too prone to look upon matters from a race angle rather than a class angle." When dissatisfaction among blacks arose at Hillhouse Farm, a union-supported cooperative in Mississippi, Mitchell called for the establishment of separate locals to deal with grievances. He also warned Sam Franklin, a Presbyterian minister who was the director of Hillhouse, against publicly using "Mr." and "Mrs." when addressing blacks.[27]

Hillhouse itself showed how Southern racial liberalism during the 1930s combined innovation with adherence to the old verities. Located between Bolivar and Coahoma counties, Hillhouse provided a refuge for a few hundred displaced white and black tenant farmers, most of whom belonged to the STFU. It served about equal numbers from both races and offered them homes, land, and equal shares of the cooperative's profits. "We are upholding the true Christian attitude toward the races," said Sam Franklin, "but not doing anything foolish." Jonathan Daniels, the liberal editor of the *Raleigh News and Observer*, called attention to the "queer compromise" that he saw occurring at Hillhouse:

> The cabins sit in two rows. . . . In one row of cabins live the white members and in the other row the Negro members. On the bank of the Mississippi the directors of the cooperative are almost as sensitive about Jim Crow as it is possible for human beings to be. Whichever way they move they may bump into their own Christian consciences or the community's dangerous prejudices. They want to take the Christian attitude toward race, but they do not want to complicate the cooperative experiment unduly by unnecessarily alarming Mississippi. . . . The Negroes and whites gather together in the community house for the cooperative meetings, but the whites have their social meetings on one night and the Negroes theirs the next.[28]

Despite internal tensions, which were real, the STFU did issue challenges to Jim Crow. In October 1936, the union's executive council even went on record against segregated schools. Obviously, the STFU was in no position to challenge Southern public education, but it did forbid its members to attend labor colleges where segregation was still the rule. This created problems for the union. The two principal Southern centers for the training of labor organizers, Commonwealth College in Mena, Arkansas and Highlander Folk School in Monteagle, Tennessee, both practiced segregation.[29]

The experiences of the STFU were not uncommon among white Southern liberals during the New Deal years. The need to include blacks in regional reform movements was recognized, but on the whole, Southern liberals tried to avoid concentrating on race. Still, they were not hidebound by the region's traditions. Spurred on by the depression, Southern liberals during the 1930s assumed more vigorous roles, speaking and acting in ways that they would not have done only a few years earlier. Those in New Deal agencies and in organized labor led the way, but there was increasing determination on the part of white liberals generally to have a greater impact on the region.

One example of this attitude was Frank P. Graham. A native of Fayetteville, North Carolina, Graham grew up in Charlotte where his father, as superintendent of public instruction, tried to see that black schools received a just share of appropriations. Aside from his father's efforts on behalf of Negro education, the major influences on Graham's racial liberalism were America's professed democratic heritage and the teachings of the Christian religion. In 1915 he joined the faculty of the University of North Carolina, where he drew more attention for his liberal views than for his scholarship. Nevertheless, Graham was an inspiring teacher who had a winning way with people, and in 1930 he became president of the university. Will Alexander referred to Graham's appointment as "one of the most encouraging things that has occurred in the South," adding that there was "great joy when the machine clicks right."

As a university president, Graham more than lived up to Alexander's expectations. In 1936 a University of North Carolina English professor, E. E. Ericson, had caused a sensation in the state by publicly dining with James Ford, a Negro who was the Communist party's vice-presidential candidate. Voices in the state demanded Ericson's dismissal. Among them was that of Jonathan Daniels of the *Raleigh News and Observer,* who felt that Ericson's action jeopardized the relatively liberal spirit that prevailed at Chapel Hill. "I may seem like a jungle creature myself now," Daniels confessed to W. T. Couch, the editor of the University of North Carolina Press, "but you know that the creatures of the intellectual jungle in North Carolina wait only an opportunity to destroy what you and I regard as the essence of the University." In characteristic style, Graham responded to Daniels's editorial criticism by arguing that despite the delicate nature of North Carolina race relations, one had to act in the spirit of Christian wisdom. He refused to fire Ericson.

A number of Southern liberals thought that Graham's defense of Ericson was excessively self-righteous, and that his identification with unpopular causes greatly endangered the influence of Chapel Hill. Even before the Ericson episode, the journalist Gerald Johnson said to Howard Odum, in reference to Graham, "the University, I fear, is in a deep, dark hole." Yet Graham somehow managed to combine controversial stands with the successful operation of a Southern state university. In the 1930s both he and the University of North Carolina stood out as symbols of flourishing enlightenment within the South.[30]

It was indeed significant that a man with Graham's inclinations had become president of the South's most prestigious university. Other Southern colleges saw Chapel Hill as a model, and the maintenance of academic freedom there was vital. Moreover, by insisting that his faculty and students had the right to participate in controversial causes, Graham facilitated the more aggressive Southern liberalism of the 1930s. In 1938 Jonathan's father, Josephus Daniels, who as Roosevelt's ambassador to Mexico kept in close touch with the administration, reminded Harold Ickes that Graham was perhaps the foremost leader of the progressive movement in the South and also a man upon whom FDR relied. "The University of North Carolina," said Daniels, "is the first institution of the South in breadth and liberalism, and Dr. Graham, its president, is the most militant liberal of all educators in America." Clark Foreman was more succinct. "Thank God for the University of North Carolina," he said.[31]

Graham's own activities won him a reputation as a crusading liberal who defended labor organizers, pointed out educational discrimination against blacks in his own state, and championed civil liberties. At times Graham's fervor bothered even his strongest Southern supporters. Still, in the end they usually stood by him. Josephus Daniels, for instance, returned to North Carolina from Mexico following the Ericson episode to help Graham do battle with the university's board of trustees. Not only did Graham survive, but as someone who could guide a state university through the depression, he could get away with much. He presided successfully over the University of North Carolina until 1948, when he was appointed to the U.S. Senate to fill a vacancy.

Graham achieved acceptance through an innate ability to justify his actions in terms white Southerners could understand. He was particularly adept at appealing to the deep religious roots of such people. It was common for Graham in answering critics to quote the Sermon on the Mount, which he looked upon as social and economic philosophy. Odum, who often regarded his university president's liberalism as overly zealous, admitted that Graham was the conscience of North Carolina. "Calling him a Communist," Jonathan Daniels once said, "would be an enterprise like trying to prove that the Kremlin was the First Presbyterian Church." [32]

Despite his militant style, Graham, like the New Dealers and the union organizers, also had to compromise with Jim Crow. In 1939 a young black woman, Pauli Murray, applied for admission to the University of North Carolina Law School. In its recent *Gaines* decision, the United States Supreme Court had ruled that, in the absence of other provisions for the legal education of blacks, Missouri had to admit a qualified Negro to its segregated state law school. Miss Murray thought that her attending the South's most liberal university would be a logical extension of *Gaines*. Graham disagreed. In denying her request, he told Murray that he was aware of the inequities that applied to Negro higher education in the South, but that "the most unfortunate thing that could happen at this time would be a popular referendum on the race issue." Graham urged her to accept his working for educational equality within North Carolina's segregation laws and to understand "the limitation under which we must work in order to make the next possible advance." Murray (who wound up attending the Howard University Law School and then went on to become a highly acclaimed poet as well as a distinguished legal scholar) replied that as a younger generation Negro she could not approve of Graham's hesitations. Like other Southern liberals during the thirties, Frank Graham, for all his liberal passions, was not yet ready to violate the Jim Crow laws openly.[33]

The depression had given Southern liberals a new sense of urgency about their mission as well as making them see the need for extending it to include the poor whites. Aiding blacks remained a high priority but was increasingly linked to the welfare of Southern whites whom, through the New Deal, the racial liberals were trying to lure away from the nigger-baiting demagogues who had been their traditional champions. Ever since Cable's protests in the 1880s, Southern liberals had been blaming these "red gallus" politicians for their region's backwardness and intolerance. The New Deal now gave them their first real opportunity to challenge the demagogues' dubious rule.

As a result, Southern liberals exhibited a new vitality. Frank Graham, though not directly involved in New Deal agencies, was an ardent supporter of FDR. Along with Will Alexander and Aubrey Williams, Graham typified the white Southern liberal as New Dealer: a militant advocate of social justice who at times violated some but not all of the old racial shibboleths while defending his break with the past as a logical outgrowth of the evangelical Christian morality presumably taught, or at least given lip service, in almost every Southern church. This attitude was also apparent among more radical liberals, such as Howard Kester, who were active in labor union activities and quite often critical of the New Deal for not going far enough. Moreover, both types of liberal, by recognizing that the federal government had a significant role to play in changing the South, were counteracting the Southern liberals' traditional fear of "outside" interference. By 1938 they were beginning to consider new ways in which they, through Washington, could have an even greater impact on the South.

CHAPTER FIVE

The Southern Conference for Human Welfare

In 1938 the search for a liberal South took on a definitely political character. Roosevelt himself rekindled hopes for a major New Deal effort in the region: in a March speech at Gainesville, Georgia he denounced the South's backwardness and declared war on anti–New Deal Southern senators. His remarks encouraged Southern liberals, especially those in his administration. "You are going to write a new chapter in the history of that whole unfortunate section of America," Aubrey Williams told the president.[1]

Clark Foreman, now with the Public Works Administration, urged Roosevelt to speak out further on Southern problems. In collaboration with Lowell Mellett of the National Emergency Council, Foreman helped produce a *Report on the Economic Conditions of the South,* which appeared in August. The report succinctly outlined the region's major problems, and it was devastating, characterizing the South as the nation's "number 1 economic problem." FDR endorsed the findings and called for appropriate legislation. Washington had issued a challenge for Southern liberals to take action.[2]

Though the *Report* was timed politically to have an impact on the congressional elections of 1938, it also coincided with efforts of white

Southerners interested in securing remedies for the misery they saw around them. In 1935 Francis Pickens Miller, a liberal Virginia lawyer who had fought against the political machine of Senator Harry F. Byrd, and H. C. Nixon, a Tulane University political scientist, had organized the Southern Policy Association to promote discussion and eventually action to deal with Southern issues. By 1937 Nixon was expressing a desire to find new avenues for reform.[3] These men subordinated the race issue to a broad concern with economic problems, reflecting the common sentiment among racial liberals that Southern blacks needed economic aid above all and would share the benefits of any regional development program. FDR's action encouraged those who wanted change in the South and convinced them that the time was ripe for the creation of a broadly based organization of Southern liberals.

Support for such a group also came from more radical elements. In 1936 Joseph Gelders, the Southern secretary for the New York–based and allegedly Communist-influenced National Committee for the Defense of Political Prisoners, had been kidnapped and severely beaten by three assailants in Birmingham, Alabama in a bloody episode related to the efforts of union organizers in the Alabama plants of the Tennessee Coal and Iron Company. Gelders came from a well-known Birmingham Jewish family and from 1930 to 1935 had taught physics at the University of Alabama. At the time of his beating, he was actively protesting the imprisonment of a local Communist party secretary. (Gelders never completely recovered from the attack, and injuries he received contributed to his death in 1950 at the age of fifty-one.) His beating was but one of numerous blatant violations of basic constitutional rights in the Birmingham area during the depression years and won for Gelders the sympathy of many Southern liberals. Early in 1938, one of them, Lucy Randolph Mason, arranged meetings between Gelders and both President and Mrs. Roosevelt on civil liberties and other regional problems. Both the president and the First Lady showed interest in Gelders's idea for a conference of liberal Southerners.

Upon his return to the South, Gelders contacted H. C. Nixon and won him over to the idea of a general conference of Southern liberals. W. T. Couch of the University North Carolina Press raised money to send Nixon around the South to do preliminary work for such a gathering. The actions of Gelders, Nixon and Couch, combined with the efforts of Clark Foreman and the president's National Emergency Council, culminated in the Southern Conference for Human Welfare (SCHW), which was scheduled to meet in Birmingham in late November 1938. "The Conference," noted Nixon six weeks before the meeting, "was not started with any idea of continuity but it seems to be taking on an enthusiasm and proportion which may not terminate with the November meeting." [4]

In bringing together Southern liberals, the Southern Conference for Human Welfare in effect became an active organization even before its first meeting. Its white sponsors believed that racism could be put aside and the New Deal extended to all the poor people of the South. This was to be the spirit of Birmingham. Moreover, the liberal South would speak as it never had before. "There are many liberal thinkers and leaders in the South," read a flyer advertising the meeting. "Their number is rapidly increasing. Progressive ideas and the desire for progressive action are spreading. Their leaders have heretofore been isolated and scattered, the effectiveness of their work limited by their lack of coordination. The Conference, by providing a meeting ground for all Southern progressives, will promote mutual trust and cooperation between them for greater service to the South." [5]

The movement for a general conference of Southern liberals generated much excitement, but there were dissenters, the most important of whom was Howard Odum. Given Odum's interest in establishing a broad liberal base among Southern whites, he should have welcomed SCHW, but such was not the case. Odum believed that the New Dealers had overlooked him. He had served on President Hoover's Research Committee on Recent Social Trends and established a reputation as a leading proponent of social planning, but New Deal policy makers had not sought his advice. "His nose has been out of joint since 1932," Aubrey Williams said of him later, "because he was not used by Roosevelt, Tugwell, and Hopkins." According to Williams, Odum was too overbearing to get along with other strong personalities in the administration. "You had to turn everything over to him or he would not play," Williams recalled. This characterization was correct in that Odum did try to mold organizations to fit his own social theories. Though he called upon intellectuals to come down from their ivory towers, Odum was himself too much the academic to feel comfortable in the political atmosphere of the New Deal.[6]

Moreover, he regarded SCHW as a rival. In 1937, at the height of his academic career, Odum had become president of Will Alexander's Interracial Commission with the express purpose of turning it into a council for Southern regional development. Here was his long-awaited chance to move beyond the classroom. His plans, however, were not going well; most white Southern liberals were more interested in a closer alliance with the New Deal, and blacks reacted coolly to Odum's willingness to play down the race issue. He resented the attention that the new organization was getting and refused to have anything to do with it. "Between the Right Honorable FDR, the Southern Conference for Human Welfare, and twenty other groups that are literally taking the lead," he said in 1938, "I think I'll go heat-wave haywire." Subsequent events convinced him that SCHW was a political agitation agency, and he advised members of the Interracial Commission to maintain a safe distance from it.[7]

Jessie Daniel Ames of the Association of Southern Women for the Prevention of Lynching also rejected the Southern Conference for Human Welfare. She confided that though Clark Foreman was as "busy as a bee in a tar bucket" making arrangements for SCHW's Birmingham conference, Foreman was a poor politician and organizer who had been ineffective in his own work with the Interracial Commission. In her mind SCHW represented a "lunatic fringe" that was trying to build support in the South for FDR at the risk of increasing racial tension.[8]

Even without Odum and Ames, SCHW's Birmingham meeting attracted a broad spectrum of Southerners. Twelve hundred people, about one-fifth of whom were black, attended. Not all the whites were racial liberals. Some came to Birmingham because SCHW reflected their opinion that the South suffered severe economic handicaps, such as discriminatory freight rates. Thus Arthur Raper and Bibb Graves, the governor of Alabama, both lent their names to the conference, though Graves, who had been instrumental in upholding the conviction of the Scottsboro boys, adhered to racial views poles apart from those of Raper. Other Southern political figures who appeared included one bona fide racial liberal, Senator Claude Pepper of Florida, and others who at least refused to engage in virulent race-baiting and who admitted that Southern blacks lived under heavy burdens. These included Senator Lister Hill of Alabama and Brooks Hays of Arkansas, a member of the Farm Security Administration who also served as the Democratic party's national committeeman for his state and who would later win election to Congress. Among the more militant white racial liberals present were Frank Graham, Howard Kester, and Aubrey Williams. Southern newspapermen also added to the luster of the conference. Ralph McGill of the *Atlanta Constitution*, John Temple Graves II of the *Birmingham Age-Herald*, and Mark Ethridge and Barry Bingham of the *Louisville Courier-Journal* all had reputations for racial liberalism and a concern for Southern problems. Six known Communists also were in attendance.[9]

The organizers of the Birmingham meeting carefully nurtured the idea that the Southern Conference represented the working as well as the professional folk of the South. Southern members of the CIO were among the delegates, as were farmers, some of whom were tenants and sharecroppers. The proceedings were to feature an address by Mary McLeod Bethune, black leader of the Division of Negro Affairs of the NYA. Still, the fact remained that SCHW was led by white, urban, middle-class Southerners, the same people who had previously identified themselves with the work of the Commission on Interracial Cooperation.

Negroes, however, hoped that the Southern Conference would represent a new, more vigorous outlook. The white sponsors of the conference furthered this feeling by continually emphasizing democracy with a small *d*. In his 1938 *Forty Acres and Steel Mules*, H. C. Nixon had concluded: "The South will never itself escape exploitation until an end is put to the exploitation of farmers, laborers, and Negroes. The South will never have economic security until these groups of Americans have economic security. The South will never be highly productive until these groups are highly productive. The South will never have its share of national income until these groups have their share of national income. The South will never be an educated democracy until these groups are educated and have democracy." The depression had given a new urgency, as well as a new twist—the inclusion of poor whites—to Lewis Blair's old dictum that Southern prosperity was "dependent upon the elevation of the Negro." Yet the exact role of blacks in any regional economic program remained unclear.[10]

One of the conference's principal organizers, W. T. Couch, exemplified the mixed feelings of white liberals who were then attempting to come to terms with the race issue. In 1934 he had contributed a chapter on Negroes to *Culture in the South,* a volume he edited for the University of North Carolina Press. Couch argued that until recently only a few Southerners—he cited George Washington Cable, Atticus Haygood, and Edgar Gardner Murphy—had demonstrated any real conception of the complexities of the race problem. "Now and then," he noted, "a southern politician would speak with frankness and insight, and a few educators and ministers stood for more justice and fair play. But for the most part, these voices went unheard." Though most white Southerners still endorsed policies of racial proscription, Couch insisted that white men and women of every class—"a much larger number than is suspected"—felt keenly about racial injustice and wanted to aid Southern blacks. He maintained that the most blatant racial outrages, such as lynching, were symbolic; they could be dramatically fought against and even removed without demonstrably altering the lives of millions of Southern Negroes. These symbols of white prejudice, thought Couch, often obscured those things that black people most needed—housing, jobs, land, and educational opportunities. The implication was clear. Southern blacks could be assisted without stirring racial controversies. They would be helped least by dramatization of incidents of mob violence and social segregation.[11]

White liberals such as Couch hoped that the economic focus of SCHW could give it a broader basis of support than the Interracial Commission had had, and at the same time allow SCHW to pursue policies of more direct benefit to Southern Negroes. "The Conference must make a mass appeal," Nixon had reiterated to Francis Pickens Miller prior to the meeting, "if it makes the grade at all." [12] It was a delicate tightrope that the Southern Conference wished to walk and, as events in Birmingham proved, an impossible one.

Some two hundred to three hundred Negro delegates, about 20 percent of the total, arrived in Birmingham to participate in the Southern Conference's first meeting. Mixed gatherings of whites and blacks in the South of the 1930s were always potentially touchy, but racial liberals usually managed to hold such affairs without raising any controversies over segregation. This often required ingenuity. In 1936, for example, Mitchell's Southern Tenant Farmers Union actually bought a run-down Little Rock, Arkansas hotel so that white and black union members could meet together without arousing the ire of curious employees or city officials. The Interracial Commission avoided trouble simply by never advertising that whites and blacks were working together on any particular project. Arthur Raper frequently bought first-class railroad accommodations for blacks traveling to and from the commission's headquarters in Atlanta, and these people would present their tickets and ride. Neither the Interracial Commission nor the railroads ever publicized the fact that a Jim Crow law had been violated. These were intentional policies on the part of the commission; had the organization formally requested permission for a Negro to travel or meet with whites, the answer almost certainly would have been no.[13]

Given the publicity surrounding the Birmingham assemblage—Mrs. Roosevelt herself was scheduled to appear—such methods could not be used. Sponsors of the conference had in part chosen Birmingham because they wanted to demonstrate that Southern liberalism could manifest itself in a city that all too often received attention only after such incidents as the Gelders beating. They hoped that even in the Deep South whites and blacks could get together to discuss problems of mutual interest. None of them sought any conflict with local authorities. Indeed, the whole point of the SCHW was to link liberalism with Southern traditions. This would be symbolized by the presentation of a "Thomas Jefferson Award" for distinguished service to the South to the Alabama-born Supreme Court justice Hugo L. Black.[14]

The conference, which was to run four days, opened on Sunday, November 20, 1938 in Birmingham's Municipal Auditorium. At first all went smoothly. Blacks and whites sat together indiscriminately at sessions dealing with such varied questions as education, civil rights, labor relations, unemployment, housing, suffrage, youth, health, prison reform, and freight rate differentials. The day's featured speaker, Frank Graham, told an audience of three thousand of the need for federal aid to education in the South. In general SCHW tried to avoid isolating the race issue from these other Southern problems. Rather than emphasize the unique injustices faced by blacks, the conference concentrated on matters that went beyond race in the hope of inspiring additional New Deal legislation to combat the effects of the depression in the South.

The following day, however, Birmingham police, led by Commissioner Eugene Connor—the same "Bull" Connor who would later achieve notoriety for his use of snarling police dogs and fire hoses against civil rights demonstrations—informed Chairwoman Louise Charlton, a local judge, of their intention to enforce segregation in the Municipal Auditorium. SCHW suddenly faced a choice of disbanding, ignoring the police, or assigning Jim Crow seating to its black delegates. Late that afternoon, fifteen policemen arrived at the auditorium and threatened to begin making arrests if the segregation ordinance were not complied with immediately. After consulting Couch and other conference organizers, Mrs. Charlton interrupted a session on farm tenancy, explained the circumstances, and asked the black and white delegates present to sit apart in the meeting room. Though a number of people protested, the order to segregate was obeyed on condition that the whole matter would be discussed later that evening. When the issue came up, the Southern Conference, without a great deal of debate, condemned the action of the police while agreeing to comply with the law for the remainder of the Birmingham meeting. Mrs. Roosevelt, though, took exception to this concession. Rather than sit on the white side of the room, the First Lady placed her chair in the aisle that now separated the two sections.[15]

The conference then resolved never to hold any segregated conventions in the future. This action immediately branded SCHW as a racial-equality organization—a label that clearly disturbed many of its white organizers. Jonathan Daniels, for example, complained that

SCHW "began in tragic mistake when action was taken which resulted in placing emphasis upon the one thing certain angrily to divide the South." [16]

The incident dealt a severe blow to the spirit of Birmingham. Neither a speech by Mrs. Roosevelt before a packed auditorium the following night endorsing the idea of federal legislation to deal with Southern problems nor one on the conference's fourth and final day by Hugo Black during which he quoted liberally from Thomas Jefferson on the need to extend democracy could erase the fact that SCHW had touched upon an issue that white Southern liberals had avoided for years. Many identified the group as militantly problack and antisegregationist. In the end this reputation, however exaggerated, proved inimical to the conference's goal of becoming the political arm of a liberal South.

The Southern Conference did manage some advances over the policies of the Interracial Commission. Officially, SCHW stood for full rights for all people under the law, abolition of the poll tax and extension of the franchise to qualified blacks, an end to wage differentials between racial groups, appropriations for graduate-school programs in state-supported Negro educational institutions, and a plea for the release of the Scottsboro boys who were still in prison.[17]

Blacks themselves applauded the new organization. Northern blacks usually looked askance upon the activities of white Southern liberals, but even Robert S. Abbott's vociferous *Chicago Defender* stated that anti–Jim Crow sentiment was more meaningful when it came from the South and described events in Birmingham as a "rare and precious moment in the social history of America." The NAACP, usually at odds with Southern liberals as a result of its policies of direct protest, featured an article in its official organ, *Crisis*, that cast SCHW in a highly favorable light. Even blacks who believed that the NAACP itself was not sufficiently militant praised the Birmingham conference and admitted that, at long last, the white South seemed to be making progress. "The hind wheel may be off and the axle dragging," said the radical literary critic Sterling Brown, "but the Old Cart is moving." Still, the almost unanimous black endorsement was more than offset by the heavy fire SCHW drew both for its alleged racial egalitarianism and for the fact that known Communist party members, even though they played only a minor role, had attended the proceedings.[18]

White liberals who wanted to expand the work of the conference tried to allay some of the criticism. Frank Graham replied to one skeptic that nothing had been done in Birmingham that had not already been done in interracial activities in North Carolina. "No action was taken," Graham carefully tried to point out, "which has anything to do with social equality or educational segregation." Mark Ethridge wrote Graham that, despite the "unfortunate injection" of the segregation issue, so long as Graham, Barry Bingham, Brooks Hays, and Francis Miller continued to lead SCHW there would be no question as to the conference's auspices. Ethridge hoped that the organization could insure that Southerners would initiate any New Deal legislative program that affected the South. Lucy Mason also justified the Southern Conference. Mason had long believed that, acting alone, middle-class liberals could not rejuvenate the South. She insisted that common cause had to be made with organized labor, the rural poor, and blacks, and that the Birmingham convention furthered the realization of such an alliance.[19]

Nevertheless, the broad coalition that liberals had envisioned immediately began to disintegrate. Some, such as Senator John Bankhead of Alabama, left the organization because of its antisegregation resolution. Others, like Francis Pickens Miller, disassociated themselves from SCHW because of the presence of Communist party members at Birmingham.[20]

Frank Graham interceded to save the Southern Conference. To do otherwise, he was convinced, amounted to desertion of "the people." Graham refused to be daunted by either the red or the race issue and believed that opponents of SCHW had deliberately tried to smear the Birmingham meeting. In 1939 he succeeded Louise Charlton as conference chairman. Though aware that the conference included Communists, he maintained that their influence was negligible. In Graham's mind, they would not inhibit SCHW from playing a major role in furthering democracy in the South—a democracy that would include Southern Negroes. But Graham's own racial liberalism, while more militant in style than that of the Interracial Commission, still fell short of opposing segregation. When queried about SCHW policies, Graham replied that they tried to promote social justice for blacks and not social equality.[21]

As the Interracial Commission had sought to deal with lynching, under Graham's leadership, the Southern Conference decided to dramatize the issue of voting restrictions. The organization's main target was the poll tax, which in 1939 remained an impediment to voting in all Southern states except North Carolina, Louisiana, and Florida. Estimates on the number of people disfranchised as a result of poll tax requirements ranged from five to eleven million. (SCHW usually cited the latter figure.)[22]

Given the nature of the conference, the poll tax should have been an ideal issue for it to focus upon. Securing the franchise for the poor was in line with the organization's professed goal of winning mass appeal. Like other liberal groups, SCHW often expressed the sentiment that the demagogic leadership of Mississippi's Theodore Bilbo or Georgia's Eugene Talmadge did not represent the "true" feelings of Southerners, many of whom could not even qualify to vote. Moreover, at a time when racial liberals still considered the disfranchisement of Southern blacks too sensitive an issue to tamper with, it could be pointed out that the poll tax affected many more whites than blacks. Some blacks would get to exercise the ballot as a result of poll tax repeal, but their number would be negligible compared with the increased numbers of white voters. White primaries and literacy test laws, the main legal methods of disfranchising Southern blacks, would not be challenged. Thus, though some members felt that even to tackle the poll tax would raise cries of white supremacy from the demagogues, sponsors of the Southern Conference hoped to present a Southern liberalism that could still win the allegiance of a good many white Southerners.

One of the leaders of the movement for poll tax repeal, Virginia Foster Durr, demonstrated once again how Southern liberals during the thirties were so often motivated by a combination of Christian ethics, living experiences outside the South, and New Deal fervor. Virginia Durr was the daughter of J. Sterling Foster, the pastor of a Presbyterian church in Birmingham that was once described as "one of the greatest churches of the South." Both she and her sister Josephine, the future Mrs. Hugo Black, were raised to be Christian ladies and taught, in a somewhat traditionally paternalistic way, that they had a responsibility to help blacks. She was married to Clifford J. Durr, a Montgomery lawyer who had come to Washington in 1933 as an assistant general counsel for the Reconstruction Finance Corporation. The Durrs were committed proponents of racial justice who easily fit into Washington's enclave of pro–New Deal Southern liberals. Indeed, Mrs. Durr's long record of outspokenness on behalf of Negro rights would, during the McCarthy era, lead to her being called to testify before a Senate investigatory committee. At that time, she explained to an Alabama newspaper how she had arrived at her liberal racial views.

> I can assure you that my father found them just as hard to understand, yet, in a way, he is responsible for them. He had a fine library and encouraged me and required me to read good books. I was brought up in the Presbyterian faith and I never got any explanation that satisfied me as to how Christian principles and race discrimination could be reconciled. And then he sent me north to Wellesley College, where for the first time in my life I came into contact with Negro girls who were just as well educated, just as smart (some a lot smarter) and just as well mannered as I was. Some of them became my friends, and it was then that my ideas began to change, but it was only when I was in Washington and came to know, through my work on the abolition of the Poll Tax, some of the great Negro women of the South, that I came to my present views.[23]

Virginia Durr and her husband would return to Alabama in 1950 and from there become involved with local civil rights activities, with Mrs. Durr constantly—apparently successfully—urging her brother-in-law, Justice Black, to take a sympathetic view of the ongoing struggle for racial justice. She was typical of the white Southerners who had found in the Southern Conference for Human Welfare a natural outlet for their racial liberalism and who in 1939 were willing to address the problem of voting restrictions.

In February 1939 the SCHW executive board established a civil rights committee. The liberal Texas congressman Maury Maverick served as chairman of the committee, Virginia Durr as vice-chairman, and Joseph Gelders as executive secretary. In September 1939 the committee issued a report calling for SCHW to help get rid of the poll tax in both primary and general elections. The parent organization was already making efforts on the federal level; in August 1939, following unsuccessful efforts to persuade a Southern congressman to introduce an anti–poll tax bill in the House, SCHW supported one sponsored by Lee E. Geyer of California that called for the elimination of the poll tax in all federal elections, and in March 1940 Maury Maverick went to Washington to testify in support of the bill. He said that poll taxes stifled true democracy among whites much more than among blacks. He characterized the opponents of repeal as "a group out to get a Roosevelt, a Maverick, or anybody who won't do his best to keep the colored people, the white sharecroppers, the whole lower third down in the dirt." Hoping the movement might meet with success if poll tax reform were freed from the stigma of being a "Negro measure," Maverick made a point of noting that he was not "out on a reforming tour to help the poor, persecuted black man." [24]

The attempt to make poll tax repeal a nonracial issue was to be a persistent policy of SCHW. When the question of whether poll tax repeal would be helpful to blacks unless other suffrage restrictions were abandoned came up at an SCHW board meeting, Frank Graham urged the conference not to work for full Negro suffrage until the opportunity presented itself. In his introduction to a 1940 pamphlet against the poll tax, Graham emphasized that all the contributors were loyal white Southerners. "Jefferson and Jackson, pioneer battlers for the suffrage rights of the people in an old Southern tradition, speak again in these pages of contemporary Southerners as they cry out against the undemocratic poll tax in eight Southern states." [25]

Barry Bingham, one of the contributors to the pamphlet, specifically denied that the poll tax mainly disfranchised Negroes, claiming that the black man was never the reason why the tax was instituted. He also maintained that statistics from the three Southern states that had abandoned the poll tax offered conclusive evidence that Negro voting did not proportionately increase after repeal. His arguments were later repeated by Moss A. Plunkett, a Roanoke attorney and chairman of the Virginia Electoral Reform League, an SCHW-sponsored anti–poll tax organization. Plunkett told the Senate Judiciary Committee in 1942 that fears of increased Negro voting following poll tax repeal were definitely unfounded. Plunkett cited figures that showed that a smaller percentage of blacks voted in North Carolina, a non–poll tax state, that in the poll tax state of Virginia. Negro advancement in Virginia, Plunkett indicated, would not be furthered by a massive increase in black voters; the efforts of a generation would be nullified by such an "extremist" undertaking.[26]

Florida senator Claude Pepper, whom the SCHW finally persuaded in 1942 to introduce a bill similar to Geyer's in the Senate, invoked his Southernness in answer to a criticism by Governor Frank Dixon of Alabama that poll tax reformers were risking disunity in time of war to lobby for their pet reforms: "My people have been southerners as long as Governor Dixon's," he said, "and since 1600 I have not had a direct ancestor who did not fight for and did not die for the South." Pepper said that he preferred to have the states abandon the poll tax, but that Congress should not abdicate its right to see that all people voted in federal elections. And when in 1944 Ralph McGill of the *Atlanta Constitution* heard that the recently elected New York Negro congressman Adam Clayton Powell, Jr., had remarked that, if not for the poll tax, a black could be elected governor of Mississippi, McGill characterized Powell as a "political jackass" whose rash statements only added grist to the mills of anti-Negro agitators. Declared McGill: "The poll tax is not a Negro question or problem, not even in Mississippi. If we permit Congressman Powell and others like him to make it so appear, we will have done ourselves harm." As late as 1948, after a commission appointed by President Harry S. Truman had issued its report on civil rights, Claude Pepper—still fighting for poll tax repeal in the Senate—carefully distinguished legislation from any endorsement of "the so-called president's civil rights program." [27]

Despite the insistence of poll tax reformers that they had the best interests of Southern whites at heart, denunciation of them was both vituperative and extensive. Conservative industrialists in Alabama, the "Big Mules," claimed that those supporting repeal wanted "nothing short of complete social equality . . . abolition of all race segregation, and a strong pressure to bring about interracial marriages." The Byrd machine in Virginia used the same reasoning as did anti-New Deal political organizations in Georgia, Mississippi, and Texas.[28]

Nonetheless, in almost every year between 1940 and 1948, SCHW helped introduce bills prohibiting poll taxes in federal elections and in other ways kept up the fight. In 1940, the CIO began to help finance SCHW's campaign, which resulted in a National Committee to Abolish the Poll Tax. In February 1941 SCHW stimulated the creation of a Southern Electoral Reform League to renew efforts on both the state and the federal level and also to keep Southerners in the forefront of the movement. As they encountered more and more opposition, the reformers became convinced that repeal would usher in a new era in Southern politics. Official organs, such as the *Poll Tax Repealer,* claimed that abolition would eliminate the "chief bulwark of the Bourbon South"—senators and congressmen from poll tax states who wielded a disproportionately large share of power in Congress. The Southern Electoral Reform League argued that unless the poll tax was done away with, the South stood in danger of becoming another India. "We have democracy with a great big 'D' in the South," Lucy Mason pointed out, "but we do not have democracy for the people." Popular rule had become a myth, asserted Jennings Perry, editor for the *Nashville Tennessean* and a leader of the anti–poll tax forces in his state. America professed to be fighting for free elections in Greece, Italy, and Yugoslavia, he noted in 1944, while restricted electorates in eight Southern poll tax states enabled Southern political bosses to make a farce of democracy at home. Perry's unsuccessful efforts in Tennessee led him to conclude that reform had to come from the top down. "The minority electorates must realize," said Perry, "that their very minority has placed *them* in the thrall to piddling political machines that could not survive the weight of all the people." At a 1944 executive board meeting Frank Graham characterized the Southern senators who fought poll tax reform as betrayers of the people.[29]

The willingness of SCHW liberals to bring up the suffrage question was an important step forward, distinguishing their organization from the Commission on Interracial Cooperation. In 1940 the commission's official publication, *Southern Frontier,* was still insisting that anti–poll tax agitation only added to racial tensions. The magazine noted that, though blacks were not involved in the movement, they would be the ones to suffer, inasmuch as the race issue could never be separated from the poll tax.[30]

But it was a small step. Despite the militantly liberal rhetoric of the poll tax repealers, the interests of blacks were given subordinate consideration. The impact of the poll tax on Southern politics was clearly exaggerated, given the reformers' own recognition that poll tax repeal would not enfranchise many blacks. Most importantly, Southern liberals channeled too much energy into what at best would have been a symbolic victory. SCHW in 1940 had financed an unsuccessful attempt to get the Supreme Court to reverse its 1937 decision upholding the Georgia poll tax.[31] Yet when the Supreme Court outlawed the white primary in 1944,[32] Southern liberals, preoccupied with their battle against the poll tax, failed to use the decision as an opportunity to work harder for black suffrage.

There was one noteworthy exception. In 1947, J. Waties Waring, a South Carolina federal district judge, ruled that his native state's efforts to maintain a white primary were unconstitutional. Judge Waring was ostracized and hounded by his fellow white South Carolinians and earned the verbal praise of other Southern liberals, but his action did not prompt the latter to campaign seriously for black enfranchisement.[33]

Finally, the anti–poll tax campaign produced little in the way of tangible results; Southern states continued the practice until it was prohibited in 1964 following the adoption of the Twenty-fourth Amendment.[34] Only Georgia in 1945 repealed its poll tax, and this was more a result of the factional dispute between incumbent Governor Ellis Arnall and the forces led by ex-Governor Eugene Talmadge than it was the work of the Southern Conference. Indeed, the Georgia committee of SCHW was conspicuously quiet during that struggle. The spirit of Birmingham, which had engendered SCHW, remained unfulfilled. The idea that white mass support could be won, a direct confrontation over Jim Crow averted, and blacks be given a greater measure of equality all at the same time proved unworkable. Though it tried, the Southern Conference for Human Welfare uncovered no massive Silent South to support its goals.

Instead of being seen as loyal Southerners, white liberals became looked upon as abettors of what one Virginia opponent of the poll tax reformers called an "amalgamated wolf-pack Confederacy of Communists, left-wingers, and ultra radicals who seek, with disguised bitterness and effrontery, to ravish the honor and sovereign integrity of the Southern states." [35] Much of this increased resistance was attributable to the controversy over Jim Crow generated by World War II. Unlike the New Deal, which had swollen their ranks and given them confidence, the war had the opposite effect. For Southern liberals, a moment of truth had arrived.

CHAPTER SIX

Jim Crow and the War

Even more than had the Great Depression, the Second World War would have a tremendous impact upon the outlook of white Southern liberals. In December 1941, while most Americans could think of little except the shock of Pearl Harbor and the entrance of the United States into the war, Southern liberals immediately saw another difficulty. "I listened with great care to the broadcasts on Sunday night," Will Alexander wrote of Pearl Harbor day to Edwin Embree, the president of the Julius Rosenwald Fund. "It seemed to me that there was too frequent reference to the color of our enemy. In my opinion the real enemy is Hitler, and to make this specific sector a race war will leave us with a very serious problem on our hands when it is all over." Alexander, who had left the FSA to become race relations director of the Rosenwald Fund, had witnessed the racial violence in the South that followed the First World War. Experience led him to believe that similar tensions and outbreaks would recur. Alexander used his influence in government circles to stop publication of a pre–Pearl Harbor pamphlet written by the novelist Pearl Buck that quoted Negro leaders as admiring the Japanese as an advancing colored race. "This is a delicate matter," he warned Embree, "and I am not sure how it can be handled. The mood of the country is that we are in for a life and death struggle, and that everything else is extraneous. I think it would make a bad impression if Negro leaders in what they say, should try to use this occasion to bring to the front, even their just grievances." [1]

Yet, the fears of Southern liberals notwithstanding, blacks did use the war to protest racial discrimination with a new vehemence. Many agreed with Horace Cayton that the "greater the outside danger to the safety of this country, the more abundant the gains for Negroes will likely to be." Before the United States entered the conflict, the black unionist A. Philip Randolph of the Brotherhood of Sleeping Car Porters had organized a massive march on Washington to protest racial discrimination in defense industries. The march, scheduled for July 1, 1941, never took place, but it held the promise of mobilizing an unprecedented number of blacks and was canceled only after President Roosevelt, acting on the advice of Aubrey Williams, issued Executive Order 8802 on June 25, establishing a Fair Employment Practices Committee (FEPC). One outraged white Southerner later called Randolph a "more dangerous enemy to the women of the South than that unspeakable Thad Stevens." After Pearl Harbor the United States professed to be fighting for democracy and against enemies whose master-race ideology made them the foe of all free people. Blacks did not forget the point. "Prove to us that you are not hypocrites when you say this is a war for freedom," said Walter White in 1942. "Prove it to us." Exhibiting an unprecedented degree of race consciousness, Negroes like White demanded immediate action against discrimination and segregation, particularly in the armed services. For the first time in its history, the NAACP began to attract a mass following. From 355 branches and a membership of 50,556 in 1940, the association increased to 1,073 branches and a membership of over 450,000 by 1946. Blacks adopted a war slogan of "double victory"—on the home front as well as abroad—and launched an all-out campaign against Jim Crow. "There never was a time in the history of the United States," noted the black Virginia newspaper editor P. B. Young, "when Negroes were more united concerning the impact of segregation on their lives." [2]

During World War II racial animosities increased throughout the country (in 1943 serious riots occurred in Detroit and New York), but the situation was gravest in the South. Southern whites feared that the war would upgrade the status of black people, and Southern politicians such as Frank Dixon of Alabama, Eugene Talmadge of Georgia, and Theodore Bilbo of Mississippi profited from white supremacist campaigns. Senator John Bankhead of Alabama introduced a bill that would allow Northern black soldiers to receive their training only in Northern army camps. Numerous incidents, beatings, and near riots occurred as whites enforced Southern segregation ordinances with renewed vigor. Southern whites also resented the operation of the FEPC in trying to alleviate racial discrimination in industry. Lynching increased, and there was talk of reviving the Klan. In July 1942 a Bessemer, Alabama attorney told his Kiwanis Club that a "League to Maintain White Supremacy" was necessary for the South, and in October a group called "Vigilantes, Incorporated" filed for a charter in Georgia. Eleanor Roosevelt's well-publicized advocacy of Negro rights during the war led one white Southern commentator to call her "the most hated woman in the South since Harriet Beecher Stowe." In 1942 the militantly liberal New York newspaper, *PM*, spoke of the "imminent possibility of bloody strife" in the South and sent one of its staff reporters to cover the situation.[3]

Such developments deflated the white Southern liberals' prewar hope of subordinating the race issue to other problems. "It makes me sick for people to push Negro equality when what the Negroes need is better pay and more hospitalization etc.," Frank Daniels told his brother Jonathan, "and what they are going to get is the loss of everything they have gained in the last twenty-five years." Mark Ethridge admitted that he was concerned that the Negroes' strategy would backfire and lead to only greater white reaction in the South. Ethridge thought that blacks were "being misled by a good number of their northern friends" and that black leaders were "overplaying their hand." Jonathan Daniels, now with the Office of Civilian Defense, also became more disturbed over race relations than ever before. "We seem to be almost back to the extreme abolitionists and the extreme slaveholders in the lines of discussion," he wrote Howard Odum. "Between them, people like ourselves seem to be left in a sort of awareness and futility together."[4]

Daniels soon got an even greater taste of wartime racial anxieties. In 1943 he became an administrative assistant to President Roosevelt, where his chief duty was to handle for the White House all problems related to blacks and the war. Once more, FDR had turned to a Southern liberal to guide his administration's racial policies. Aided by a white member of the Office of War Information and a black reporter from the *New York Evening Post,* Daniels, working with the FBI and military intelligence agencies, watched for potential trouble spots, especially on military bases and in adjacent areas, in order to prevent violence. He also tried to persuade the armed services to commission more black officers, but his main task was to "keep the lid on." Daniels made it clear to a number of his fellow Southern liberals that official Washington shared their concerns. He informed them, for example, that a proposed National Committee on Race Relations was scotched by those who feared that antisegregationist Northern Negroes would occupy positions of leadership.[5]

Though they may have been upset, white Southern liberals recognized the fundamental cause of the current wave of racial unrest—continuing discrimination against blacks at home and in the armed forces at a time when the United States was fighting a war against totalitarianism. As Herbert Agar, the English-born editor of the *Louisville Courier-Journal* and a former confidant of the Vanderbilt agrarians, noted in a flash of patriotic idealism, the war had "ordained" the United States with the responsibility of "taking the lead in bringing a spiritual sense of equality to the world." And, added Agar apprehensively, Southern Negroes lived so far from "equality" with white Americans that to them the very word was a joke. Julian LaRose Harris, a Columbus, Georgia newspaperman who had long battled against the Klan in his state, described the contradiction between American ideals and practices as the "weak joint in our armor." "You can imagine the conversation between a Northern Negro soldier and a Southern Negro," Harris pessimistically informed the Richmond editor, Virginius Dabney. But Southern liberals, rather than dwell upon the status of Southern blacks in a democratic society, frequently blamed tensions on the "extremists" at both ends of the racial controversy—an attitude that equated the NAACP with the Ku Klux Klan and Walter White with Eugene Talmadge.[6]

Trying to steer a middle course amid heightened wartime racial feelings proved difficult for white Southern liberals. In 1940 Mark Ethridge had incurred the wrath of many Southerners by accepting the chairmanship of the FEPC. In June 1942, at FEPC hearings in Birmingham, Ethridge tried to mollify whites hostile to the committee by declaring that its creation reflected a war order rather than a social document and that "no power in the world," including the combined Allied and Axis armies, could force Southern whites to abandon segregation. Ethridge's remarks were widely quoted, and he received a flood of criticism from black leaders and newspaper editors. Walter White attacked Ethridge's attempt to appease the Bilbos, which, he contended, succeeded only in infuriating blacks. "The highest casualty rate of the war seems to be that of Southern white liberals," said White. "For various reasons they are taking cover at an alarming rate—fleeing before the onslaught of the professional Southern bigots." The criticism perturbed Ethridge. He insisted his statement did not represent his racial outlook and that he was the victim of "gross misrepresentation." He had also pointed out in those same hearings, Ethridge explained to Virginius Dabney, that even though racial segregation existed, FEPC meant to see that blacks received fair treatment in industry. But the racial situation in the South was so explosive that Ethridge became discouraged. "Since I have never tried to be a hero to either Negroes or whites," he concluded, "it didn't make a hell of a lot of difference what either side thought of what I had to say." [7]

If white liberals in the South failed to appease the so-called extremists, it was not because they did not try. Liberals went out of their way to play up the contributions of blacks toward the war effort in a manner designed not to antagonize whites. Some attempts strained credibility. In 1943 *Southern Frontier*, the official organ of the Interracial Commission, carried a front-page story on the heroic saga of a blind Negro peanut vendor in Greenville, Mississippi who saved the nickels and dimes he earned from selling peanuts—though he had to support a wife and four children from his earnings as well—in order to buy the first war bond in his county's latest sales drive. Other efforts had a saccharine quality about them. In July 1942 racial liberals in North Carolina sponsored a "Win the War" rally in Raleigh featuring white and black speakers who emphasized the biracial nature of the war by extolling the Pearl Harbor heroics of Colin Kelly, a Southern white aviator, and Dorie Miller, a black messboy on the *USS Arizona* who had manned an anti-aircraft gun during the attack and shot down a Japanese plane. Frank Graham specifically wanted the rally held on July 14, Bastille Day, because the conflict was, in Graham's words, a "people's war." When in June 1945 Senator James O. Eastland of Mississippi declared that black soldiers in Europe had been an "utter and dismal failure" and had "disgraced" the flag of their country, Southern liberals led a concerted effort to publicize the creditable war record of black GI's.[8]

But, compared to the genuine dread that an all-out race war was impending, optimistic statements were few. If Southern liberals expected to see the emergence of a Silent South, it was now the Silent South of their nightmares rather than the one of their dreams. It was the bigots who were becoming more and more vocal, and with increasing race consciousness, the majority of the South's people, white as well as black, would suffer. As one observer put it in 1943, the current wave of Bilboism and Talmadgism represented a recrudescence of the "decadent medievalism" that had frustrated the South for eighty years. "Demagoguery," reported the *Southern Frontier*, "bids fair to reach a peak equal to if not higher than in the nineties when the Southern states finally disfranchised Negroes." Thomas Sancton, a Louisiana native who wrote for the *New Republic*, characterized the Southern racial situation as "fertile soil for Axis propaganda" and asserted that continued racial violence would amount to a "domestic Pearl Harbor." Sancton also revealed the white Southern liberal's traditional contempt toward the racists. "I believe it can and should be shown," he said, "that white bigots and rumormongers and brutal demagogues are doing the South—the South which they possess and others love—the tragic disservice they have always done it." [9]

The difficulties of white racial liberals during the war years resulted from the fact that the entire Jim Crow system had finally come under attack. Ever since the unsuccessful efforts of George Washington Cable, Southern liberals had avoided the segration issue and instead concentrated on such problems as Negro education, lynching, poverty, and the poll tax. In 1930 publicity director Robert B. Eleazer had summed up the general attitude of the Interracial Commission on the subject by pointing out that, though the commission did not advocate either the extension or stiffening of Jim Crow laws, its members did not deem it either "wise or desirable" to fight segregation.[10] When it came to segregation, Southern liberals generally had little to say.

For some, a segregationist position represented a tactical stance; for others it demonstrated their own commitment to racial separation; and for still others it reflected divided sentiments. Arthur Raper never believed in segregation and personally violated its strictures on numerous occasions, but in the 1930s he felt that to campaign for its abandonment would have made the Interracial Commission less effective. Virginius Dabney, on the other hand, believed that justice for blacks could be achieved under segregation so long as services and opportunities for Southern Negroes were raised to levels substantially equal with those for whites. In 1936, W. T. Couch had chided: "Do you really believe that no white person can eat with a Negro without injury to someone?" Yet in 1944, because of his disagreement with most of the black contributors to a volume explaining Negro wartime demands, Couch added a special "publisher's introduction." According to Couch, the elimination of segregation would be "disastrous for everyone and more so for the Negro than the white man." The white Southern writer David L. Cohn believed that though it would be possible for Southern blacks to gain voting rights, justice in the courts, and equitable shares of tax money for health, education, and public services, on segregation there could be no compromise. Cohn insisted that if the federal government interceded to end segregation, "every Southern white man would spring to arms and the country would be swept by civil war." The war years, however, made it difficult for Southern liberals to sidestep segregation; for segregation and all it represented had finally become *the* race issue in the South.[11]

Howard Odum found the war years particularly trying. It seemed that the destructive sectionalism of the past was triumphing over the potential regionalism of the future. He saw racial passions stifling the progress that had slowly but surely been taking place in the South:

> Just a few years ago we almost had unanimity in plans for cooperative arrangements, in which Negroes and whites were enthusiastic and in which representatives of nearly all phases of the South were participants. We had worked into entirely new patterns of fellowship and

> participation, and there were many evidences that the South was beginning to be proud of this progress. Today, as far as I know, there is practically none of this left. The South is becoming almost unanimous in a pattern of unity that refers to white unity. The thousands of incidents and accidents in the South are being integrated into the old pattern of southern determination against an outside aggression. . . . We know that a South which was just coming into its own, getting ready for an enriched agriculture, a more balanced economy, a more liberal viewpoint will sacrifice all this in a pathetic blood and sweat episode reminiscent of the Civil War and Reconstruction.[12]

Thirty years of studying race relations had not changed Odum's basic approach. After 1940, as Jim Crow came under more direct attack, he found it increasingly difficult to present the race issue as a scientific rather than an ethical question. Nevertheless, Odum tried to prevent those whom he considered irresponsible emotionalists from exerting influence. "In life as in football," he once said, "we must after all have a strategy," and for Odum, a winning strategy had to be arrived at dispassionately. At the height of wartime Negro-white antagonisms, Odum would claim that his criticism of racial agitators stemmed from "conclusions growing out of long days' work of trying to be scientifically honest and American." He easily regarded the two positions as inseparable.[13]

If the war and the racial controversy it generated never swung him from his tenacious scientism, however, it did convince him that he had been wrong in relegating black-white relations to a back burner within his regionalist view of the South. In 1943 Odum, who only a few years earlier had been anxious to lose the tag "Negro expert," returned to his region's racial situation with the publication of *Race and Rumors of Race*.

As its title indicated, *Race and Rumors of Race* aimed to show that a good deal of white Southern perception of what blacks were doing in 1942 and 1943 lacked validity. In particular, Odum devoted much attention to widespread but groundless stories about the activities of the so-called "Eleanor Clubs" of Southern blacks who sang hosannas to their "Great White Angel" and willfully sought to get "uppity" with white folks. The rumors usually alleged that black domestics made secret pacts with each other not to work for white employers unless they were granted "social equality," but in some cases they even accounted for the flagrant actions of zoot-suited young black males whose rank in their local Eleanor Club could be presumably told by the number and size of feathers they wore on their wide-brimmed fedoras. Odum argued that, preposterous as such beliefs seemed, they reflected the commitment of an overwhelming majority of white Southerners to segregation and their bitter hostility to outside demands that the South change its racial customs overnight. Only a minority of Southern whites, according to Odum, actually desired to brutalize blacks, but most still subscribed to the "Southern credo" that "the Negro was a Negro and always would be that and nothing more." Characteristically, he termed such feelings "organic" to the South.[14]

Though he clearly sympathized with the defensiveness of Southern whites, Odum nevertheless demonstrated much empathy for the point of view of blacks and their Northern liberal supporters. He openly admired blacks for their growing racial consciousness and admitted that in any theoretical debate they were most right and the white South least right. But policies had to be based upon reality, not debating points. Discussing wartime racial discrimination in the North, Odum wondered if "with all the efforts of all the liberals and progressives and reformers and propagandists the thing [desegregation] cannot be done in New York or Seattle or Los Angeles, what sort of intelligence is it that reasons that it can and must be done in the South, where there are these cultural complexities and conditionings over long periods of time?" Publicly, in *Race and Rumors of Race,* he again called for a "scientific" approach that would acquiesce in segregation. However, privately Odum recognized the limitations of even social science. In 1943 he confessed to Virginius Dabney that one "necessarily" had to "feel inadequate in a situation which has no satisfactory solution in the sense of here and now, yes or no, white or black, North or South, you or me."[15]

In 1944 Gunnar Myrdal's highly influential *An American Dilemma* was published and in Odum's view added fat to the fire. According to Odum, the Swedish scholar, who had characterized the treatment of blacks as America's "greatest and most conspicuous scandal," showed a typically European attitude toward the United States in relying upon "new objectivists and Freudian analysts" for the framework of his book and largely ignoring the valuable work of American social scientists. "Nowhere," said Odum, "does he sense the contribution of our great historians and nowhere is there hardly a mention of the cultural, organic, and evolutionary tragedy of reconstruction." Although Myrdal brilliantly showed the race question to be essentially a moral problem, Odum believed he had overlooked much good work that whites and blacks had done in the South before the war. Myrdal's critical sketch of white Southern liberals—particularly those connected with the Commission on Interracial Cooperation—proved especially disturbing to Odum, who argued that such people were far more forward-looking than the Swedish scholar maintained. Furthermore, Myrdal added insult to injury. Odum was peeved over *An American Dilemma's* failure to mention even once his own magnum opus, *Southern Regions of the United States.* Moreover, in arguing that the "American Creed" would soon consign segregation to oblivion, Myrdal had failed to take into account how the heritage of white Southerners enabled them to resist rationality. Consequently, Myrdal was excessively optimistic, and *An American Dilemma* was not the problem-solving book it purported to be. Pro-Negro sentiment, Odum concluded, had seriously affected Myrdal's sociological judgment.[16]

The majority of Southern liberals shared Odum's skepticism about *An American Dilemma.* Rupert Vance, Odum's colleague at Chapel Hill and himself a leading sociologist of the South, declared that Myrdal had naively dumped the race issue into the dismal arena of politics. Still more critical was W. T. Couch, who believed that Myrdal's work was written under "gross misapprehension of what such ideas as equality, freedom, democracy, human rights have meant, and of what they can be made to mean." Virginius Dabney, writing in the *Richmond Times-Dispatch,* acknowledged the book rather lamely. He characterized *An American Dilemma* as a "thorough and exhaustive" study of race relations but did not go into details. Dabney, though, went farther than most of his fellow Southern liberal journalists. The *Atlanta Constitution,* the *Raleigh News and Observer,* and the *Louisville Courier-Journal,* for example, failed to mention Myrdal's work.[17] Nonetheless, the book became an instant classic in the North and made life more difficult for those Southern liberals who were still trying to avoid a reappraisal of segregation.

The wartime racial situation spelled the end for the Commission on Interracial Cooperation. The organization had been in decline since 1935 following Will Alexander's departure for Washington. Blacks resented their token representation in the commission and their lack of influence over its actions. According to one Memphis Negro, white members tried to be broadminded, but none of them dared speak bluntly. Instead, they drifted on "clouds of sentimentality" and passed meaningless resolutions. The blacks blamed much of this on Howard Odum, who, ever since he had become president of the Interracial Commission in 1937, had been trying to transform it into a regional planning association. Interested in obtaining financial support from private foundations (or perhaps even the federal government), Odum played down the race issue. In 1938 he informed Jackson Davis of the General Education Board of the Rockefeller Foundation that what he had in mind for Southern blacks was planned agrarian communities—"some little Denmarks . . . American Negro style," he called them. He also toyed with the idea of a black community center for the Chapel Hill area. For a time Odum even considered moving the Interracial Commission from Atlanta to Knoxville, where as a Southern regional organization it would act in coordination with the National Resources Planning Board and the TVA. His plans, however, came to naught. Commission members discussed Odum's ideas but did little to implement them, and SCHW with its more militant style siphoned away support. W. E. B. Du Bois said in 1939, referring obliquely to Odum, "It does not reduce Negro ignorance or poverty by calling the plight regional and proceeding to give the whites better schools and higher wages." [18]

By then even white members of the organization knew it was at a low ebb; in 1939 Emily Clay, a secretary in the commission's Atlanta office, wondered if it was "time to begin to look around for a suitable location for a peanut or hamburger stand" inasmuch as expectations did not appear very promising for the continuation of the commission's work. A few months later M. Ashby Jones pointed out that the commission had not met in more than a year and that he also had grave doubts about its future.[19] Aside from helping Howard Odum publish *Race and Rumors of Race* and issuing *Southern Frontier*, a monthly newsletter edited by Jessie Daniel Ames, the commission had taken no action to deal with the current wave of racial unrest. In 1943 the commission hired William E. Cole, a University of Tennessee sociologist, to investigate its status. Cole concluded that the organization had grown inefficient and suggested a revival of Howard Odum's plan for a council on Southern regional development. Odum himself believed that the commission had stagnated under the direction of people like Mrs. Ames and M. Ashby Jones. Yet even Ames knew that the end was near. Though she belittled Odum's leadership, explaining to Virginius Dabney that Odum's only role was to provide ideas and then depend on others to carry them out, she admitted that the commission's greatest weakness was that it had neither a policy nor a well-defined program.[20] It was symbolic of the times that the Interracial Commission, the major organization of Southern racial liberalism within the confines of segregation, formally came to an end in October 1943.

Jessie Ames tried to salvage some influence for white Southern liberals amid the wartime tensions by promoting a conference of black leaders. In April 1942 she wrote Gordon Hancock, the black president of Virginia Union College in Richmond, and explained that Negroes could not consolidate their old gains and achieve new ones without the help of Southern whites. Mrs. Ames, unsure of the future of black people in the South, hoped that white and black leaders could agree on objectives and strategy that they would then work for both jointly and separately. She wanted Hancock and two or three others to call a conference of a dozen or so blacks who in her words were "not dependent on the Federal Government for their living," so that they could arrive at some consensus on ways in which Southern whites could help them. Cognizant of the declining influence of Southern liberals, Ames did not want her idea publicized; she insisted that Negroes act as if the initiative were their own. "Any other procedure," she advised Hancock, "would . . . leave the whole plan open to attack by members of your race on the grounds that 'Bourbon' white people of the South were already planning to reenslave Negroes."

After Hancock had responded favorably to her plan, Mrs. Ames provided him with more specific instructions. She said that the black conference should draft a "New Charter on Race Relations in the South." Such a charter should not be too specific, lest a potential following fall apart in disagreement over what should and should not be included. Segregation would be implicitly recognized, but neither attacked nor affirmed. Ames's attitude reflected many years of Southern liberal thinking on race, especially the desire to aid blacks without antagonizing whites. A charter on race relations, she asserted, must "convince the blind, selfish and greedy people that material benefits will derive from a changed course. It must give the Negroes assurance that they are not going to be the recipients of racial paternalism if they go along with us."

Ames's proposal amounted to a last-gasp measure to make separate-but-equal workable in the South. Convinced that white liberals would be caught in the middle of any struggle, she again emphasized the credo of Southern liberals that those closest to the problem ought to be the ones to deal with it. This exclusionary attitude now even extended to white Southerners who had left the South to work in Washington and other parts of the country; people such as Will Alexander and Clark Foreman were regarded as being out of touch with local situations and no longer capable of dealing with Southern racial questions. Ames still believed that there was a liberal South that, if organized, could improve the status of Southern blacks. As late as 1941, she pointed out that Southern whites generally sympathized with the goals of blacks but were afraid to take public stands so long as the race issue was infused with controversy. She characterized this "conspiracy of silence" as a "bottleneck" to progress that had to be broken. A "sane" approach, Ames insisted even during the war years, could break the bottleneck.[21]

On October 20, 1942 a group of Southern blacks met in Durham, North Carolina and joined Hancock in drafting a statement. The group included Charles S. Johnson of Fisk University, Frederick D. Patterson of Tuskegee, Benjamin E. Mays of Morehouse College, Rufus E. Clement of Atlanta University, Horace Mann Bond of Fort Valley State College in Georgia, and P. B. Young, editor of the *Norfolk Journal and Guide.* Claiming to speak in "candor and wisdom," they called for equal pay and opportunities for blacks in industry, a federal antilynching law, equality in public services, the hiring of Negroes by Southern police departments, and the abolition of poll taxes and white primaries. They also stressed that it was a "wicked notion" to suggest that the struggle for Negro rights contradicted the best interests of a nation at war. They voiced criticism of segregation but did not demand its immediate abolition. "We are fundamentally opposed to the principle and practice of compulsory segregation in our American society," ran the carefully drafted statement, "[but] we regard it as both sensible and timely to address ourselves to the current problems of racial discrimination and neglect and to ways in which we may cooperate in the advancement of programs aimed at the sound improvement of race relations within the democratic framework." [22]

White Southern liberals, many of whom did not know of Jessie Daniel Ames's role in the conference, enthusiastically supported the Durham statement. Thomas Sancton, usually more militant in his opposition to racial discrimination than many of his fellow Southern liberals, praised the Durham blacks for their realism. According to Sancton, it was a "far cry from the Booker T. Washington line which accepted permanent humiliation and segregation as the basis for race relations." Ames herself was pleased with the Durham statement and worked to live up to her end of the agreement with Hancock by establishing a special committee of Southern whites to respond to the Durham blacks. She received a setback when the Birmingham newspaperman James E. Chappell refused to head such a committee. Though he sympathized with the blacks' demands, the mere mention of segregation caused Chappell to feel, in his own words, "obliged to duck and run." Ralph McGill, however, chaired the white committee, which finally met in Atlanta on April 8, 1942. At Atlanta the whites affirmed their solidarity with the signers of the Durham statement and agreed to form a committee to bring the two groups together. The whites emphasized their intent to distinguish segregation from other forms of racial discrimination. "Many conservative white people are fearful that such movements as this have the destruction of segregation as an ultimate objective," Virginius Dabney explained to P. B. Young, "and I had hoped to allay such fears." [23]

In June 1943 the two groups came to Richmond to adopt a common platform. The meeting did not go well. Ralph McGill, the designated chairman of the proceedings, said he could not break away from his duties with the *Atlanta Constitution*. To the consternation of the blacks who attended, M. Ashby Jones responded to Gordon Hancock's moderate opening address with an impassioned lecture on how blacks were demanding too much too fast, and that only a continuation of the policies of the Interracial Commission could assure racial progress in the South.

Howard Odum saved the Richmond meeting from turning into a complete disaster. Odum objected to Jones's remarks and stated that the blacks at Durham had made an outstanding gesture that deserved a positive response from white Southerners. He urged the white delegates at the meeting to act, first to show blacks that some Southern whites were capable of receiving their protests with an open mind, and second to serve as an advance guard that could help Negroes achieve as many concessions as possible. Odum also believed that any organization resulting from the Durham, Atlanta, and Richmond meetings should be along the lines of his earlier plans for a council on Southern regional development. The promoter of regionalism, however, now accepted the fact that race relations had to be the first priority of any new organization. For his plans Odum had the moral as well as financial support of Will Alexander, whose position with the Rosenwald Fund offered prospects for financial assistance. Dr. Will endorsed the project so long as Odum rather than Ames and Jones—people whom Alexander had concluded were backward looking—drew up the guidelines. Through Odum's efforts, the Richmond conference finally resolved that American Negroes were "entitled to and should have every guarantee of equal opportunity that every other citizen of the United States has within the framework of the American democratic system of government." [24]

In October 1943 the Interracial Commission formally disbanded, and the following February the Southern Regional Council (SRC) was incorporated in Georgia. No effort was made to make the SRC an organization with mass appeal. Sponsors of the new organization, however, hoped that it would be more broadly based than had the old Interracial Commission; both Alexander and Odum wanted to attract business and professional people as well as the usual coterie of academics, clergymen, and newspaper editors. Odum became the first president of the council, and for executive director secured the services of Guy B. Johnson, a white Texan and fellow sociologist at the University of North Carolina who specialized in the study of black folk culture. Alexander heartily welcomed Johnson's appointment.[25]

The search for a Silent South had led to the formation of a new white Southern liberal organization. Though blacks would have a measure of influence in the Southern Regional Council that they had not had with the Interracial Commission, the Regional Council represented one final effort on the part of white Southerners themselves to deal with racial injustice. The new group, formed in an atmosphere of racial crisis, would have the important task of coming to terms with the issue of segregation.

The creation of the Southern Regional Council reflected the difficulties that white racial liberalism in the South faced during the war years. For the first time, the entire nature of the Jim Crow South received national attention as, potentially, America's leading domestic problem. During the depression it had been possible to lose perspective on Jim Crow amid the poverty of the South. The boom generated by the war, however, made it clear that rising prosperity alone would not alleviate racial discrimination. Segregation, the issue dreaded by most white Southern liberals, was now becoming the test of their commitment to the struggle for Negro rights.

This development would make heavy inroads in the ranks of Southern liberals. One of the leading casualties was the Richmond newspaperman Virginius Dabney.

CHAPTER SEVEN

Virginius Dabney: Publicist for a Liberal South

Any list of white Southern liberals between 1920 and 1950 would reveal a high percentage of newspapermen; almost every major city in the South contained white newspapermen who campaigned against racial intolerance. Men such as Louis I. Jaffee of the *Norfolk Virginian-Pilot*, Julian LaRose Harris of Georgia's *Columbus Enquirer-Sun*, Grover Hall of the *Montgomery Advertiser*, John Temple Graves II of the *Birmingham Age-Herald*, Barry Bingham and Mark Ethridge of the *Louisville Courier-Journal*, Hodding Carter II of Greenville, Mississippi's *Delta-Democrat Times*, Jonathan Daniels of the *Raleigh News and Observer*, W. J. Cash of the *Charlotte News*, and Ralph McGill of the *Atlanta Constitution* were the publicists for a liberal South and frequently took an active role in the major liberal organizations. Prominent among these men was Virginius Dabney, frequent contributor to many national magazines and from 1939 to 1969 editor of the influential *Richmond Times-Dispatch*.

Dabney's background was patrician; he was born into one of Virginia's leading families, including in its ranks numerous planters, lawyers, doctors, and college teachers. His mother was a collateral descendant of no less a Virginian than Thomas Jefferson. His father,

Richard Heath Dabney, was a long-time history professor at the University of Virginia, where from 1905 to 1923 he also served as dean of graduate studies. The elder Dabney was a highly respected historian who wrote books on John Randolph of Roanoke and the French Revolution, and who for many years carried on a close personal correspondence with Woodrow Wilson. After his death in 1947, a eulogizer wrote that Richard Dabney had "embodied all that was most admirable and pleasing in the Old-School Virginia gentleman, with whom honor came first, and human kindness close behind." Virginius's paternal grandfather, for whom he was named, was a well-known literary critic and the author of two novels. But probably the most famous Dabney of all was Virginius's great-grandfather, Thomas Smith Gregory Dabney, who in 1835 had moved his family and slaves from Virginia to Mississippi where he established Burleigh, a cotton plantation running to more than 40,000 acres and ultimately holding over 500 slaves.[1]

Thomas Dabney was a model planter, the kind from whom legends are made. He was progressive both in the way he ran his plantation and in the way that he treated his bondsmen. A deeply religious man, he encouraged his slaves to learn to read and write, recognized the sanctity of black families, and whenever possible purchased spouses of his own slaves who were owned by another master. Until the Civil War Burleigh flourished. Dabney was a Whig who opposed secession and even considered migrating to England once the conflict began, but since this would entail parting with his beloved servants and leaving them to some unknown fate, he rejected the idea. The saga of Thomas Dabney, including his travails during the Civil War and Reconstruction, was recorded by his loving daughter Susan Smedes in her 1887 *Memorials of a Southern Planter*, which she wrote specifically to counteract the malevolent image of the slaveholder popularized by such works as Harriet Beecher Stowe's *Uncle Tom's Cabin* and Fanny Kemble's *Journal of a Residence on a Georgia Plantation*. The book was a success; seven editions were published within a space of twelve years. An English edition appeared in 1890, and another American one in 1914. Though biased, *Memorials of a Southern Planter* stands out as a first-rate historical source, undoubtedly one reason why it was reprinted again in 1965.[2]

It was to such a heritage that Virginius Dabney was born in University (now Charlottesville), Virginia in 1901. Growing up in the intellectually congenial atmosphere of a college community, he received an excellent education. Dabney was an outstanding student. He was graduated Phi Beta Kappa from the University of Virginia in 1920 and went on to receive his master's degree in 1921. After teaching French for a year at a high school near Alexandria, Dabney became a reporter with the *Richmond News Leader* in 1922. He remained with the *News Leader* until 1928, when he joined the editorial staff of the *Richmond Times-Dispatch*, a position he would hold for the next thirty-three years.[3]

There was little in his early years to indicate that Virginius Dabney would eventually concern himself with the problems of Southern blacks. Dabney's father, though his education set him apart from most white Southerners, had been conservative and entirely orthodox. Virginius's own comfortable background insulated him from many of the blatant racial injustices of the era, and not until much later in his life did he fully comprehend them.[4] Even at the height of his fame as a progressive-minded newspaperman, Dabney's racial liberalism never quite moved beyond a highly articulate—and undoubtedly sincere—separate-but-equal position. However, what distinguished him from his father was a willingness to criticize openly members of Virginia's political and ecclesiastical establishment. For example, in 1926 his coverage of the trial of a Negro woman sentenced to thirty years in prison for stealing less than $200 led to public indignation against the ruling judge.[5]

In taking periodic whacks at the Southern status quo, Dabney unquestionably reflected the great impact that H. L. Mencken had upon young, educated white Southerners whose views matured during the 1920s. Illustrative of his intellectual debt to Mencken was Dabney's long interest in one of the more enigmatic figures of Southern history, Bishop James Cannon, Jr., a Virginia Prohibitionist and one of the driving forces behind the Anti-Saloon League's successful effort to secure passage of the Eighteenth Amendment. The anticlerical Mencken once described Cannon as "the most powerful ecclesiastic ever heard of in America." Dabney undertook a probing investigation of Cannon's life and work, beginning in 1929, that culminated in the 1949 publication of a scathing biography appropriately titled *Dry Messiah.* Though Dabney showed a grudging admiration for Cannon's high-handedness and efficiency, the book was devastating; Dabney was brutally frank about his distaste for the hypocrisy he thought his subject represented. He characterized Cannon as "one of the most significant and most ominous figures of his time, a man whose tempestuous career holds lessons for us all." [6]

By exposing men such as Cannon, Dabney showed his willingness to acknowledge the South's seamier side, but like other Southern liberals, he did not believe that the Bishop Cannons truly represented the region. Dabney had his own vision of a Silent South. For him it consisted of the spiritual descendants of Thomas Jefferson—an elite of educated humanists who exercised a liberalizing influence far out of proportion to their numbers. It was a radically different kind of Silent South from the noble white yeomanry perceived by Howard Odum.

In 1932 Dabney outlined his views in *Liberalism in the South,* a four-hundred-page volume dealing with enlightened white Southerners since the eighteenth century. Dabney believed that the defense of slavery had retarded the development of the region's otherwise liberal impulses, but that once the trauma of the Civil War era was over, the South's liberal heritage reasserted itself. The book chronicled the work of native Southerners such as Jabez Lamar Monroe Curry, who from the end of the Civil War until his death in 1901 had continuously campaigned for greater educational opportunities for both white and black Southerners. Dabney asserted that the influence of men like Curry was increasing and making the South a better place in which to live. "The South may rejoice," he wrote, "that the social attitudes of its leaders and its people are coming to be more and more shot through with liberalism." According to Dabney, Southern white men with liberal proclivities were chiefly responsible for the progress that had occurred since antebellum times and their continuing activities could bring about the "future greatness" of the region.

Though it focused on numerous nonracial areas, *Liberalism in the South* tried to show that advances had also been made in black-white relations. Despite the demagoguery of some Southern politicians and the activities of the Ku Klux Klan, Dabney insisted that there was "a growing awareness on the part of the dominant race that the Negro is not a serf or a helot, but a human being with legitimate aspirations . . . which are slowly being realized." Dabney even detected a "growing conviction" on the part of a "substantial body of Southerners" that Jim Crow laws were excessively severe. However, he made it a point of noting that the prevailing view among the white majority was that segregation should be strictly maintained.[7]

Liberalism in the South demonstrated the young man's yearning to find a liberal traditon in his region's turmoiled past. At times he strained to prove his thesis. Arthur Raper thought well of the work but pointed out that Dabney tended to label almost anything "liberal." Clarence Cason, an Alabama writer, was more blunt. He thought the book "entirely too long, because there simply never had been that much liberalism in the South." [8] At any rate, in his own way Dabney had tried to prick some holes in the idea that the South was a blight upon the rest of the nation. Its past was not totally dark; its future was bright. These were the book's principal contentions.

Like other liberals, Dabney pointed to the futility of Reconstruction. In a 1936 article for the *American Mercury,* he speculated that if the South had won the Civil War it would have at least been spared the "ordeal to which it was subjected at the hands of thieves, cutpurses, and picaroons from the North." Only white Southerners, implied Dabney, could solve the region's problems. Yet he did not lament the Confederacy's demise. According to Dabney, if the Confederacy had been successful, the poor whites might have risen to power sooner and more assertively than they ultimately did, with the end result a South ruled by some "Führer Huey Long." It was an unusual point for a Southern liberal to make; such a view, for example, would have been unthinkable to Howard Odum.[9]

During the mid-thirties Dabney's reputation as an outspoken Southern liberal continued to grow. Particularly daring were his editorials denouncing the 1933 conviction in Atlanta of a nineteen-year-old black Communist, Angelo Herndon, who received a sentence of 18–20 years at hard labor for having organized a demonstration of unemployed white and black workers to protest the inadequacy of Fulton County's relief programs. Though the lily-white court considered its judgment merciful (the obscure Georgia insurrectionary law under which Herndon was tried could have demanded the death penalty), the case would become second only to Scottsboro as an example of "Southern justice." Yet in openly criticizing the outrageous verdict, Dabney was only one of two white Southern journalists, the other being W. T. Anderson of the *Macon Telegraph*. Moreover, after attending a May 1936 meeting of the Southern Policy Association, the predecessor of the Southern Conference for Human Welfare, he publicly denounced the poll tax and began to write editorials against it in the *Times-Dispatch*. It was a bold move for the editor of Virginia's leading newspaper to take, for Virginia in the heyday of the Byrd machine was probably the most tightly run and narrowly ruled of the Southern states. The political scientist V. O. Key characterized it as a "political museum piece," so much under the control of an oligarchy that its politics resembled those of England prior to the Reform Bill of 1832 more closely than they resembled those of any other American state.[10]

The following year Dabney again went out on a limb. In February 1937, after an NAACP-sponsored antilynching bill was introduced in Congress, Dabney wrote a strongly supportive editorial in the *Times-Dispatch*. Only federal action could wipe out lynching, he insisted, while urging other Southern liberals to support the measure. He later wrote additional editorials as well as an article for the *Nation*.[11]

Walter White was elated. "Like a pebble dropped into a still pond," he told Dabney, "the repercussions of your superb editorial stand." White sent reprints to every member of Congress and to the press. He believed that Dabney would deserve much of the credit if the antilynching bill passed and told Carl W. Ackerman, the dean of Columbia's journalism school, that the *Times-Dispatch* editorial marked "one of the most significant positions taken by an American newspaper since the Civil War." According to White, Dabney deserved a Pulitzer Prize. White wrote to each of the thirteen members of the Pulitzer committee, a move that made even Dabney suspect that he was carrying things too far. Nevertheless, for almost a year White kept up his one-man campaign to get Dabney the Pulitzer. In the end, he failed, and he also lost his fight for federal antilynching legislation.[12]

White's lionization of Dabney showed how desperately the NAACP director wanted Southern liberals to support his efforts. For the most part, he was unsuccessful. Committed to protest and legal action, White wanted federal help to deal with Southern racial issues, which conflicted with the aim of the majority of Southern liberals. Moreover, as the Pulitzer Prize episode demonstrated, White's attempts at influence were at times heavy handed, and he made numerous enemies, black as well as white. Although White was in reality a cautious leader who fulfilled an important and necessary role, his style, plus his visibility as head of an established organization, made him seem more radical than he was. Walter White, to many Southern liberals, was the archetypal black agitator. Eventually, Dabney would join the chorus of White's critics. In 1939, to White's great disappointment, Dabney opposed the NAACP's attempts to integrate Southern professional and graduate schools following the Supreme Court's decision in *Missouri Ex Rel. Gaines* v. *Canada*.

In November 1938 Dabney expressed a desire to participate in the Birmingham meeting of the Southern Conference for Human Welfare. But when he discovered that known Communist party members would be included in the conference, he refused to go to Birmingham or have anything further to do with SCHW. Yet he generally shared most of the group's early goals. This was particularly true of the organized campaign against the poll tax. Dabney lent his name and prestige to the anti–poll tax movement with editorials, articles, and speeches. "From the crags above Harper's Ferry to the mesa fringing the Rio Grande, a revolt is brewing against the poll tax," he happily reported for the *New York Times* in 1939. Dabney argued that the poll tax was a relic from the Reconstruction era and that universal white manhood suffrage had been a tradition in Virginia ever since 1619. Moreover, since the measure disfranchised many more whites than blacks, Dabney did not hesitate to call for its immediate repeal in Virginia as well as elsewhere in the South.[13]

Dabney's outspoken views on such controversial matters aroused the ire of many white Southerners. When in 1941 he called upon defense industries to hire Negroes and pay them equally with whites, one outraged reader referred to the "BLITZKRIEG" that Dabney had started against the "decent white worker." The following year he waged practically a one-man campaign in the state to save Odell Waller, a convicted black Virginia sharecropper, from a death sentence for the murder of his white landlord. Dabney later remembered having "caught hell all over the place" for maintaining that Waller, whose landlord had been cheating him, should not be executed.[14]

In 1942 Dabney published his second major work, *Below the Potomac*, a book about the status of the South on the eve of the United States' entrance into World War II. As he had done in *Liberalism in the South*, Dabney once again defended the region from its image and tried to demonstrate that it was making substantial progress in many areas. "It should be emphasized," he wrote, "that the demagogues are distinctly in the minority here. . . . They merely make the most noise, and consequently are the recipients of the most publicity." Dabney also asserted that portrayals of the *Tobacco Road* type did not do justice to poor Southern whites. Only a few were as "filthy and depraved as Jeeter Lester and his libidinous entourage." Dabney assured his readers that they would not necessarily find such people every time they traveled South.

Predictably, much of the book was devoted to race. Dabney had extensive praise for the Commission on Interracial Cooperation. He contrasted Will Alexander's group with what he termed the divisive "pugnacity" of the NAACP, which he considered detrimental to the interests of the vast majority of Southern Negroes. Dabney called lynching "the greatest of all blots on the good name of the South," but he modified his own position regarding a federal antilynching law, arguing that a decline in lynchings and actions on the state level made such a measure less necessary than it had been a few years earlier. Dabney believed that any new attempt to present Congress with an antilynching bill would trigger Southern filibusters rather than reduce mob violence. He insisted that a federal law should be enacted only as a last resort. In general, Dabney maintained that Southern race relations were not as terror-prone as people would think from reading newspapers. Tuberculosis, he pointed out, was a more serious threat to Southern blacks than lynching. In the traditional manner of a Southern liberal, he also noted that blacks were still discriminated against and segregated in areas outside the South. "Obviously the Negroes of Mississippi suffer under serious disabilities," he wrote, "but how much worse is their condition than that of their racial kinsmen in Harlem or the Chicago Black Belt?"

Dabney was particularly enthusiastic about the progress in black education in the South and impressed with what he saw as the increasing tendency of whites to facilitate rather than hinder efforts in this area. He called for federal funds to help Southern states advance black education. Unaided, the South could not upgrade Negro schools to a level of substantial equality with white ones, and this had to be done in order to rid education of discrimination. The alternative would be to admit blacks to white schools. However, since only an "infintesimal minority" of white Southerners would agree to an abolition of the dual school system, Dabney surmised that such an approach was unlikely in the foreseeable future. In fact, he did not favor admitting blacks to white Southern educational institutions under any circumstances, even on the graduate level. Despite the Supreme Court's ruling in the *Gaines* case, Dabney believed that the time was not yet "propitious." He maintained that the one or two blacks in a state who sought to exercise their undoubted legal right for an equal education might endanger the lives and welfare of hundreds of Negroes in the violent white reaction that would almost certainly follow. Given the situation, the most positive step would be for several Southern states to pool their resources and establish quality regional institutions for black higher education. But he admitted that the Supreme Court's possible refusal to sanction such a program presented a major obstacle.

Dabney, though not a hard-core opponent of Supreme Court decisions against racial discrimination, was a middle-of-the-road Southern liberal. He believed in justice for blacks but insisted that proponents of change still had to recognize the racial sensitivities of the vast majority of white Southerners. "Americans must candidly admit that the democratic ideal is at war with the thesis that American citizens can be placed in separate pigeonholes and given varying educational and social advantages, depending upon the color of their skin," he could write in one sentence, while in the next: "Yet sight must not be lost of the fact that the modern South inherited a problem of tremendous complexity and difficulty at the close of the Civil War."

For Dabney and for Southern liberals in general, such a position proved increasingly difficult to maintain.

Like other Southern liberals, and despite his own genteel heritage, Dabney denounced traditional white paternalism. He regarded the racial outlook of William Alexander Percy, a Mississippi planter and poet who was an articulate exponent of paternalism, as unfit for the twentieth century. "Mr. Percy was led into the unfortunate error," said Dabney, "of assuming nearly all other large Southern plantations were like his 'Trail Lake' and that other Southern landlords were like himself. Would that they were!" [15]

But, in his own way, Dabney still asserted that the future of Southern blacks lay in the hands of an elite group of Southern whites. "In that great future which awaits the South," he wrote somewhat self-righteously, "its alert and uninhibited editors may be expected to join with its colleges and universities, its public-spirited professional men, its socially conscious women, and its articulate and progressive business and labor leaders in building below the Potomac and the Ohio a grander civilization than that storied land has ever known." The *Times-Dispatch* editor made it clear that he regarded the press as vital to this heretofore Silent South:

> How, for instance, would Louisiana have got rid of the Huey Long machine, and its assorted crooks and thieves, without the courageous New Orleans newspapers? Who but the Atlanta press is leading the opposition to Talmadge in Georgia? Where in the South does one find a more insistent and effective advocate for fairness and justice for the Negro than in the white press? Where have the better schools, better roads, better health, and better penal institutions had more tenacious champions than among Southern publishers and editors? . . . The press of the South frequently is the spearhead leading the advance to new frontiers, the panzer division which breaks a path for the slogging infantry. There is at least one large, influential, and forward-looking newspaper in every Southern state.

Below the Potomac, though it defended the theory behind segregation, inveighed against any further browbeating of Southern blacks. Dabney argued that the education and uplift of Negroes created useful citizens without leading to that "oft debated, and somewhat nebulous concept," social equality. White Southerners who still clung to what he described as "out-moded ante-bellum notions" of race relations would have to give them up. Dabney's argument was a familiar one to white liberals: "Ultraconservative Southerners whose chief thoughts on the race problem revolved about the business of 'keeping the Negro in his place' seem unable to explain how the white population is ever to be reasonably healthy and prosperous if for every two white persons there is a diseased, poverty-stricken and illiterate, if not criminally inclined, Negro." [16]

The entrance of the United States into World War II changed the racial situation throughout the nation so dramatically that the views expressed in *Below the Potomac* seemed outdated even as the book was being released by its publishers in 1942. The wartime militancy of American blacks and their sympathizers, plus the resulting white anxieties, particularly in the South, severely tested the racial liberalism of Virginius Dabney. He soon became one of the leading critics in the country of what he regarded as the excesses in Negro demands. Dabney applauded the statement of FEPC chairman Mark Ethridge to the effect that the white Southerner would never countenance the abolition of legal segregation. "You are dead right, and I am glad that you said it," he told Ethridge. He railed against those who he felt were misleading blacks. "My considered judgment," he informed John Temple Graves, "is that Mrs. Roosevelt, Pearl Buck, Herbert Agar and a few others are doing tremendous harm. In fact, I believe that they have had as much to do with stirring up the Negroes as anybody." Dabney took special umbrage at the militant tone of such leading black newspapers as the *Chicago Defender*, *Pittsburgh Courier*, *Baltimore Afro-American*, and New York's *Amsterdam News*. "I believe that it will be obvious to you," he wrote the editor of *Reader's Digest*, "that when supposedly responsible Negro opinion compares Mark Ethridge to Gene Talmadge that things have come to a pretty pass, and we are in danger of wholesale race riots." And Southern blacks, Dabney added, would be the major losers in any confrontation.[17]

Dabney hoped that his reputation as a liberal would enable him to speak freely and influentially on wartime racial tensions. In January 1943, he outlined his views in an *Atlantic Monthly* article entitled "Nearer and Nearer the Precipice." "A small group of Negro agitators and another small group of white rabble-rousers," he wrote, "are pushing this country closer and closer to an interracial explosion which may make the race riots of the First World War and its aftermath seem mild by comparison." Dabney severely criticized A. Philip Randolph for his intention to lead a Negro protest march on Washington, D. C. and Roy Wilkins of the NAACP for remarking that American blacks did indeed desire social equality with whites. Such militancy, insisted Dabney, only inspired the South's demagogues to new mischief. He once again had harsh words for the "radical element" of the black press, particularly concerning the harm done through attacks on Southern liberals. The Richmond editor did not believe that Southern blacks could make progress unless they had the support of men like himself. Dabney hoped that to relieve the South's current sense of racial crisis and avert bloodshed, both the Randolphs and the Talmadges could be silenced for the duration of the war.[18]

"Nearer and Nearer the Precipice" received wide attention and caused an immediate outcry from blacks and some of their white supporters. The distinguished black writer Langston Hughes wondered whether the American dream for which the nation was fighting was just for whites. "Mr. Dabney's article as a whole," said Hughes, "implies that Negroes, segregated, Jim-crowed, and lynched as we are, should still not seek to disturb the *status quo* of racial oppression." Criticism of Dabney was not confined to Northern blacks. P. B. Young, the editor of the relatively moderate *Norfolk Journal and Guide*, told his long-time Richmond friend that the *Atlantic Monthly* piece had failed to point out that Negroes were under tremendous pressure and had to fight bitterly for every bit of humane treatment they received. Said Young: "You seem to fail to realize that what is actually going on is a determination on the part of many that the Negro shall have no part in this war, and subsequently no part in the fruits of victory. . . . You fail to see that the Negro is being reduced to a menial or common laborer; that organized labor is excluding him from any skilled work—except what it has been forced to by a presidential executive order." Young also took strong exception to Dabney's assertion that no black man in the South could win election to Congress in the foreseeable future. He informed Dabney,

"It is the same thing that Messrs. Rankin, Talmadge, Bilbo and others say with the difference that their language is always coarse and their attitude brutal, while your language is always cultured and your attitude dignified. The result is the same." [19]

Dabney's views, which a great many other Southern liberals shared, contributed to a growing chasm between Southern and non-Southern liberal blocs. *The New Leader*, an organ of the non-Communist left, ran an article entitled "What's Happened to the Southern 'Liberals'?" Cy Record, the author of the piece, said that wartime changes in the South bewildered Southern liberals more than any other group. According to Record, white Southern liberals—he mentioned by name, in addition to Dabney, John Temple Graves, Mark Ethridge, Jonathan Daniels, and Jennings Perry—had been "caught woefully offguard, unprepared to measure the impact of the war . . . and unable to channel their general humanitarian impulses into the stream of rapid social and economic change." *The New Leader* also took Southern liberals to task for insisting that only they could bestow progress upon poor whites and blacks. "The thought . . . that Negroes, organized and led by their own leaders, might make immediate demands for certain rights and prepare to implement such demands is shocking to the liberal temperament, not to say terrifying," wrote Record.[20]

Dabney did not take such criticism lightly. He regarded himself as a sincere friend of Southern blacks and did not argue, as John Temple Graves did, that blacks had to drop all their wartime demands. He vigorously endorsed the Durham statement, and he played an instrumental role in the formation of the Southern Regional Council. Only the controversy resulting from his *Atlantic Monthly* article caused him to decline to serve as chairman of the June 1943 interracial conference in Richmond. If for no other reason than to quell Negro militancy, Dabney thought it absolutely essential to establish a dialogue between blacks and liberal Southern whites. "I am sure you can see that if our group keeps on manifesting relative indifference in the face of the Negroes' great eagerness to cooperate," he wrote to one wavering Regional Council supporter, "they will become convinced that we are not serious . . . and will conclude that Southern whites are a hopeless lot." Dabney feared that the end result of such inaction would be that Southern blacks would increasingly look up to the "radical Northern leadership of the Walter White caliber." [21]

During 1943 Dabney worked hard to promote a coalition between blacks and white Southern liberals. In October he wrote of the "Dynamic New South" for the *New York Times*, arguing that, rather than following Tobacco Road to its logical end of misery, disease, and poverty, the former Confederacy was on "a broad highway which may well lead to the greatest prosperity it has ever known." A month later, writing in *Survey Graphic*, Dabney addressed himself more directly to the issues raised by the newly created Southern Regional Council. He noted that the white South still had plenty to answer for in its treatment of blacks and that segregation constituted a tremendously thorny problem. The principle of racial separation, according to Dabney, could only be defended if "absolutely equal" facilities were provided for both races, and such was obviously not the case in the South. Segregation had instead come to mean "discrimination and a whole series of hateful oppressions." Dabney insisted that the Southern Regional Council recognized this fact and meant to deal with it. He added that if he himself were a Negro, he would wish segregation abolished, but would realize that to do so in the face of the overwhelming hostility of white Southerners would do more harm than good. In Dabney's view many white Southerners were prepared to make reasonable concessions to some black demands, particularly if they came from the black South rather than from sources above the Mason-Dixon Line. However, he detected "a deliberate conspiracy of northern extremists to picture the entire South as the abode of lantern-jawed lynchers, tobacco chewing hillbillies, and bigoted ignoramuses with no humane instincts or decent sensibilities." He regarded this as the single greatest obstacle to racial progress. [22]

Dabney believed that Southern liberals had to come up with some dramatic gesture to demonstrate that their empathy with blacks was not confined to rhetoric. He envisioned something both symbolic and substantive and decided to take a bold step. In November 1943, in two *Times-Dispatch* editorials, Dabney urged that Virginia repeal its segregation laws in regard to servicing blacks on streetcars and other common carriers. His chief argument was that enforced segregation on public conveyances was an irritant to both whites and blacks and, especially when administered by uncouth whites, a source of frequent interracial friction. Furthermore, according to Dabney, Jim Crow streetcar laws defeated their own intention in that they more often than not forced whites and blacks to push their way past each other and thus come into more actual contact than they would if left to sit wherever they pleased. He characterized a statewide abolition of such laws as a "conservative course in race relations," for it would offer tangible evidence to Southern Negroes that their best interests lay in renewed cooperation with their white fellow citizens rather than with outside groups. "We white Southerners," Dabney concluded, "can remedy the evident injustices in the treatment of the Negroes, and thereby win their confidence, respect and cooperation, or we can refuse to do anything, and repeat the old nonsense to the effect that 'the problem will solve itself, if people will only stop talking about it.' " [23]

Despite his labeling of this proposal as "conservative," Dabney's views prompted an outpouring of praise from the militant Negro press, the NAACP, and Northern liberals—the very groups that had so roundly denounced him only a few months earlier. The *Pittsburgh Courier*, one of the papers Dabney usually referred to when he spoke of "sensation-mongering" black publications, ran a laudatory editorial about Dabney's "Sanity in the South." The *Courier's* executive editor, P. L. Prattis, congratulated Dabney for his stand and maintained that no matter what the *Times-Dispatch* editor chose to call his action, it represented a radical step forward. "You are tampering with the foundation of racial chauvinism," said Prattis. "Should you succeed, the super-structure must of necessity become less secure." Roy Wilkins informed Dabney that Negroes outside the South greeted his proposal with happy amazement and said that the NAACP did not mind being cast in the role of "bogey man" in order to secure such concessions. "It has been more of a tonic than you can imagine," he wrote. Writing in the *Progressive*, Oswald Garrison Villard, an ogre to many white Southerners, called Dabney's position on bus segregation a "statesmanlike and far seeing stand." [24]

More significant than the accolades was the fact that Dabney's effort to eliminate Jim Crow on buses aroused much more white Southern hostility than support. No other white Virginia newspaper defended his proposal; indeed, the only other white paper in the entire South to agree with Dabney was a small weekly in Kinston, North Carolina. Even Ralph McGill's *Atlanta Constitution* refused to stand with him. Dabney found himself trying to explain his editorials to disbelieving readers and friends. He told one worried Virginia woman that he did not propose abolishing segregation anywhere but on common carriers.[25]

Louis I. Jaffe, an editor for the *Norfolk Virginian-Pilot* who in 1929 had received a Pulitzer Prize for his criticism of the Ku Klux Klan and the Byrd machine, could not understand how his Richmond colleague could call for the abandonment of Jim Crow on public transportation without giving up the entire theory behind segregation. Dabney replied that the war had increased racial tension in the South and that the elimination of segregated buses and streetcars would give Negroes a psychological lift so that they would feel "we are not stalling them off with nothing but fine words." Since the law would be repealed on the basis of its ineffectiveness, Dabney foresaw no major threat to institutionalized racial separation. Nevertheless, no city, county, or state agency in Virginia considered Dabney's plan.[26]

Despite his advocacy of an idea that, by his own admission, "set the whole South on its ear," Dabney felt uncomfortable in the role of militant. R. M. Golightly, coordinator of the Detroit-based National Committee to Abolish Jim Crow Transportation, offered Dabney his group's assistance, but Dabney flatly rejected the suggestion, arguing that Northern interference would only decrease the already slim chance that his proposal had for adoption. Dabney may have been sympathetic to the problems of Southern blacks, but as the urbane and sophisticated scion of one of Virginia's more prominent families, he was also a close associate of Richmond's banker-lawyer-merchant elite. He did not appreciate Richmond women telling his wife, who had a black cook, "If V would stop talking so much we might have some cooks in *our* kitchens." [27]

The truth of the matter was that Dabney, nurtured in a South where segregation was at its peak, was too much a product of Southern gentility to shift his views easily on this touchy issue. Though he represented the best of his tradition, he had limits. Thus Dabney could be "impressed" by the letter of an army major stationed in Washington who complained of the "cocky insolence" of the city's blacks and who wrote that "unless the Negroes are immediately forced out of their Virginia toehold and a stop is put to this equality octopus, Virginia and the whole South . . . will soon be enmeshed in its tentacles." Dabney answered that he did not soft-pedal the importance of maintaining racial separation, and that the *Times-Dispatch* frequently ran editorials criticizing Mrs. Roosevelt and the NAACP. "It seems to me that we must take a stand somewhere," said Dabney, "and unless we take it now, the whole structure of segregation will crumble." [28]

Dabney never could comprehend what blacks thought they could possibly gain by undertaking a militant campaign against Jim Crow. He could not understand why so many of their leaders became immediately incensed when white Southern liberals stated the necessity of segregation even though they offered other reforms and concessions. For Dabney, push was beginning to lead to shove, and that could not be tolerated. "I am entirely sure that the colored people ought to have a good many things that they haven't got," he wrote to one fearful Southern white, "but I am also sure that we ought to maintain the segregation of the races." In June 1943 he heard that blacks were planning to take their cause into the streets. His reaction was total apprehension: "It appears that Negroes are to be told to go into restaurants reserved for whites and take seats, to go into the theatres and do likewise, and to sit in the section set aside for whites on streetcars and buses. Furthermore, they are supposedly being told not to fight back, if there is any trouble, but to emulate Gandhi and his followers in India by resisting non-violently. I do not have to tell you how disquieting this sort of thing is, even when there may be no truth at all in it." Thomas Sancton's *New Republic* articles on racial injustice in the South rankled Dabney so much that he suggested that FEPC chairman Mark Ethridge should use his influence in Washington to have the lid put on Sancton.[29]

A series of exchanges between Sancton and Dabney revealed the differences between a white racial liberal who had left the South and one who had chosen to remain. During the war Sancton, a native of New Orleans who made his home in New York, believed that whites had for too long appeased the "understandably rebellious" blacks with empty promises. "In communication with family and friends," he wrote Dabney, "I see the same old rationalized prejudices and selfishness in full sway and I have a sickening feeling that it is these qualities which win out time after time when the issue of Negro justice comes to a real showdown." Dabney replied that Sancton's position paralleled the ultimately destructive one taken by Northern Abolitionists in the 1830s.

> I think the issues posed by the war have focused so much attention on the Negro's present disabilities, that too little attention is paid to the slow, steady and constructive progress that has been made through the joint efforts of white and black in the South. My fear is that thoroughly sincere and honorable persons like yourself who insist on forcing matters to a showdown are going to wreck what we have accomplished heretofore, and drown the good-will which has been created in violence and bloodshed. . . . Much as I deplore many of the phenomena which exist in the sphere of race relations today, I cannot believe that these matters are going to be righted by anybody who insists on an over-night reversal, implemented by federal authority.[30]

Sancton answered by assuring Dabney that he was not a "white rabble-rouser," but rather a Southerner who loved the South and who had more faith in the mass of whites and blacks in the region than did Dabney. Sancton noted that he got the impression from reading Dabney's books, articles, and editorials that Dabney was "not quite sure lint-heads and ignorant blacks—even though they were deserving of reform measures like the New Deal's—would in the long run turn out any differently; except perhaps a little healthier." Sancton believed that Dabney's argument that Negro and white agitators had the South on the brink of race war was too simple, and that he should instead turn his passion on the majority of Southern whites. Said Sancton:

> I think someone has got to drive it into the heads of well-to-do housewives who sit around talking their snide talk about Mrs. Roosevelt and the beastly servant problem that the New Deal is causing by paying Negro husbands such wages and sending the mothers of Negro soldiers all that money—I think someone has got to tell these people straight to their faces even though it means insulting them that . . . a change of attitude is damn well demanded of them by virtue of every soldier who is risking and giving his life to keep this country worth living in.

He maintained that though gains made by Southern blacks with the encouragement of white liberals might look impressive on paper, they had not raised most Negroes from almost "complete social and economic serfdom," and that in general Southern whites did not intend to give black people a thing unless forced to by external pressure.[31]

Dabney respected the sincerity of Sancton's views but thought him thoroughly misguided. He admitted that Southern whites were overwrought, antagonistic, and not very anxious to talk about the rights of blacks. Yet, as Dabney saw it, this was precisely the point. In such a charged atmosphere it would be difficult to achieve small advances for Negroes, let alone a complete breakdown of Jim Crow. He expressed astonishment over Sancton's assertion that Southern whites never did anything for blacks. Though indifference toward the plight of blacks was no doubt the feeling of the vast majority of Southern whites, according to Dabney, many "prominent white Southerners" did care, and their prestige and influence had helped Negroes achieve genuine advances in education, health, and economic well-being.[32]

Like Thomas Jefferson, whom he admired greatly, Dabney was an upper-class Virginian who celebrated the virtues of democracy. He was more willing than most white Southerners to extend the fruits of democracy to blacks. He thought that this could be done through the activities of people like himself without unduly shocking white Southern sensibilities, and he devoted himself to publicizing liberal trends in the South. But Dabney's way failed to alter significantly the status of black Southerners. Not only did Southern Negroes, assisted at first by white and black Northerners, begin demanding their own version of racial justice, but they did it without consulting Virginia gentlemen. Dabney's genteel heritage, the source of many of his views about the necessity for change in the South, was undoubtedly one of this greatest strengths. But for a white liberal striving to comprehend the meaning of genuine racial justice in the South, it was also a major weakness. Dabney believed too strongly in the wisdom of his white elite. Despite his brief campaign against segregated public transportation, Dabney's wartime stand against black militance tarnished his reputation as a liberal. In continuing to insist that separate could be made equal, he would not win it back.

Liberals amid Dixiecrats

There were white Southern liberals during the war years who, unlike Virginius Dabney, did try to accommodate themselves to a changing racial situation. After periods of internal conflict over the issue, both the Southern Conference for Human Welfare and the Southern Regional Council eventually adopted antisegregationist positions; Southern liberalism finally came to represent white dedication to the breakdown of Jim Crow in the region. This process, however, was a painful one. After many years of insisting that racial liberalism was possible in the South if white Southerners were appealed to in the correct manner, liberals increasingly found themselves becoming isolated as a group.

In 1940 SCHW secretary Clark Foreman had hoped his Southern New Dealers could work and even perhaps merge with any new organization that developed from the Commission on Interracial Cooperation. However, SCHW's reputation for unpredictable racial militancy and its connections with known Communists made such a coalition impossible. A few individuals, such as Will Alexander, could manage to feel comfortable associating with both groups, but for the most part, the members of the two organizations were on uneasy terms. Howard Odum frequently expressed displeasure over what he regarded as the Southern Conference's pretentious racial liberalism; he believed SCHW used the race issue to attract publicity for itself, and that it was not as genuinely interested in helping blacks as was his own group. Clark Foreman cast similar aspersions on the Interracial Commission–Regional Council faction and once described *Southern Frontier* as a magazine fit only for a Sunday school audience. Ironically, probably through the influence of Will Alexander, Foreman served on the board of directors of the newly formed Southern Regional Council, a position that made him a source of irritation to men like Odum, Virginius Dabney, and Guy Johnson. Despite these antagonisms, the two organizations at least managed to avoid public criticism of each other.[1]

Foreman had hoped to revive the spirit of Birmingham by scheduling a second mass SCHW meeting for April 1940 in Chattanooga. In line with SCHW's emphasis on poll tax repeal, the general theme of the meeting was to be popular democracy in the South. Foreign policy issues, however, overshadowed all others. Chattanooga conference participants were divided over whether to condemn the Hitler-Stalin pact, Nazi Germany, or the Soviet Union's invasion of Finland; the conference became a battleground between interventionists, isolationists, and pro- and anti-Communists. The conference's inability to stick to Southern issues dismayed Foreman and Frank Graham. Yet, on the race issue, a consensus was reached. SCHW still refused outright opposition to segregation, but the Chattanooga conference took the position that it was the duty of Southerners "to work toward the general equalization of opportunity in all spheres and toward the development of the friendliest of relations between our two racial groups."[2]

The 1939–1941 period was a low point for SCHW. Until the Nazi invasion of Russia settled the foreign policy question, the Communists, hoping to keep the United States out of the war, attempted to influence SCHW. The struggle for control between them and the interventionist liberals hamstrung the organization and left bitter feelings on both sides. Later, during the Cold War years, the organization's enemies would exploit these differences and charge that SCHW had been, all along, a Communist group.

Communists did not dominate SCHW, but the red taint stuck with it. Frank Graham, whose enthusiasm for SCHW exceeded the attention he gave to it, repeatedly told worried friends of the conference that Communists never determined its policies. Graham stood 100 percent behind the organization. "I refuse to run in the face of Communist intrigue on one side," he said, "or smearing by powerful and privileged groups on the other." Graham thought that SCHW represented Christianity and democracy and that white Southern New Dealers who took these principles seriously were apt to be called Communists and thus should not concern themselves unduly with the label. Nonetheless, Graham's reassurances failed to prevent a number of people from leaving SCHW because of its alleged Communist connections. In 1941 Barry Bingham, Mark Ethridge, and Louise Charlton all resigned from the conference over the red issue.[3]

Other issues were also dividing conference members. Financial support from the CIO, whose leader John L. Lewis was now feuding with FDR, proved embarrassing to Southern Conference stalwarts like Clark Foreman and Maury Maverick who were close to the Roosevelt Administration. Southern liberals who joined SCHW to overcome their own sense of isolation were discouraged by its apparent breakup. "It does make me sick to see the few liberals in the South split four ways for Sunday," a disappointed Virginia Durr told Bingham.[4]

After the United States entered the war, SCHW hired James A. Dombrowski as its executive secretary in the hope that he could work toward unification. The son of a successful Tampa, Florida jeweler, Dombrowski had served with the army ambulance service in France during the First World War. After graduating from Emory University in 1923, he went on to the University of California, Harvard, Columbia, and the Union Theological Seminary in New York, studying under such luminaries as Alfred North Whitehead and Reinhold Niebuhr. Dombrowski became a dedicated Christian Socialist. In 1932 he helped form the Highlander Folk School in Monteagle, Tennessee and served as the school's staff director until he joined the Southern Conference. In 1937 the CIO supported Highlander as its training school for Southern union organizers. Dombrowski was an excellent administrator who brought SCHW leadership that was genuinely and open-mindedly radical without being unnecessarily dramatic. SCHW leaders such as Graham, Lucy Mason, and Foreman carefully screened Dombrowski and found no Communist party connections. But as one whose views frequently paralleled the Communist party line, Dombrowski was not the person who could eliminate the red cloud that still hung over SCHW, though it became less menacing during America's wartime alliance with the Soviet Union.[5]

Under Dombrowski's leadership, SCHW held its third general meeting in Nashville in April 1942. The theme this time was staunch support for an Allied victory, but the race issue was not overlooked. To symbolize the biracial nature of the war effort, SCHW awarded its Thomas Jefferson honors to a white and a black. Frank Graham, who had resigned as chairman in 1940 but who still maintained close ties to the organization, was the white recipient, and Mary McLeod Bethune the black. Instead of criticizing the vehemence of Negro protest during the war, Frank Graham praised American blacks for leading the fight against fascist trends in the United States.[6]

Late in 1942, under the editorship of Dombrowski, the conference began publication of the *Southern Patriot*, a modest monthly newspaper whose title reflected conference leaders' enthusiasm for the Allied cause. But Dombrowski also hoped to reignite some of the zeal of Birmingham in reaching out to a liberal South. As he explained to Foreman, the paper would be "directed at the mass of unconverted Southerners who economically and patriotically have every reason to support a liberal war policy, but whose ideas have been distorted by sentiment and prejudice." Each issue of the *Patriot* stressed victory, with reform in the South to be achieved both through and after the defeat of Germany and Japan. The paper portrayed Southern race-baiting politicians as misleaders of the people who were contributing to Axis goals rather than American ones.[7]

The Southern Conference, now influenced by wartime rhetoric about extending democracy, tried hard to affirm the belief of Southern liberals that the white South was not as racist as it appeared to the average observer. A combination of education, organization, and propaganda, conference spokesmen indicated, could make "unconverted" white Southerners adopt more enlightened attitudes toward blacks. In 1943 the conference began forming local committees in every Southern state. In the words of the Georgia newspaperman Tarleton Collier, SCHW wanted to reach the "little people." A January 1944 executive board meeting described the actions of those who gave racial reasons for opposing anti–poll tax and soldier vote legislation as a "betrayal of the Southern masses." Lucy Mason tried, unsuccessfully, to secure Rosenwald support for SCHW by telling Edwin Embree that the Southern Conference was a vital "symbol and rallying point" with roots "deep in Southern Soil." [8]

By the end of the war, SCHW leaders claimed that the continued existence of the organization could mean the difference between the South's finally emerging as a racially just, prosperous, and genuinely democratic region or reverting to racial reaction, even greater poverty, and "neofascism." According to Clark Foreman, with victory in the war assured, SCHW had to spread the "creed of tolerance and humanity" and work against the "vile prejudice" of men such as Mississippi's Congressman John Rankin and Senator Theodore Bilbo. When in April 1945 SCHW presented another Thomas Jefferson award to Justice Hugo Black, Claude Pepper told the audience that "Hugo Black represents the South for in its heart the South feels as Hugo Black feels. Yes, it has been shocked, stifled, and it has been belied and misunderstood, but the throbbing heart of the South is proud of Hugo Black and down deep they cherish the aspiration that his tribe may increase." [9] Though conference members could afford to make bold statements at Washington dinners, however, back home their voices were more subdued.

Such was the case in Georgia. In 1942, the moderate forces of Ellis Arnall had won a gubernatorial victory over the race-baiting demagoguery of the "wild man from Sugar Creek," Eugene Talmadge, and heartened all Southern liberals. With Arnall in the governor's office, SCHW leaders pinned great hopes upon its committee in Georgia. In 1945, Arnall brought about the repeal of Georgia's poll tax law, but to the dismay of Clark Foreman, the Georgia SCHW committee led by Margaret Fischer failed to stand publicly behind Arnall. Fischer believed that SCHW's racial unorthodoxy would hurt Arnall if his name ever became connected with her organization. Whatever aid SCHW gave Arnall was behind the scenes.

This attitude of restrained support carried over into the bitter 1946 gubernatorial race in which Talmadge defeated the candidate of the Arnall forces (Arnall could not succeed himself) through a campaign against "niggers" and "reds" that was extreme even by Southern standards. When Talmadge died prior to his inauguration, however, Georgia's chaotic politics reached new depths in confusion and animosity. The state legislature chose Talmadge's son Herman for the office, while the outgoing Arnall appointed the Lieutenant Governor-elect, M. E. Thompson. A near civil war atmosphere pervaded Atlanta. Although clearly in sympathy with Arnall, the Georgia SCHW remained silent. Since the Georgia committee was the best organized and most financially secure state affiliate of SCHW, its reticence proved especially disheartening.[10]

The sad truth was that, despite its emphasis on being a genuine representative of the Southern masses, SCHW never uncovered any deep base of Southern support. The conference depended heavily on outside sources of revenue, particularly from the CIO, to sustain its activities. After 1946, when the CIO began to look upon the Communist-tainted Southern Conference as a hindrance to its own organizing plans in the South and withdrew its aid, SCHW suffered a financial blow from which it could not recover. From a peak membership in mid-1946 of 10,000, including Northern as well as Southern supporters, SCHW rapidly dwindled to 5,500 by the end of 1947. Moreover, only 269 delegates showed up at its November 1946 New Orleans convention—a drastic reduction from the 1,200 who had assembled in Birmingham back in 1938. In 1945 and 1946 conference president Clark Foreman engaged in extensive financial campaigns in New York and Washington for his supposedly Southern organization, a virtual admission of his group's weakness in the South. To justify his actions, Foreman used the tenuous argument that, since Southern racists and reactionaries always received backing from outside the region, it made sense for Southern liberals to do the same.[11]

Undoubtedly the onset of the Cold War scared many people away from SCHW, which in 1947 was investigated by the House Un-American Activities Committee. American Communists had participated in conference affairs, but the committee grossly exaggerated their influence. In a lengthy analysis of the committee's report, Walter Gellhorn of the Columbia School of Law characterized the investigation as a legal fiasco and said that the committee's assertion that SCHW was a Communist front was "not founded on credible evidence." [12]

But the race issue rather than the red scare contributed the most to SCHW's downfall. The war years had convinced conference leaders to take an increasingly militant stand on behalf of Negro rights. Men such as Foreman and Dombrowski abhorred segregation, which they now equated with the racism of the Nazis. SCHW literature stressed the wartime contribution of blacks, the arguments of social scientists against racial differences, and the facts of widespread discrimination. Such activities caused Mississippi Senator Theodore Bilbo to refer to SCHW as an "Un-American, negro social equality, communist, mongrel outfit" that was the South's number one enemy. Bilbo declared his intention to filibuster until the organization disbanded. Nonetheless, the conference, concluding that it was time for Southern liberals to ignore such neanderthals as Bilbo, began increasingly to support what had been an old bugaboo for the seekers of a Silent South: outright federal intervention on behalf of blacks. In March 1945, for example, Clark Foreman testified before the Senate in favor of a permanent Fair Employment Practices Committee. Echoing the words that Lewis Blair had written sixty years before, Foreman said that "the economic prosperity of the South depends upon the economic and educational welfare of its Negro citizens as well as its white citizens." Moreover, after the war, SCHW fought for the hiring of blacks by Washington's Capital Transit Company and worked openly with the NAACP—an organization white Southern liberals usually tried to steer clear of—in defending blacks indiscriminately arrested when local police invaded the Negro section of Columbia, Tennessee. In November 1946 Walter White himself appeared in New Orleans at what was to be the last general convention of the SCHW and spoke out against segregation.[13]

These events cut deeply into SCHW's Southern support. The New Orleans gathering proved disappointing compared to past conventions. Foreman's opening speech once again emphasized that SCHW reflected a genuine Southern tradition; he characterized the conference as a "conservative organization, reserving and cultivating the finest traditions of our forefathers, the tradition of democracy and tolerance toward the belief of others." In addition to the usual names of Jefferson and Jackson, Foreman cited George Washington Cable for recognizing "so early and so boldly that the human resources of the South were its greatest assets and should not be wasted by prejudice of color or creed." The organization's Thomas Jefferson Award went to former Georgia Governor Ellis Arnall, whose own political demise belied his statement that the South's "little people" supported the goals of the conference. To complicate SCHW's problems further, in December 1946 a serious disagreement developed between Foreman and Dombrowski over the management of the organization. The internal dissension boded ill for the continued existence of the conference, which lacked effective local action and was short of funds. One SCHW executive board member reported to Dombrowski, "These things are killing us." [14]

A memorandum prepared by Lucy Randolph Mason for an April 1947 SCHW board meeting revealed that SCHW had debts of $35,000–$40,000. It had never developed strong state committees, and conference leaders, according to Miss Mason, had to deal realistically with the fact that SCHW had failed as a mass political movement. She hoped it would continue to operate, but only as a "small, militant, standard-bearing organization" that could possibly influence other groups in the South. On some issues, it would have to work quietly, "like leaven," and not take public credit for its advancement of every cause. Also, the conference should try to become more indigenous and self-supporting in the South, even if doing so required a drop in outside revenues. Mason also advised the conference to adopt more specific and longer-range programs than it had in the past. "If what I have to say seems too drastic," she concluded, "I can only remind you that the Conference is facing slow death at its Southern roots. . . . We have no choice but to come to grips with these problems." Her recommendations were not followed.[15]

In debt, and with a number of its principal sponsors, such as Clark Foreman and Virginia Durr, heavily involved in Henry Wallace's Progressive Party movement, in November 1948 the organization formally dissolved. Its only lasting heritage was yet another Southern liberal organization, the Southern Conference Educational Fund (SCEF).

The Educational Fund had been established in January 1946 after SCHW had been rechartered in order to separate its political and educational functions. James Dombrowski administered SCEF and stayed with it even after his falling out with Foreman caused him to leave SCHW. Since only the Educational Fund could receive tax-exempt donations, it managed to operate at the same time that its parent organization was dying. In 1947 SCEF took over the publication of *Southern Patriot*.

Dombrowski's years of work in the South had convinced him that no fundamental reforms would take place without the elimination of segregation. In 1947 he was among the minority of Southern liberals who were openly calling for the end of *de jure* racial separation. Dombrowski wanted the Educational Fund to produce detailed statistics about the evils of segregation, for despite SCHW's difficulties, he still believed that there was significant white support in the South for the advancement of Negro rights, even on this issue. Accordingly, he requested $10,000 from the Adele R. Levy Fund in New York so that SCEF could undertake an extensive study of the racial attitudes of Southern whites in either Virginia or North Carolina. Dombrowski indicated that evidence existed questioning the widely held belief that any tampering with traditional racial patterns would necessarily meet with either opposition or violence. He did not succeed in getting the grant, but SCEF nevertheless conducted some polls. One survey of Southern state university faculty members revealed that 70 percent supported the admission of blacks to graduate and professional schools.[16]

Assisting Dombrowski with the SCEF was Aubrey Williams. After Congress had ended the National Youth Administration in 1943, Williams had become organizing director for the National Farmers Union, a liberal group well suited to his Populist outlook. He also continued his ties with the Southern Conference. Williams, in short, was still highly visible as a crusading liberal when in January 1945 President Roosevelt named him to head the Rural Electrification Administration.

The nomination led to a bitter struggle between pro– and anti–

New Deal forces. Senator Kenneth D. McKellar of Tennessee, the leader of those opposed to Williams, was by 1945 a crusty and determined foe of the New Deal. He had played a large role in killing the NYA and was unwilling to allow the administration to resurrect his old nemesis. McKellar presided over a lengthy investigation of Williams and charged him with being a Communist, while Bilbo added harangues against his racial views. New Deal liberals fought back with a publicity campaign. A "Friends of Aubrey Williams Committee" was formed, and its chairman, Eliot D. Pratt, referred to the nominee as "a symbol of the old fight between those who want a square deal . . . for all the people, as opposed to the system of special privileges for the few." Finally in March, the Senate voted decisively not to confirm Williams. The episode was a bitter defeat both for Williams personally and for American liberals generally.[17]

Following the Senate's rejection, Williams returned to his native Alabama. Still active in the National Farmers Union, he moved to Montgomery and began publishing *Southern Farm and Home*, a family rather than politically oriented magazine that proved to be profitable. From Montgomery he also tried to prevent SCHW from disintegrating and, failing this, began working closely with Dombrowski on the Southern Conference Educational Fund. In 1947 Williams became its president.[18]

Under Williams and Dombrowski, SCEF became a small but militantly antisegregationist organization. It strongly endorsed the controversial 1947 report of President Truman's Committee on Civil Rights,[19] criticized Southern Dixiecrats, and called for a strong civil rights plank in the 1948 Democratic party platform. On November 20, 1948, two hundred black and white Southerners led by Williams and Dombrowski gathered in Richmond to issue a declaration. To demonstrate that the South had liberal roots, Williams took forty of the group over to Thomas Jefferson's Monticello home and from there called for the passage of federal, state, and local civil rights legislation. The old New Dealers saw in defenders of segregation the same groups that had fought FDR most strongly. Truman, said Williams, had inadvertently "put a good club in their hands when he announced his civil rights program." [20]

President Truman's civil rights program had begun in 1946. Blacks and white Northern liberals had appealed for federal action in response to several brutal instances of white violence against Southern Negroes—a black veteran beaten and blinded in a South Carolina bus incident, a race riot in Columbia, Tennessee during which Negroes were attacked and then imprisoned, and the lynching of four black men and women in Monroe, Georgia. On December 5, Truman issued an executive order appointing a President's Committee on Civil Rights to investigate these and other abuses and to recommend remedial legislation.[21] The fifteen-member committee was chaired by Charles E. Wilson, the president of General Electric, and included what a correspondent for the *Nation* called a "Noah's Ark": two corporation heads, two labor leaders, two college presidents, two Jews, two Catholics, two women, two Negroes, and two white Southern liberals. The white Southerners were Frank Graham and Dorothy M. Tilly of Atlanta, a race relations activist in Methodist women's groups who, as a part-time field secretary for the Southern Regional Council, had been trying to revive the Association of Southern Women for the Prevention of Lynching. Graham and Tilley were deliberately chosen to add balance to the carefully selected panel.*

The Civil Rights Committee issued its book-length report, *To Secure These Rights*, in October of the next year. It called for vigorous federal efforts and, in all probability, went well beyond anything Truman had envisioned when he appointed the committee. Among the recommendations were an antilynching law, abolition of the poll tax, laws to prevent discrimination in voter registration, an end to segregation in the armed services, the prohibition of Jim Crow in interstate public transportation, the outlawing of all forms of segrega-

* The other members were Charles Luckman, the president of Lever Brothers; James B. Carey, the secretary-treasurer of the CIO; Boris Shishkin, an economist with the AFL; John Dickey, the president of Dartmouth; Sadie T. M. Alexander, a black woman lawyer from Philadelphia who was on the board of directors of the National Urban League; Channing H. Tobias, the black head of the Phelps-Stokes Fund and a member of the board of directors of the NAACP; Morris Ernst, a well known civil liberties lawyer; Francis P. Matthews, an Omaha lawyer active in Catholic charities; Roland B. Gittelson, a New York City rabbi; Francis J. Haas, a Catholic bishop from Grand Rapids, Michigan; Henry Knox Sherrill, the presiding bishop of the Episcopal Church of America; and Franklin D. Roosevelt, Jr.

tion in the District of Columbia, and a cut-off of federal funds to recipients practicing segregation. Walter White called the report "the most uncompromising and specific pronouncement by a government agency on the explosive issue of racial and religious bigotry." The *New Republic* summed up the reaction of most Northern racial liberals: "For those who cherish liberty, freedom and forebearance; for those sickened by the sight of reaction riding in the land; for those who feel alone and for those who feel afraid, here is a noble reaffirmation of the principles that made America." As white Southerners, Graham and Tilly received special praise for lending their names to the document.[22]

Most observers were unaware, however, that, during the preparation of *To Secure These Rights,* schisms had developed between the two Southern liberals and the other members of the committee. On the whole, these differences were old and familiar.

Graham and Tilly had objected to both substantive measures and what they perceived as the generally anti-Southern bias of the report. They opposed, for example, the recommendation that federal funds be withdrawn from school systems that practiced segregation. "I agree with you in principle" Tilly told her non-Southern colleagues, "but at the same time I see . . . the reaction of the South." She believed that many Southern school administrators would refuse money that was conditional on desegregation, and black and white children would be the ultimate losers. Graham, for many years an advocate of federal aid to education, agreed. Rather than end segregation, he believed, attaching such a string would result in the South's losing badly needed educational financing. Graham and Tilly also admonished the committee to tone down its report. Tilly said of a proposed draft, "Can't we soften it a little? Try to understand us a little bit and don't rub it in quite so much." At one point, she presented her case directly to Robert Carr who, as the committee's executive secretary, was responsible for coming up with an acceptable draft. Tilly warned Carr to avoid raising a "whip-hand" against the South. Graham remarked, "Throughout this report every time anything is wrong with the South . . . we always say the 'South,' but when we come to the North and the West we put it in a locality or an institution, we never say the 'North' or the 'West!' " In the final version, examples of Northern discrimination were substituted for some of the Southern ones and, at Graham's insistence, a reference to discrimination against Jewish students was expanded to "particularly in the North." [23]

The continual arguments about the language of the report reflected a growing estrangement between Northern and Southern liberals over civil rights. James B. Carey, the secretary-treasurer of the CIO, was particularly opposed to Tilly's pleas for the committee to "be careful and go slow." Both expressed their opinions forcefully in a discussion of the final draft:

CAREY: *We are going to define whether or not we will take issue with the abuses. I don't know why we should monkey with the words.*

TILLY: *I think you are missing the point. The South is making progress rather fast, but we are going to highlight some things here that will . . . retard it.*

CAREY: *That is the accusation that is directed against anyone who agitates the [race] question. . . . I don't think that it would help in meeting the problem if we join forces with the opposition.*

TILLY: *I am not asking that we join forces. I think that we have to be careful of the way it is approached. There has to be an understanding. The South had the largest minority group and has the biggest problem, and it is hard for anyone who doesn't live in the South to really understand the heart throbs on both sides. . . . Mr. Carey, you are too far away from the South. You just don't feel it.*

CAREY: *I suppose you are right, but I am not quite far enough from the South on this particular issue.* [24]

The final report was a clear victory for the Northern approach. During the Truman years, Northern liberals, closely allied with an increasingly well organized and politically potent black protest movement, were gaining the upper hand. For the first time since Reconstruction, they, more than white Southern liberals, would determine federal policies.

The Southern Regional Council also found contending with the new racial politics difficult. The council had been organized in 1944 ostensibly to enable Southern liberals to face the growing outcry against racial discrimination. For five years SRC maintained a nebulous stand on segregation in the hope of drawing support from people with differing views on the issue.

The Regional Council soon became a battleground between critics and defenders of Jim Crow with each side seeing the new organization as serving its own interests. Virginius Dabney tried to persuade a Southern official of the American Medical Association to join the council, implying that SRC posed no threat to segregation. "Unless we in the South are willing to work with our colored friends . . . to channel interracial advancement in the directions we desire," warned Dabney, "relations between the races may well take a violent turn with incalculable consequences." [25]

But to others the council represented a significant effort to deal Jim Crow a death blow without risking the direct confrontation that Southern liberals so greatly feared. In 1944 the Southern-born journalist Stetson Kennedy undertook a study of SRC for the Rosenwald Fund. According to Kennedy, a vigorous campaigner against racial injustice, the council was correct in assuming that reforms in race relations in the South would have to stop short of the immediate abolition of segregation. "The best way to rid the South of segregation," he concluded, "is to set out to rid the segregation of discrimination." He believed that an emphasis on equality would eventually make segregationists recognize the futility of their position. As Kennedy saw it, their only legal options would be either the very expensive one of upgrading services for blacks or the unthinkable one of lowering them for whites. Thus, while the activities of the council should be kept under close scrutiny, according to Kennedy, the SRC merited Rosenwald support.[26]

Yet the council's evasive stand on segregation served to provoke rather than dampen controversy. In the spring 1944 issue of *Common Ground*, a publication of the Common Council for American Unity, two writers, J. Saunders Redding, a young black man, and Lillian Smith, a Southern white woman, attacked SRC for its failure to oppose segregation. Redding argued that the council's position was "potentially more harmful than beneficial." According to Smith, SRC represented an effort of white Southerners to alleviate tensions that embarrassed them rather than a genuine effort to secure full human rights for blacks. SRC director Guy Johnson termed Redding's attack "skunkish" and felt that Smith's criticism, atypical coming from a Southern liberal, was also unfair. In a subsequent issue of *Common Ground*, Johnson rebutted their criticism with the contention that it was "more realistic" not to restrict the council to those willing to denounce segregation but powerless to do anything about it. He reasoned that it was better to "capture the foothills" before "storming distant peaks." Johnson believed the exchange in *Common Ground* would benefit the council. Not that it would please the "all or none crowd," he explained to Virginius Dabney, but it would "boost the morale" of those who thought the council had strong possibilities. Nevertheless, there would be increasing sentiment among some Southern liberals, Will Alexander among them, that segregation could not so easily be isolated from other racial issues.[27]

Alexander had always tried to be pragmatic in his approach to the South's racial problems. In 1935 he summed up his philosophy of race relations in the question, "what can liberal-minded white people and constructive-minded Negroes do to create a better racial atmosphere?" Alexander often expressed displeasure with "special pleaders," men like Walter White of the NAACP, and once counseled a group of black college students against becoming "professional colored persons." While race relations director at the Rosenwald Fund, Alexander found people interested in ideologies rather than action to be time-wasters, forever involving themselves in discussions.[28]

Early in 1945, however, Alexander broke a long public silence and spoke out against segregation. In the January issue of *Harper's*, he characterized education and segregation as "conflicting" racial policies inasmuch as segregation negated the purpose of education. "Unless the problem of segregation can be resolved," wrote Alexander, "there is no hope for any alleviation of the race problem in America." Though he stopped short of calling for an immediate end to segregation, the veteran racial liberal made it clear that he thought the policy unsound. He maintained that Jim Crow not only degraded blacks but also kept the mass of Southern whites poor. Alexander emphasized that equal services would defeat the symbolic purpose of segregation—keeping the Negro aware of his inferior place—and viewed the movement for genuinely equal services as a step in the right direction. Nonetheless, Alexander recognized that such a goal was unfeasible as a long-run solution and would not serve as a substitute for the eventual abandonment of segregation. This fine distinction did not help the Southern Regional Council, which had difficulty deciding whether to circulate reprints of Alexander's article. The council finally did so but only after indicating that the contents did not represent its own policy.[29]

The segregation question hamstrung SRC. At its December 1944 board meeting, Virginius Dabney introduced a resolution that would put the council on record as accepting segregation as the "law of the land." Howard Odum in particular opposed this motion, believing that SRC should not commit itself to segregation. Of the blacks at the meeting, only Carter Wesley, the editor of the *Houston Informer*, supported Dabney. Even though Wesley's own newspaper opposed segregation, he insisted that the council could not do any positive work so long as it hedged on the issue. To complicate matters further, Benjamin Mays of Morehouse College offered an antisegregation statement. No clear-cut position emerged from the meeting.[30]

Guy Johnson found the wrangling irksome. "We've got to dispose of this segregation dilemma as soon as possible or it will keep blocking the future of the Council," he wrote Odum shortly after the exasperating meeting. Johnson favored endorsing a prosegregation statement on the ground that it was wiser to lose some Negro support in order to attract whites; otherwise, he argued, SRC would "degenerate into a propaganda and agitation agency." He also took Odum to task for what he regarded as muddled thinking. Johnson could not understand how Odum could oppose Dabney and Wesley and at the same time wish to bring additional Southern whites into the organization. In his year as director of the Southern Regional Council, Johnson found "a continuing malaise" over the council's policy on segregation.[31]

The "continuing malaise" clearly disturbed Odum. He believed that the controversy over segregation had caused some of the council's originally enthusiastic white liberal supporters to drag their feet. Odum had hoped that the inclusion in SRC of such well-known critics of Negro wartime demands as Virginius Dabney, Ralph McGill, Mark Ethridge, Jonathan Daniels, and John Temple Graves would induce a significant number of cautious but realistically liberal white Southerners to join his organization. By January 1945, however, Odum wondered what had happened to "that brilliant coterie of liberals that we had counted on?" Save for a few dissident voices, no newly potent Silent South emerged after World War II, not even one committed to the advancement of Negro rights within the framework of segregation.[32]

In 1945 Odum received the Edwin L. Bernays award from the Federal Council of Churches for his contributions toward improving black-white relations in the United States. The honor must have seemed slightly ironic to Odum, whose views on the current racial situation were becoming increasingly pessimistic. The failure of his Southern Regional Council to deal adequately with the segregation issue proved a heavy disappointment. More and more Odum came to sense himself as a man whose views on the problem differed significantly from those of the controversy's main principals—blacks, Northern liberals, and, most sadly of all, the mass of white Southerners. In 1946 he ruefully admitted to one hardline segregationist that his own conclusions were "unacceptable to a large proportion of the people in the South, particularly to my own kin folks." Added Odum, "I don't see why one who has been entrusted with the opportunity to do research and work hard should give back to the people only the things that they believed a hundred years ago." [33]

In 1948 Odum reported that the South, in the midst of growing hostility to civil rights, was a "different South," a South even less enlightened than it had been during the 1920s. Recognizing the injustices wrought by segregation, Odum saw that Jim Crow stood on an increasingly shaky foundation and that it might soon be eliminated in many areas. He spoke of the need to desegregate but characteristically added this could only be done in a "framework of reality and achievement rather than in ideology and agitation." [34] As much as he agreed with the essential justice of the cause of blacks, he concluded that they were in the process of pursuing their rights in destructive ways. Odum's explanation of black demands revealed a curious blend of sympathy and disapproval.

> We Negroes [wrote Odum] want equal opportunity to live in this the best land in the world. We want a chance to do the best work and

> get the best pay. We want to express ourselves fully, and as youth in a youthful race perhaps we are considerably bumptious and noisy. We want the right to travel, to trade, to work without embarrassing segregation laws and customs, and we would like to live anywhere in the community whenever we can make the grade. In more specific instances and cases, we like to go into the drug stores, in the markets, and in other public places as a matter of fact just as other people do; perhaps we want this more because we have not had it, and we are a little immature and naive about it.
>
> And we like to dream of unreasonable things to be done and ideals to be attained, and we want to do this even as other people do without being considered presumptuous. In the long life line of human beings waiting their turn for service, achievement, privilege, and obligation we want to take our place regularly and not be always slipping back to the end of the line and giving away always to someone else. We are in a transitional stage, boisterous, vocal, unreasonable, and we don't give a damn if we are; we will be heard. And don't blame us even if the best of us talk big about what we are going to do when and if we do get what we want, and if we don't get it. And don't blame us permanently if in this stage of new transition and learning some of us do lose our balance and if we lose our patience and run amuck. We are eager, ambitious, and we get hypnotized with the feeling within ourselves.[35]

Though Odum could be critical of black protest, inside the Southern Regional Council Virginius Dabney was the main voice for refusing to compromise on segregation. Dabney regarded Odum as much more flexible on the issue than himself. As early as 1945 Dabney predicted that the Jim Crow controversy within SRC was "the rock on which we are going to crash" but nevertheless decided to remain with Odum's group because, as he explained to one distraught white member who resigned, the council was the only organization "to stand between us and leadership from Northern radicals." Yet Dabney sensed all along that the council was moving toward an avowedly antisegregationist stand. Guy Johnson once offered him the presidency of the council only to have Dabney decline on the grounds that if SRC ever came out against segregation, it would "finish" him. Dabney made it absolutely clear that he intended to leave the organization in such an event.[36]

Dabney became increasingly uncomfortable in dealing with the subject of race relations. By the end of the war he regarded himself as a sincere friend of blacks, but one to whom they no longer seriously listened. In June 1945 he denounced those who wanted to continue the FEPC as a permanent agency after the war. He wrote in the *Times-Dispatch*, "No law which is strongly opposed by the overwhelming majority will ever be effective or will ever achieve the results which it seeks to achieve." Yet Dabney urged his fellow white Southerners to take positive steps to improve the lives of black people. "Merely to say that Negroes are getting 'uppity,' and that this must be stopped by force . . . is absolutely no solution," he contended. "Thousands of colored people are now well-educated, ambitious and sensitive. They have aspirations, some legitimate and some not, and if we deny those aspirations entirely, we shall have a constant source of friction in the middle of our society with violent outbreaks a continuous possibility." [37]

He interpreted black and Northern criticism of Southern liberals like himself as part of a delusionary and self-defeating campaign to blame the nation's ills on the South. In an April 1946 *Saturday Review* essay on the question of whether the South was that bad, Dabney answered an emphatic no. He argued that the Detroit and New York race riots of 1943 indicated that the North offered more promises than opportunities for ambitious Negroes and that black frustration was consequently greater there than below the Mason-Dixon Line. Furthermore, he insisted that it was not fair to judge the entire South solely by the actions of its well-publicized racial fanatics. The whole state of Texas, contended Dabney, could not be dismissed as reactionary merely because a "gang of hatchetmen" led by Senator W. Lee "Pappy" O'Daniel had forced the 1944 firing of the liberal University of Texas president Homer P. Rainey. After all, Rainey, too, was a Texan. The white Virginian decried what he saw as the emergence of a fashionable cult dedicated to denouncing the South. For Dabney, the anti-Southern tone had negative historical implications:

> The greatest danger confronting the South today lies in the possibility that the attacks being made upon it from other sections in a mounting crescendo will have the effect of stifling the authentically progressive movements which are under way in the region. Just as in the 1830's

> the unbridled attacks of the Northern Abolitionists drove the entire Southern people into a defensive position from which they were never able to extricate themselves, and killed the promising indigenous effort for the elimination of slavery, so the assaults being delivered currently upon the South and many of its more enlightened leaders tend to discourage, and even to crush, movements which otherwise might bring important and far-reaching advances. Let it be remembered that the Southern people are a proud people. They can be persuaded but they can never, under any circimstances, be driven.[38]

When the South was attacked by outsiders, Dabney, like Robert E. Lee before him, stood ready to defend the region of his birth even if doing so would require him to side with causes that he did not fully accept. Eventually, Dabney would become identified almost wholly as a segregationist and would abandon the Southern Regional Council.

The first major program undertaken by the Southern Regional Council after the war had aimed at assisting black veterans. From 1944 through 1949 the Rosenwald Fund and the General Education Board respectively gave the council grants of $227,000 and $46,000. To help finance the veterans program, which ran from July 1945 to May 1947, the council on its own raised an additional $55,000. It employed eight black veterans and one white veteran to travel around the South to inform returning black soldiers of their benefits under the G. I. Bill of Rights and the Veterans Administration. This was done without challenging segregation. Council literature, for example, emphasized that the excellent combat record of black troops had caused many white Southern soldiers to question their long-held prejudices. Southerners could not "abuse the colored people any more," noted one white army sergeant from Texas. Though he suggested that it might be "best" to maintain segregated schools, the man gave an otherwise impassioned plea for racial justice on the grounds that Negroes as well as whites had given their lives for their country. In accordance with this line of argument, the council called for the employment of black veterans by Southern police and fire departments.

The SRC's veterans program was a new departure, but for the most part the agency still resembled the Interracial Commission that it had supposedly replaced. It endorsed the Supreme Court's decision against the white primary but made no significant effort to register black voters. The council revived interracial groups in ten states, called for greater equality in public education and transportation, and provided informational services.[39]

Yet even limited goals seemed unrealizable in the postwar South. Guy Johnson, noting in his annual director's report the reelection of Bilbo and the comeback of Talmadge, characterized 1946 as a "period of reaction." "Yes, the trend is discouraging," Johnson insisted, "and we may as well face the fact that it will probably get worse." Privately he expressed the opinion that the council was going nowhere. During Georgia's contested governorship fight, Johnson told Will Alexander that the "sickening" political situation had made the operation of the SRC difficult. "All this is exciting, challenging—but virtually futile," he noted. Alexander was displeased; the council's failure to live up to expectations now convinced him that SRC should become more openly critical of Jim Crow.[40]

Alexander himself tried to give Southern liberalism some antisegregationist direction. As usual, he was cautious. He thought that desegregation should begin only in the District of Columbia, in the armed services, and in the Protestant churches. But Alexander was not tentative. At a special conference on race held by the Federal Council of Churches in Columbus, Ohio in March 1946, he used his role as chairman to fight vigorously for a statement denouncing segregation as "unnecessary and undesireable and a violation of the gospel of human love and brotherhood." In 1947 Alexander toured several Southern cities, where he spoke out against segregation. This position estranged him from many of his former colleagues. His onetime secretary Emily Clay sarcastically referred to him as the "great Dr." in a letter to Guy Johnson and expressed her disagreement with his views. "It is a strange thing," she said, "that a man who lived and worked so long in the South and who used to know the problems so well would think, after living outside the region for a few years, that all barriers could be broken down immediately. They haven't been in Chicago, where he has been spending most of his time since leaving Washington and they haven't been in other cities of the North. Why should he think that a miracle could happen down here?"[41]

In April 1947, largely through the influence of Alexander, George S. Mitchell, the head of the council's Negro veterans program, replaced Guy Johnson as SRC executive director. Before joining SRC, Mitchell had been a board member of the SCHW but had resigned over its failure to take a more explicitly anti-Communist stand. The council also had a new president, Paul D. Williams, a Richmond publisher active in Catholic social action groups who had replaced Odum in 1946 when Odum thought it prudent to have a Southern businessman head the organization.[42]

Under Mitchell and Williams, the Regional Council gradually adopted a more antisegregationist posture. In May 1947, *New South*, which had succeeded *Southern Frontier* as SRC's official organ, featured an article by the Negro sociologist Charles S. Johnson calling upon Southern whites to abandon segregation as a sacred principle. Johnson, who for many years had cooperated closely with white Southern liberals, accepting the limitations under which they operated, now contended that no upstanding black man could endorse segregation. "For the Negro to accept segregation and all of its implications as an ultimate solution," said Johnson, "would be to accept for all time a definition of himself as something less than his fellow man." The council also praised the report of President Truman's Civil Rights Committee and urged Southerners to give it "thoughtful consideration." Truman's January 1948 request for civil rights legislation moved the council even closer to the Northern liberal and black stand. Following the president's message, Ralph McGill had asserted on a national radio broadcast that neither the black nor the white leaders of the Regional Council favored federal legislation in the area of civil rights. The NAACP's Walter White immediately wired George Mitchell, asking if McGill had correctly stated the council's position. The council's executive committee replied that McGill had not represented SRC's views. Though it preferred to have the Southern states guarantee the civil rights of all their citizens, the SRC did not oppose federal civil rights legislation.[43]

To be sure, there was still ambiguity in the council's position. Late in 1947 Paul Williams contributed some of his own in replying to queries over SRC policy. Williams believed that SRC had dealt with segregation through action rather than words, pointing out that the council was composed of Southerners, without any further classification. "The question before us is not whether . . . segregation is right or wrong, which is like saying whether or not we are against sin," Williams explained to his fellow council members, but rather "to convince other Southerners . . . that the way of life followed by the Southern Regional Council is right and proper." He thought that white council members were more likely to recognize the "injustice and unworkability" of segregation through rational argument and personal observation than by listening to people with a "holier than thou" attitude. Williams explained the council's function as one of "education and persuasion, by word and deed, so that more and more of our fellow Southerners will come to think and act as we do for the same reasons we have found to be liberating." [44]

Williams still hoped that the council could represent a rational middle way and avoid a showdown between civil rights advocates and Dixiecrats. Rarely had white Southern liberals felt more squeezed than they did during the charged presidential election campaign of 1948. At its September meeting in Atlanta, the council's executive committee declared that the situation had degenerated to the level of the controversy over slavery during the 1850s. At that time, according to the SRC, many spoke about the slavery problem but only a few managed to advance beyond accusation and counteraccusation. White liberals in the South of 1948 identified with those disregarded voices. "Today the old issue is back, in new guise," said the SRC, "and we are performing in the same old way."

The Regional Council wished to examine the situation dispassionately. The organization described civil rights as a misunderstood issue that applied only to the right of black Southerners to vote, to have legal protection of their persons and property, and to achieve education and employment commensurate with their abilities. The council pointed out that civil rights had "nothing to do with swimming pools and dating places," and thus it was irrelevant to argue that civil rights laws would lead to the immediate abolition of segregation and the establishment of social equality. SRC took the position that the denial of basic rights to Southern blacks justified the passage of federal legislation. However, it argued that civil rights proponents placed too much emphasis on legal remedies while overlooking the economic aspects of discrimination. "Until the South enjoys a standard of living comparable to that of the rest of the nation," declared the council statement, "it appears likely that political democracy will also lag behind." Realizing that its stance would meet the approval of neither Dixiecrats nor civil righters, SRC nevertheless called for "intelligent disagreement, reasonable compromise, and a fruitful working solution." [45]

But time was running out for Southern liberals to be evasive. Blacks and Northern whites had succeeded in making segregation the point about which all discussion of Southern racial problems revolved. Federal action in one form or another was inevitable, and white liberals in the South would have to take sides. For the Southern Regional Council, this pressure proved decisive.

In 1949 the SRC finally adopted a clear position. Late that year *New South* declared that legally enforced segregation "in and of itself constitutes discrimination and inequality of treatment." The statement emphasized that segregation was detrimental to white Southerners in that they had to adjust themselves to the hypocrisy of a double standard in violation of the "American Creed." The SRC now classified separate-but-equal as a "constitutional anachronism" and said: "It is neither reasonable nor right that colored citizens of the United States should be subjected to the humiliation of being segregated by law, on the pretense that they are being treated as equals." [46] As the Supreme Court continued to consider the constitutionality of segregation in public education, the SRC undertook studies to show the unworkable nature as well as the injustice of Jim Crow.

Once committed to the breakdown of segregation, the SRC lost a number of its traditional supporters. In his November 1950 annual address, council president Paul Williams went so far as to denounce Southern "gradualists" who opposed any federal action that affected race relations. Williams now believed that such men, though they considered themselves realists, neglected the larger implications, "the doubt and criticism of two-thirds of the world's people who are not convinced that our kind of democracy is available to people of their color." As Williams saw it, the gradualist's emphasis on education as a cure-all for Southern racial problems represented a convenient sidestepping of the issue.[47]

Williams's argument demonstrated how the Cold War was changing the context of American race relations. With the United States championing global anti-Communism and asserting moral leadership of the "free world," Jim Crow became difficult to ignore. Both blacks and Northern liberals, in demanding civil rights measures, raised the international implications of segregation in the South.

In April 1947 Walter White had asked President Truman to speak at the Lincoln Memorial following the upcoming annual conference in Washington of the NAACP. White reminded Truman how Communists were utilizing acts of racial discrimination to denounce the United States. Truman accepted White's offer, which was not surprising considering that, according to one State Department estimate, almost 50 percent of the Soviet Union's anti-American propaganda focused on race. At any rate, the president got the message. He pointed out that the "top dog in a world which is over half colored ought to clean its own house first." When blacks and whites failed to live together in peace, he said on another occasion, "the failure touches not us, as Americans alone, but the cause of Democracy itself in the whole world. This we must never forget." But the Cold War was not the only factor that prompted Truman to support black rights more than had any previous American president.

Truman also recognized the growing importance of the black vote in national elections. In 1932 the majority of black votes had been Republican, but in 1936 fully 76 percent of black voters had cast ballots for Roosevelt. Though the New Deal had already weaned Negro voters away from the Republicans, World War II, which quickened the pace of Southern black migration into Northern cities, made their potential influence greater. In November 1947 presidential adviser Clark Clifford gave Truman a forty-page memorandum on how to conduct the 1948 campaign. Prophetically, Clifford held that, along with the farm vote and the labor vote, the Negro vote could lead Truman to victory. Moreover, Clifford believed that black voters, because they were concentrated in swing states such as Illinois, Ohio, Pennsylvania, and California, would more than offset Truman's loss of strength in the South resulting from his pro-Negro stands. Along with Cold War idealism, then, practical politics was making segregation expendable to the Truman Administration.[48]

The first breaks came in 1948. In February, acting in accordance with advice of his Civil Rights Committee, Truman recommended to

Congress the passage of a battery of civil rights legislation: the creation of civil rights bodies in both the legislative and executive branches, an antilynching law, a permanent FEPC, laws against discrimination in interstate transportation, and laws protecting the right to vote. When the legislation did not materialize, Truman promoted civil rights through executive orders. In July, he banned segregation in the federal civil service and in the armed forces.[49]

The trend against segregation during the Truman years made it impossible for white liberals in the South to operate within a segregationist tradition. By 1950 they either opposed segregation or no longer were looked upon as liberals. In this respect the transformation of the SCHW and the SRC was significant. Broadly conceived by Southern liberals during the 1930s, each had hoped to subordinate segregation to other problems. The experience of the two groups, however, affirmed the impossibility of this approach. Both organizations evolved into small groups of white Southerners committed, above all, to racial integration in their native region.

The year 1950 was a turning point for white racial liberalism in the South. In that year George Smathers soundly defeated a political hero of Southern liberals, Claude Pepper, in a nigger- and red-baiting Florida primary campaign, thus ending Pepper's fourteen-year senatorial career. More portentious, yet, was the senatorial primary defeat of Frank Graham, who a year earlier had been appointed U. S. senator from North Carolina following the death of the incumbent. Willis D. Smith, after one unsuccessful red-baiting primary (Graham received a plurality of 53,000 votes and came within a hair of getting the majority needed to win the election) harangued often and loud during the subsequent run-off against his opponent's long record of racial liberalism. Smith passed out circulars with the simple mesage: "If you want your wife and daughter eating at the same table with Negroes, vote for Graham." Smith won by 18,000 votes. Graham's defeat, together with Florida voters' rejection of Pepper, represented a crushing setback for Southern liberalism. At a time when a direct questioning of the entire caste system had finally surpassed black education, lynching, disfranchisement, and even fair employment practices as a major issue in the South, racial liberalism became fatal to political careers.[50]

As the South entered two decades of racial turmoil, white liberals could no longer assert that they represented the key to change in the region. Southern liberals, recognizing themselves for the small minority they were, now either engaged in direct confrontations with segregationists, often making great personal sacrifices for the cause of the civil rights movement, or watched powerlessly as events took their course. Gone were the days when liberals could point to "progress" in Southern race relations and emphasize the good work being done by white Southerners. Instead, Southern liberals witnessed a new wave of white hysteria as blacks and Northern whites, through their own action, achieved a federally enforced racial revolution. This was precisely the situation that white liberals had hoped to avoid.

The mid-century South was an uncomfortable place for many white Southern liberals. Between 1950 and 1954 membership in the Southern Regional Council dropped from 3,400 to 1,800, and the organization survived largely because George Mitchell used his own funds to keep it alive.[51] Among the disillusioned were Howard Odum and Virginius Dabney.

Prior to his death in November 1954, Odum registered pessimism over developments in the South. Though publicly he called for a "scientific and statesmanlike" Southern response to the Supreme Court's ruling against segregation in public education, privately Odum doubted the wisdom of the *Brown* decision. He believed that no organization in the South, including the SRC, was adequately prepared to deal with the breakdown of Jim Crow. When North Carolina's State Superintendent of Public Instruction requested his help, Odum, whose life-long philosophy had been that academic intellectuals had a moral obligation to deal with social problems, meekly responded that "this whole matter of integration is so clearly one of administration and politics that . . . I would do more harm than good in suggesting procedures and specifications." He later wrote his old friend Gerald Johnson that the Supreme Court's reasoning had been "naive and amateurish" instead of "structured in the bed rock of factual reality." Odum confessed he did not know where to turn. "I just don't know anything to recommend," he told Johnson, "except to adapt ourselves as solidly as possible . . . and then charge all the rest up to transitional society and the hazards of immature stages of development." To his last days, Odum retained his faith in science. He was less sure, however, of his faith in a liberal South.[52]

Virginius Dabney, who by his own admission became a racial "conservative," had not changed as much as the times had changed. He remained remarkably consistent in urging his fellow white Southerners to provide blacks with genuinely equal—though segregated—facilities, in denouncing outsiders who demanded a revolution in Southern racial patterns, and in working quietly to create more opportunities for Virginia Negroes.

Yet it was in the role of segregationist that Dabney continued his dignified journalistic career—a career that finally won him a Pulitzer Prize as an editorial writer in 1948 for his criticism of the poll tax and the South's one-party politics. He left the Southern Regional Council once that group came out against Jim Crow. By 1950 Dabney was openly praising the arch-conservative Virginia Senator Harry F. Byrd. In the *Saturday Evening Post* he noted that many responsible Virginians formerly critical of the senator now realized that Byrd's stands against increased federal bureaucracy, higher taxes, and labor unions—stands that outraged liberals schooled in New Deal and Fair Deal policies—had their merits. Though acknowledging some disagreements with Byrd, particularly over the poll tax, the *Times-Dispatch* editor maintained that Virginia's political boss was "one of the most scrupulously honest men in American public life." In extolling the virtues of the Byrd machine, Dabney once again revealed his class-consciousness:

> [There is not] a Bilbo, a Heflin, a Talmadge or a Huey Long in office anywhere in the Old Dominion. More, there hasn't been one in our time. Candidates for office in Virginia don't always discuss the issues frankly, but neither do they remove their socks or their shoes in front of country audiences, as has been done in other states, solely for effect. There are no race baiters in Virginia, and race relations are exceptionally good. The overall average of salaries of colored public-school teachers last year throughout the state was slightly higher than the average for white teachers. (Northern papers please copy.)

V. O. Key declared that, compared to the way in which Virginia was run, Mississippi was a "hotbed of democracy," but according to Dabney, the Byrd organization was giving the majority of Virginians the kind of government they wanted.[53]

During the school desegregation crisis of the 1950s, Dabney reacted in much the same way as he had to wartime racial tensions. Comparing blacks who could not stand the sight of a Confederate flag to white Ku Klux Klanners, he once again admonished the "extremists" on both sides to silence themselves. The Supreme Court's ruling against segregated public education in the South disappointed Dabney, who opposed the decision on both legal and moral grounds. Though he urged compliance with the court, he left the door open for legal, nonviolent circumvention and delay of integration. In 1955 Dabney supported the relatively moderate (compared to what came later) plan of a special commission appointed by Virginia Governor Thomas B. Stanley, which called for limited integration in the state on a "local option" basis. However, he thought that even this would retard progress in race relations. After Senator Byrd called for "massive resistance" to racially mixed schools in 1956, Dabney defended the South's reluctance to desegregate.[54]

Dabney believed that desegregation was an ill-advised policy that Negroes opted for only after the failure of Southern whites to demonstrate a genuine willingness to rid segregation of discrimination. He insisted that, even though it was a matter of too little too late, progress in the South made prior to 1954 was sufficient to make race relations in Dixie better than those in the North. He repeatedly alluded to such facts as that in 1953 Chicago police had to provide twenty-four hour protection for black families who had moved into a Trumball Park housing development and regarded it as hypocritical for Northerners to force white Southerners to do what they themselves neither believed in nor practiced. Moreover, Dabney thought that wholesale integration would lead to miscegenation, a prospect he regarded as harmful to both races. Though he never used the white fear of "commingling" to engage in race-baiting, he opposed racial admixture as much as any diehard defender of white supremacy. In 1958 Dabney declared in a national magazine article that, given the explosiveness of the issue of court-ordered integration of their state's public schools, white Virginians, by closing schools, had taken a "peaceable" and "honorable" stand that had avoided riots such as had occurred in Little Rock, Arkansas the previous fall. Byrd himself told

Dabney that this piece represented "the very best and most convincing article that has yet been written in behalf of the South in our present crisis." [55] Though not an outright defense of massive resistance, Dabney's stand represented the closest thing to it.*

Dabney's retreat contrasted with the behavior of Aubrey Williams. If anything, Williams campaigned even harder against racial injustice in the postwar era. Remaining in Alabama, where he continued to work for the Southern Conference Educational Fund, Williams denounced the "gradualists" who wanted anything less than an immediate breakdown of segregation. "I am sure I am very unreasonable," he told one skeptical white Southerner in 1950, "but I am so fed up with the milk and water stuff that I just can't take it any longer." Still, he recognized that it was a "sad hour" both for America and for the South. Early in 1954, as the Supreme Court was listening to final oral arguments in the *Brown* case, Williams traveled to Washington to speak before the court on behalf of school desegregation. While in Washington, Williams engaged in a radio debate with Senator Herman Talmadge of Georgia, a virulent defender of segregation. [56]

Williams's outspokenness made him an isolated and persecuted figure. In March 1954, along with fellow SCEF members James Dombrowski and Virginia Durr, he was called to testify before the Senate Internal Security Subcommittee, which held hearings in New Orleans that were chaired by Senator Eastland of Mississippi. Once again, Williams was smeared for his alleged red leanings. The investigation led to the decline of his farm journal, which was abandoned by advertisers and subscribers after the American Legion made a determined effort to crush what it regarded as an example of "Commu-

* During the 1960s, Dabney voiced sentiments similar to those that had made him a leading white liberal before the Second World War. Once the Supreme Court overruled Virginia's last-ditch legal efforts against mixed schools, Dabney urged Virginians to begin integration. Despite the fact that most white Richmonders opposed desegregation, he contended in 1964, the quiet methods of the city's "sane and reasonable" Negro leadership were making great progress in achieving integration while actually reducing interracial tensions. Dabney attributed this to the "traditions of genteel behavior, of courtesy and fair dealing for which Richmond has been known." "Richmond's Quiet Revolution," *Saturday Review*, 47 (February 29, 1964), 19. For Dabney's growing acceptance of integration see "Next in the South's Schools: 'Limited Integration,' " *U.S. News & World Report*, 48 (January 18, 1960), 92–94; "With All Possible Speed," *Saturday Review*, 45 (August 18, 1962), 43–44; "The Pace Is Important," *Virginia Quarterly Review*, 41 (Spring 1965), 176–91.

nism in Agriculture." Moreover, many Northern liberals and black civil rights leaders, afraid of becoming tainted, failed to defend Williams, even though the evidence against him was flimsy. Instead, they ignored him and avoided any cooperation with SCEF.[57]

Williams's experiences during the 1950s left him embittered. The era of massive resistance, he concluded, was harder on white Southern liberals than on blacks, for most people believed that any white Southerner who opposed segregation must be either a Communist or crazy. "The rank of the 'liberal white Southerners' has been considerably thinned," wrote Williams in 1958. "All have receded somewhat and a great many have gone underground." [58]

Will Alexander shared Williams's sense of frustration. In 1948 Alexander had retired to a farm in North Carolina located about fifteen miles from Chapel Hill, wanting to spend his last years close to what had long been one of the vital centers of Southern liberalism. Instead, he ran into rumors suggesting that he had been sent back to the South by Jews and Mrs. Roosevelt to purchase land in Durham and Orange County in order to give it to blacks. As a result, he found himself shunned by many university people who were afraid of openly associating with him. Even Frank Graham had hesitated to allow Alexander to participate actively in his attempt to win the 1950 senatorial primary. The founder of the Commission on Interracial Cooperation had to sit on the sidelines and witness a campaign so racist that he later said the notorious Senator Bilbo could have taken lessons from it. Alexander was certain that Willis Smith had exacerbated prejudice in North Carolina to a dangerous extent. His prophecy proved only too true. The Ku Klux Klan, insisting that North Carolina had to be "straightened out," grew rapidly in what many had presumed was the most racially enlightened of the former Confederate states. (By the 1960s, North Carolina would have the dubious distinction of having more dues-paying Klan members than any other state.) All this made Alexander despondent. In 1951 he wrote Howard Odum of his fear that he had become an embarrassment to the university. Though Alexander went so far as to break off contacts with his Negro friends, his white neighbors still talked about his being engaged in secret work. Alone and dispirited, Will Alexander died in 1956.[59]

Also paying for their liberalism were Clifford and Virginia Durr.

The Durrs had returned to their native Alabama only to find themselves ostracized for their work on behalf of the SCEF. In January 1954 Virginia informed her brother-in-law, Justice Black, how painful it was to keep going. "We live among and with people who don't agree with us on any single thing or even on the basic premises of our thought," she told him. Although she did not feel that she and her husband were as outspoken as their Montgomery neighbor, Aubrey Williams, this made no difference. "I am afraid that we will have to occupy the same position that Aubrey Williams does," she said, "which is completely outside the community." Two months later Virginia Durr was called, along with Williams, to testify before Senator Eastland's witch-hunting subcommittee. She survived the harassment and continued her civil rights activities. But it was not easy. In 1959 Mrs. Durr, again writing to Black, told him that segregationists brooked no dissent: "I am seeing down here this deathlike conformity building up, when to speak out, to take action of any kind, to protest, to write a letter, to hold a meeting, brings down on your head both social and economic ruin and there is no recourse in the law." Such was Alabama in the 1950s. George Washington Cable had used similar words to describe Louisiana in the 1880s.[60]

The isolation that Williams, Alexander, the Durrs, and other antisegregationist white Southerners complained of during the 1950s was real. Not since Reconstruction had the white South felt so threatened. Northern commentators, like Samuel Lubell, observed that there was a "totalitarian quality" to the South's refusal to tolerate those who supported civil rights. Southern liberals agreed and, in some cases, took Lubell one step further. "Today even silence does not afford protection against the fanatics," said Harry Ashmore of the *Arkansas Gazette* in 1958. "Unless a man goes the whole way with fervid condemnation of the United States Supreme Court and all its works, he is subject to charges of disloyalty and heresy." Operating in a hostile climate, white Southern liberals, if they spoke out at all, undertook the unenviable task of opposing Southern school boards, sheriffs, politicians, White Citizens Councils, and resurrected Ku Klux Klans in their own bailiwicks and at unfavorable odds. Theirs would be a lonelier, more dangerous struggle than the one Southern liberals had faced when Jim Crow had appeared impregnable.[61]

Lillian Smith: The Southern Liberal as Evangelist

Before 1954, Southern liberalism as a whole was essentially moderate in its approach. When the Commission on Interracial Cooperation fought against the lynching of blacks, it did so in the manner least likely to offend conventional white attitudes. Neither the commission nor the Association of Southern Women for the Prevention of Lynching directly criticized the caste system that underlay the protected murder of blacks by white mobs. Similarly, suffrage reformers expended surprisingly little energy on behalf of black enfranchisement and instead concentrated on poll tax repeal because poll taxes affected many more whites than blacks. The Southern Regional Council, which had been formed at a time when black protest was making segregation a matter of national concern, skirted the issue for as long as it could. Even in the late 1940s, most Southern liberals, whether they believed in segregation or not, agreed that a direct confrontation over the issue would do more harm than good. From George Washington Cable to the embattled members of the Southern Conference Educational Fund, Southern liberals who unequivocally opposed Jim Crow too often found themselves either in exile from their native region or, if they remained in the South, ineffective and ostracized.

Under the circumstances, it is legitimate to ask whether, during the Jim Crow era, one could be both a Southern liberal and a militant antisegregationist. The answer is yes. A minority of Southern liberals did take an uncompromising stand against caste.

What distinguished such people both from their fellow Southern liberals and from Northern advocates of civil rights, white and black, was their emphasis on religion. Links to the New Deal and experiences outside the South helped to motivate them, but like Southern blacks, they also believed that color caste was a violation of basic Christian ideas. Stressing "regeneration" of the South, these people found in evangelical Christianity not only an answer to the region's long dilemma over race but a possible bridge between racial liberalism and the concerns of the typical white Southerner. They would end up supporting the civil rights movement in the 1950s and 1960s.

The importance of evangelicism to Southern liberalism can hardly be overemphasized. Religion played a dominant role in the careers of many, and one is struck by the number of white Southern liberals who pointed to simple Christian pieties as the essential element of their thinking. "I have never lost faith by what I seemed to glimpse in the New Testament," said Will Alexander in 1951. "I have been influenced more by this than by anything I have ever known." For Aubrey Williams, the Sermon on the Mount ranked alongside the Constitution and Lincoln's Second Inaugural Address as having had the greatest impact on his views. Frank Graham, in defending a minister whose civil rights statements had outraged his congregation, stated: "We should make clear that we will not retreat from the faith in programs based on the Fatherhood of God and brotherhood of all peoples for which Jesus lived, preached, and gave his life." In describing Graham, Senator Wayne Morse of Oregon called him "the most Christlike man I've ever known." Howard Kester, asked what had prompted him to work as a union organizer and lynching investigator during the 1920s and 1930s, replied that it was, above all, Christian love. "The kind of healing the region and the nation needed wouldn't come through politics or economic organization," he said, "there had to be an ethical orientation, a moral confrontation based on the teachings of Jesus." Nearly all Southerners were, in the opinion of one of them, "haunted by God." This seems to have been especially true for liberals.[1]

The religiosity of Southern liberals did not necessarily mean that they were active in churches. Will Alexander, for one, had left the ministry after deciding that the Methodist Church was incapable of dealing with the South's racial problems. Indeed, he came to believe that the majority of the South's churchmen lacked the "divine compulsion" without which they could not properly serve as Christian leaders.[2] But many discovered, as did Alexander, other outlets for their religious enthusiasm.

Some found a pulpit in the editorial pages of Southern newspapers. Hodding Carter II and Ralph McGill regularly used their respective columns in the *Delta Democrat Times* and the *Atlanta Constitution* to denounce white chauvinism and demand a genuinely Christian relationship between the races. Carter wrote in 1949 that "the time must come when the way of Christ will be the way of the world; when men of every faith and every tongue will be as equal in the sight of each other as they are in the sight of God." In 1963 Harry Ashmore praised the *Constitution* for contributing to Atlanta's relatively peaceful desegregation and noted that McGill, who gave his readers "hell-fire-and-brimstone denunciations of their prejudices," was "more a preacher than anything else." [3]

One can only speculate as to how large a part McGill's religious outlook played in his plea for white Southerners, outraged by the *Brown* decision, to abandon Jim Crow. Virginius Dabney, whose views on the race problem prior to 1954 had closely paralleled McGill's, wound up implicitly endorsing "massive resistance"; unlike McGill, Dabney had a Menckenesque dislike for evangelism. Is it possible that the differing attitudes of the two men toward religion accounted for their dissimilar reaction on this most difficult issue for liberals to confront? At any rate, it can be said that the white Southern liberals who eventually adopted antisegregationist outlooks were more often than not the ones who exhibited a strong evangelical orientation. This was certainly true of one of the South's earliest, most outspoken, and best known white opponents of Jim Crow—Lillian Smith.

Lillian Smith was born on December 12, 1897 in Jasper, Florida, a small town just a few miles below the Georgia line. It was a typical Deep South community; its population was evenly divided between whites and blacks, and subservience was the lot of the blacks. Lillian, the seventh of nine children, spent her first eighteen years there. Her parents, Anne Simpson and Calvin Warren Smith, were both from slaveowning families in Georgia and were among the grandees of Jasper. Lillian's father had made a fortune in the naval stores industry, which until the First World War was immensely profitable in the swamp and piney woods region of southern Georgia and northern Florida. Mr. Smith owned mills that employed several hundred white and black workers. A shrewd businessman, he did not play his employees high wages, but his paternalistic outlook and devout Methodism led him to take a personal interest in their welfare. Nor did he neglect his family. An appreciation of literature and music was an integral part of the Smith children's upbringing. They were also taught the virtues of religion, democracy, and good manners.[4]

But the parents also schooled them in the intricate rituals of white supremacy—something that Lillian sensed was contradictory to the other teachings. Once, when she was still a young child in Jasper, the Smiths brought a little orphan girl of about the same age as their daughter to stay with them until a home could be found for her. Lillian and the orphan soon became fast friends. After about a month, however, Mr. and Mrs. Smith discovered that the little girl staying with them was a mulatto; they immediately dispatched her to the local orphange for black children. Lillian's parents' explanation of why she had to be separated so suddenly from her new playmate—"you are white, she is colored"—proved unsatisfactory, both to herself and to her departing friend. It was an incident that would have a significant impact upon her racial outlook.[5]

By 1912 Calvin Smith's various businesses were doing so well that he bought some land in Rabun County near Clayton in the north Georgia mountains and constructed a summer home for his large family. However, when World War I broke out during the summer of 1914, the European market for naval stores closed, and Smith's fortunes declined drastically. In 1915 he closed out his many businesses, sold the house in Jasper, and turned his place in Clayton into his family's new permanent home. For a time he operated a summer hotel and eventually founded Laurel Falls Camp for Girls on top of Old Screamer Mountain, the site of the Smith home.

The change in her father's financial status threatened Lillian's formal education. She graduated from high school the same year the

Smiths moved permanently to Clayton and enrolled at Piedmont College in Demarest, Georgia, a town about thirty miles south of Clayton. The following year she dropped out of school completely to help her father manage his new businesses in the Georgia mountains and a Daytona Beach, Florida hotel that he leased and operated. While in Daytona Beach, Lillian met a violinist who encouraged her to pursue a musical career. In 1917 she enrolled in Baltimore's Peabody Conservatory to study piano, but World War I patriotism soon caught her up. She stayed at Peabody only one year, leaving Baltimore in 1918 to join the Student Nursing Corps.

After the armistice, Miss Smith, upon the urging of her father and Rabun County school officials, went to work at a two-teacher mountain school in Tiger, Georgia, a tiny town a few miles from Clayton. The young girl now found herself in a world that was not only far removed from the Peabody Conservatory but remote from her Southern childhood. She lived with a mountain family during the week and commuted home only on weekends. Despite the Spartan living conditions, she found herself delighted with the mountain people, especially the children, and instituted creative activities to enrich their otherwise drab winter existence. She organized school plays, games, singing, and even Saturday night parties for families. Her few months as a school teacher were an unusually fulfilling initial experience with the world of children. Lillian, however, had too many ambitions to remain a rural school teacher, and in the fall of 1919 she returned to Baltimore to resume her musical studies at Peabody. Until 1922 she suffered financial hardship to stay in Baltimore and become an accomplished pianist only to decide in the end that she lacked sufficient talent for the concert stage.

An important influence upon Southern liberals was their experiences outside the South. Even when they returned home, they found that residence elsewhere had added new dimensions to their views about the South's racial situation. Almost invariably, the perspective gained from having lived in different settings stiffened the resolve of a Will Alexander or an Aubrey Williams to oppose the rigid customs of their native region. The same would apply to Lillian Smith, except that, in her case, the break away was more severe.

In 1922 she accepted a position as head of the music department at the Virginia School in Huchow, China—a Methodist mission school for well-to-do Chinese girls. Though not herself a missionary, she strongly identified with mission work then being done in China, for her older sister and brother-in-law had gone to China as missionary-teachers as early as 1910. Lillian's decision, therefore, seemed quite natural and had the full approval of her devout Methodist parents, who had tried to teach all their children to employ their talents in socially useful ways.

For the next three years she lived in China, and the strange land was a revelation for her. While in China she found both the time and the stimulation to pursue reading in areas that eventually became the consuming interests of her life—children, psychology, and racism. She delved extensively into Freudian literature and also acquired a familiarity with Gandhi's ideas.[6]

The young lady from the South was intrigued both by Chinese attitudes toward one another and by Westerners' reactions to the Chinese. She found the Chinese people to possess great dignity and, in line with her own religious upbringing, admired them for believing that man's spirit was more important than his body. She believed that Westerners misunderstood these attitudes as the Oriental's desire to "save face." Most of all, however, Lillian Smith was shocked by white foreigners, including the missionaries, who established enclaves in China that excluded Chinese. She drew an immediate connection between what was occurring in China and life in her own native South. Years later she remembered:

> I was young then. Young and inexperienced, and from a South where I had practiced segregation since I was born. But I saw what was happening. Seeing it happen in China made me see how ugly the same thing is in Dixie. I can never forget my deep sense of shock when I saw Christian missionaries from the South (and North, and England) impose their ideas of "white prestige" on this people who were living on their own soil. Here were intruders, staying there only on sufferance, yet forever preening and priding ourselves on our white superiority and calling ourselves followers of Christ. It was the kind of thing which makes a young person sick. And I was young and honest, and I was sickened by what I saw.

From her observations, Smith concluded that white foreigners had "sinned" against China.[7]

In 1925 she returned to Georgia and took over from her aging father the directorship of the Laurel Falls Camp for Girls. To help with the camp, she employed Paula Snelling, a young woman from a well-to-do Georgia family who had taught mathematics in a Macon high school and who was as interested in psychoanalysis and literary criticism as was Lillian. From then until Lillian's death in 1966, they remained close companions. During the next five years Lillian ran the camp in Clayton; worked two winters as a secretary for an older brother who was city manager of Fort Pierce, Florida; and managed to spend one year studying child psychology at Teacher's College, Columbia University. In 1930 her father died and left Lillian with heavy responsibilities—unpaid debts and an infirm mother—that she unhesitatingly assumed.

Under Smith and Snelling's direction, Laurel Falls soon won a reputation as one of the finest girls camps in the South. It was an exclusive place; the campers who came regularly belonged to the white South's more prominent and wealthy families. While Snelling led the girls in physical activities, Smith oversaw the writing and production of plays, dealt with the problems of girls growing up, and in general urged each youngster to seek identity. Income from the camp was used to pay off her father's debts.

In the off-months when camp duties lagged, Lillian escaped some of the drudgery of having to take care of a sick mother by turning to creative writing. Between 1930 and 1935 she drafted three manuscripts. One was a novel about China, "And the Waters Flow On," that sought to demonstrate the connection between racism and sexual attitudes in a Chinese setting. A second novel, "Tom Harris and Family," was about the South. She also completed a novella, "Every Branch in Me." None of these works was ever published and, unfortunately, they were all destroyed, along with many other valuable possessions, by a fire that struck Smith's Clayton home in 1944.

As Lillian Smith began her writing career, it is probable that her racial views had become interwoven with her ideas about sex. She had apparently given up romantic involvement with men. Possibly the family burdens that she assumed after returning from China contributed to this. But her subsequent statements on the subject were evasive. Speaking before a group of college women in 1963, Smith commented on the difficulties that women of her generation had in trying to pursue a career and meet men at the same time. "We often found both," she told them, "but it was easier to find interesting men in the professions and in the business world than in the home. We had many interesting men for friends. Let it go at that."

Despite this unwillingness to discuss her personal life, Smith's published writing about sex would be, to say the least, avant-garde. She would deal frequently with the need to encourage children to feel proud rather than guilty about their sexuality, with the feminine side of nature, with the potential healthiness of masturbation and homosexuality, and with Protestantism's failure to appreciate a "mature genitality." Of course, as W. E. B. Du Bois, John Dollard, and William Faulkner demonstrated, one did not have to be a Southern white woman to make the connection between sexual attitudes and racism. Still, few would do so with the fervor and explicitness of Lillian Smith. Perhaps she thought that white Southerners were more likely to be, if not changed, at least shocked by such arguments when they came from one of their own women. At any rate, it seems clear that Lillian Smith's sexual outlook merged with the more visible influences of Christianity and China and contributed to her unorthodox racial views.[8]

By 1935 Lillian Smith was thinking about racism, sex, child development, and what it meant to be a white woman in the South. Still, except to her family, friends, and camp patrons, her ideas were totally unknown. She needed a vehicle of expression. That winter she and Paula Snelling decided to publish a small magazine devoted to topics related to the South. They chose the unlikely name *Pseudopodia* for their new journal but soon changed it to *North Georgia Review*.

In this magazine, Smith showed that she approached the South's problems differently than did most Southern liberals. She made it clear, for example, that in her opinion most of their efforts to come to grips with the region's injustices only amounted to "scratching the topsoil." Smith confessed that she herself had no magic prescription but welcomed all to join her in searching for "truth." This pursuit of "the truth" would, as she read and pondered, lead Lillian Smith to concentrate most heavily on caste.[9]

At first, rather than attack segregation directly, Lillian employed literary, cultural, and psychological criticism to condemn the debilitating effects of caste. In a 1937 essay about black writers, she lamented the ones like Paul Lawrence Dunbar who could not use their talent to "rise above the silly drool" of racism while praising those like Du Bois, James Weldon Johnson, and Claude McKay who attacked racial injustice. Smith also believed that whites should stop treating blacks as if they were debased. In 1938 she argued that many racial tensions would "fade away" if school readers for both white and black children contained stories about blacks as well as whites, black history along with white history, and studies on African culture to complement those on European culture. She was greatly influenced by John Dollard's *Caste and Class in a Southern Town,* which held that white racial chauvinism was a sickness. With Dollard's views fresh in her mind, she wrote in 1938 that the Southern senators then filibustering against an antilynching bill manifested the "compensatory mechanisms of Nordic bluster and paranoiac destructiveness." Such "maladjustments" could best be corrected, she declared, "by a psychiatrist with the insight of a Karl Menninger in collaboration with a southern sociologist possessing the objectivity of a Rupert Vance." [10]

A further indictment of caste appeared in the fall 1939 edition of *North Georgia Review* in Smith's introduction to "Drums," a play about black sorrow and anger that had been written by her girl campers. She compared white and black Southerners to the strands of two intertwined grape vines, saying that to cut one was to sever both. Like other Southern liberals, Smith was not yet calling for an immediate end to Jim Crow—it would take the racial issues generated by World War II to lead her to that—but she left little doubt over her ultimate position. [11]

Because of her moralistic outlook, Lillian Smith had an evangelical conception of an artist's role. In *Pseudopodia,* she wrote a debunking review of Margaret Mitchell's *Gone with the Wind* in which she chided the author for not using her talents to tell the truth about the South. Smith implied that, like a good preacher, a good writer comprehended the social, economic, and intellectual assumptions of his audience but maintained sufficient critical detachment to tell its members truths about themselves. By concentrating on "trivial social snobbery" instead of on the making of a caste society, Mitchell had failed to do this. This review affirmed a point that Smith would make throughout her career: A *true* artist needed social commitment, and the purpose of art was to explicate, as creatively and brilliantly as possible, the greatest problems that confronted human beings, so as to enable them to live more justly and more in accordance with Christian ethics.[12]

As a result, Smith abandoned quite early some of the assumptions that hampered other Southern liberals. In particular, she did not believe that the Civil War and Reconstruction demonstrated the futility of supporting civil rights for blacks. These historical experiences, she maintained, could not be used to excuse current injustices.

Accordingly, she disapproved of James G. Randall's *The Civil War and Reconstruction* and Paul Buck's *The Road to Reunion* in a 1937 review. She found the two Northern historians' sympathies with the South disturbing and contended that the Southern homogeneity of which they wrote so approvingly consisted largely of racial fears and hate; in her mind the tie that bound white Southerners together resembled "a rope with a noose at one end." She expressed only "tempered appreciation" for Randall's influential study. Arguing that his approach was too detached, empirical, detailed, unphilosophic, and amoral, she also criticized Randall for ignoring the rights of blacks and the black man's contributions during Reconstruction. "Matching sectional sin against sectional sin," said Miss Smith, "may be a nice game for elderly ladies of the U.D.C. to play, but it seems singularly inadequate as a technique for interpreting one of the world's greatest tragedies to minds eager to understand in order to avoid a worse tragedy." [13]

Early in 1938, following the death of her invalid mother, Smith found herself with more time to devote to her work. During the winter of that year, she and Snelling traveled to Brazil where Smith did much of the writing for what ultimately was to become *Strange Fruit*. It is likely that Brazil, where race relations allowed mulattoes more freedoms than was the case in the American South, influenced the author.[14] Upon their return to Clayton, Smith and Snelling continued to operate Laurel Falls Camp and publish *North Georgia Review*.

Late in 1938, the two women applied for a joint fellowship from the Julius Rosenwald Fund to help them pursue their interests. Lillian—more dynamic and more at ease with people than the relatively quiet Paula Snelling—wanted to complete the book she had begun and expand the scope of the little magazine. She also had vague ideas about turning the Clayton house into a center for the promotion of creative arts in the South. As Southern women who combined innovative ideas with old-fashioned manners, Smith and Snelling were able to muster recommendations on their behalf from such extreme poles as W. E. B. Du Bois and the Lions Club of Clayton, Georgia. Du Bois had nothing but praise for the two women, calling *North Georgia Review* "stunning and courageous," and M. L. Harper, the secretary of the Clayton Lions Club, informed the Rosenwald people of the brilliant manner in which the two ladies ran their girls camp and also vouched for their high character.[15]

The Rosenwald Fund had a sharp eye for talent, especially when it related to the South and race relations. During the 1930s and 1940s, the fund, directed by Edwin R. Embree, awarded fellowships to many Southern whites and blacks who became famous in later years. Recipients included such figures as Ralph McGill, the poet Margaret Walker Alexander, the photographer Gordon Parks, the novelist Ralph Ellison, and the historian C. Vann Woodward. It is not surprising, therefore, that the fund not only awarded Smith and Snelling a fellowship, but tried to induce Smith to write a "*Grapes of Wrath*-type" novel about the collapse of cotton tenancy in the South. Embree explained to her, "If we are to move the region and the nation we must state the case in more powerful terms than a sociological treatise." [16]

Lillian declined Embree's invitation, explaining that she was already at work on a novel that dealt with the relationships between white and black families in a small Southern town. She stated that she was using college-educated blacks in the story inasmuch as she did not want to carry on the "old tradition of quaint Negroes." Smith emphasized that she was "intensely interested" in exploring the family relationships of Southern blacks. "I tend always to think first," she said, "of interpreting characters in terms of their many and complex relationships with their family, as these affect and are affected by their economic problems, their religious beliefs, and their sexual and racial ideas."

In August 1939 Lillian Smith again wrote the Rosenwald Fund of her desire to get away from camp obligations and devote full energy to studying the South, doing creative writing, and turning the little quarterly into a monthly publication. "It happens," said Smith, "that I am the kind of person who has to give as much creative energy to a child as to a book—and sixty little girls, each with her emotional problems, can by the end of the summer have a desiccating effect on the spirit." Rather than continue the camp, she and Paula wanted to travel about the South meeting people. "We sound like missionaries with a powerful solemn purpose," Lillian Smith confessed, "but we do own up to a love for the South that makes us want to do a little to help pull it up by its own bootstraps."

She once again appealed to the fund for financial assistance the following December. Writing to Edwin Embree, she praised him for a pro–Negro rights speech he had delivered at West Georgia College in Carrollton. She informed the Kentucky-reared Embree that his words gave her "that psychic release which comes from hearing a Chicago southerner say all the things a Georgia southerner still fears to say to an unselected group." Smith told of her intense pleasure at watching the faces of rural Southerners who heard aloud thoughts "which they know so well in their hearts are there but will not admit without invalidating qualification."

She went on to explain to Embree that income from her girls camp was the only means of support for *North Georgia Review* and stressed that the magazine was not breaking even. Nevertheless, she hoped to increase interest in it by adding such features as a "Do You Know Your South" contest with a $250 first prize; offering $100 for the best article on what the church could do to improve race relations; and awarding $50 for the best essay on the South by a high school student. Smith added that though the purpose of *North Georgia Review* was to stimulate creative writing about the South, a number of established Southern writers did not like the magazine because it had reviewed some of their work unfavorably and that they consequently dismissed it as a "merely sociological" journal. According to Smith, most Southern writers of her generation or older were "sunk too deeply in their own self-pity and nostalgic dreams for us to expect much more than an occasionally good local-color book out of them." (Her opinion of William Faulkner, for example, was that he possessed great imagination but lacked common sense, especially in his portrayal of women.) All of this made Lillian feel that she stood at a crossroad:

> As the magazine and my writing become better known (Miss Snelling's writings are more scholarly, less controversial than mine) my camp will inevitably be ruined, for I draw my children from the South's wealthiest and most conservative families. God knows they've taken plenty from me already. My camp patrons and I are friends, and our warm personal feelings have made it possible for me to get away with almost the impossible in social philosophy, sex education and religious skepticism. But I have had good luck so far. As everyone tells me, the time will come . . .

Smith also expected that her soon-to-be-completed novel was "going to make many people angry." If she could raise the money, she would rather turn the camp into a creative center for the arts.[17]

Smith applied for and received a renewal of her fellowship for 1940–41. She failed, however, in her effort to get the Rosenwald Fund to underwrite the *North Georgia Review* and her prospective art center. Embree wanted very much to help Miss Smith's ambitious enterprises, but he concluded that direct financing of her work by a "Yankee organization," would, if the fact became known, jeopardize its character and influence. Hence, Smith oversaw the publishing of the literary quarterly, operated her girls camp, traveled about speaking to YMCA and college groups, and diligently worked on her novel. During the summer of 1941 she informed a friend, "As for honors: the biggest honor I have received was an anonymous letter threatening my life after a talk on the South which I made to the students at Blue Ridge." [18]

In ensuing issues of *North Georgia Review,* Lillian Smith denounced segregation in increasingly harsh terms. When in a 1941 review of Richard Wright's *Native Son,* the white Mississippian David Cohn argued that, despite the disastrous impact of caste on Wright's black protagonist, blacks could not expect the breakdown of segregation, Miss Smith wondered how white Southerners could consider themselves a gentle people yet "lash out explicitly and implicitly with caste prejudice of the toughness and crudity of rawhide."

On the other hand, when Southern whites and blacks did get together in a non–Jim Crow spirit, she hailed the occasion as a new beginning. Speaking of the integrated 1940 meeting of SCHW, Smith declared that this was "not simply an unusual happening but the symbol of a changing South, a good South. And the fact that it happened at Chattanooga is to some of us like hearing the thin fine sound of horns across the hills. We know that we shall hear them again and we prize the knowledge." [19]

The entrance of the United States into World War II stiffened Miss Smith's resolve to campaign against Jim Crow. She believed that the threat to freedom from abroad made it more incumbent than ever upon Southern whites and blacks truly to understand each other, and that whites presented a greater obstacle to progress than did blacks. She was particularly critical of Southern liberals like Virginius Dabney who insisted that Negroes should not use the war to fight against segregation, for to do so would only enhance the already excessive influence of racial demagogues. Smith declared that it was absurd to equate A. Philip Randolph with Eugene Talmadge as a "racial troublemaker." To Smith such attitudes symbolized a liberal South that once again was choosing reticence over action.

> If the liberals in the South do not turn to the constructive act, if they continue to "solve" deep fundamental conflicts by silence and evasion, pep talks, quiet pressures, or by criticism of Negroes who are attempting to pull their race toward freedom, much of the responsibility for the violence which may result will be theirs—as it has been theirs in the past. . . . If we profoundly believe that the Negro is as important as the white man, that his happiness and security are as essential as ours, we shall not be so quickly alarmed about "race trouble" by which is meant trouble for the white man. The Negro is always in trouble, a trouble which does not seem to concern many white people until the contagion spreads from the Quarters to White Town.[20]

Mark Ethridge's statement in June 1942 to the effect that segregation was here to stay greatly disturbed her. She regarded it as a prime example of the negative approach of many Southern liberals. In August 1942 Smith informed Virginius Dabney that she understood the pressures that induced white liberals to adopt such a line but made clear that she deplored Ethridge's words as a betrayal of racial liberalism.

> We decent southerners can have a tremendously moral and quieting effect upon the more irresponsible group not by appeasing them but by taking a firm stand against them. They will not dare carry out their designs if they think the liberal forces are standing for the rights of the Negro. They will bluster and make a big noise but they will be afraid to take the thing too far. That famous paragraph of Mr. Ethridge's must have sounded "just right" to Japanese and German ears. I confess that I could have sat down and cried in the traditional feminine manner when I read it, had I not felt too much pity for the Negro for tears.

Though she realized the critical nature of the wartime racial situation in the South, she called upon Southern liberals to seek new approaches.[21]

Early in 1943, Smith and Snelling published a special issue of *South Today*, as *North Georgia Review* was now called, that dealt exclusively with the racial crisis generated by the war. In a long article Smith declared that fighting for freedom while maintaining Jim Crow was like "trying to buy a new world with old Confederate bills." She once again criticized her fellow Southern liberals for refusing to stand up against the injustice of segregation.

Miss Smith went on to probe the Southern liberal outlook. "Symbolized by the southern liberal and focused in him," she argued, "are the pressures, fears, dreams, and conflicts of the South." As children, nearly all white Southerners had developed genuine affection for the black nurses, servants, and friends who formed an integral part of their early lives. However, in adolescence their own white families schooled them in white supremacy or, as Smith put it, taught them not to esteem a group of people whom they had already learned to love. What distinguished racial liberals from the mass of white Southerners, however, was that in later years, as a result of education, Christian sensibilities, and common sense, they discovered that it was foolish to advocate white supremacy to the point of denying the humanity of black people. But—and here lay the tragedy of Southern liberals—by this time it was too late for most of them to respect fully these people whom they had once loved but had later been taught were inferior. This experience, which Smith believed was common among white Southerners of her generation, left scars of fear, anxiety, and guilt. It accounted for the "troubled depths of their spirit" and was the main reason why so many of them were incapable of doing more than what she described as "concocting little recipes for sweetening the old segregation." Hers, to be sure, was an exaggerated portrait, but it revealed her belief that most Southern liberals were unprepared to meet the South's racial dilemma. She would have to show the way.[22]

The same issue of *South Today* contained guidelines through which "intelligent white Southerners" could deal with current racial tensions. Among Smith's suggestions were avoidance of words like "nigger," "coon," and "darky"; use of courtesy titles when speaking to or about educated blacks; sending letters on behalf of racial justice to politicians, newspapers, and radio stations; subscribing to Negro magazines; becoming acquainted with blacks of a relatively high social status; quietly refusing to obey segregation laws; rebuking those whites who were rude to blacks. Miss Smith thought that almost any upstanding white Southerner could undertake such actions without risking his person or property.

However, she also had advice for the few, like herself, committed to a genuinely new way of life in the South. She urged them to take bold, admittedly dangerous steps required to shock the South into realizing the destruction wrought by caste. There is little doubt that she regarded this as her own role. In a subsequent issue of *South Today* she wrote:

> As a white Southerner, born in a Deep South town whose population was predominantly Negro, reared under the segregation pattern, still living under it, I know the fears by heart. I know the placid taking for granted of a way of life so wounding, so hideous in its effect upon the spirit of both black and white. I know the dread of change; I know all the rationalizations by which the white man eases his guilt and conserves his superiority; how he concentrates—as if *he* were unchangeable, as if *he* and *his* pattern can never be changed—*not* on his own sick obsession with skin color, but instead on the Negro, hoping somehow that the Negro can be changed to fit the pattern more

harmoniously. That is what most of us mean when we talk of race relations: a more harmonious adjustment by the Negro to the white man's pattern.[23]

Because of her outspokenness, Georgia officials, hounded by such groups as the Ku Klux Klan and Vigilantes, Incorporated, began to harass her. They tried to pressure the Post Office into revoking the second class permit of *South Today*, having gotten what Lillian called a bunch of "frigid old hens" in Atlanta to testify that the magazine was indecent. She was even threatened with an investigation by the Georgia legislature, a prospect that did not dismay her in the least. Such an investigation would provide a forum for her, a respectable Southern white woman, to state emphatically that she believed in social equality for Negroes. Her only worry was that authorities might try to stifle her through a sex scandal or by charges of income tax evasion. "I rapidly surveyed the last twenty years and found poor pickings in sex," said Lillian, "so I don't think they can get far there; they might catch me on income tax . . . as neither Paula nor I . . . are experts in accountancy." [24] Despite her fears, *South Today* continued publication until 1944, when Smith, suddenly a celebrity because of *Strange Fruit*, no longer needed her own journal to state her views.

Strange Fruit finally appeared in February 1944. Though she had completed the novel in 1941, Smith had to fight to get it published intact. Seven publishers had rejected the manuscript on her terms before Reynal and Hitchcock agreed to take it. The book's title reflected her view that the South's contemporary culture and people, both white and black, were the "strange fruit" of white supremacy. Also, the blues singer Billie Holiday had recently made popular a lament about lynching that bore the same name.[25]

Set in the imaginary town of Maxwell, Georgia (a place very much like Lillian's old hometown of Jasper) shortly after World War I, the book centered on the complications resulting from a clandestine love affair between a white man and a black woman. It was a carefully constructed and gracefully written novel, dramatic in theme, explicit in language, and psychologically probing. Somewhat to the surprise of its author, it quickly became a best seller. It was banned in Boston and produced as a play on Broadway. Overnight it turned Smith into a spokeswoman for racial justice. It eventually sold over three million copies and was translated into sixteen languages. So great was its notoriety that during the 1940s the phrase "strange fruit" became synonymous with interracial love affairs.[26]

Strange Fruit was primarily an examination of segregation and white supremacy, which underlay all action in the story and determined, with naturalistic predictability, the sad outcome. The two lovers were victims of a system that made them feel guilty about what otherwise would be a normal relationship. This was particularly ironic, for it was their inability to function within their respective black and white worlds that had drawn them to each other in the first place. The black woman, though a graduate of Spelman College, the most distinguished Negro women's school in the South, could only find employment in Maxwell as a domestic. She was unable to relate to the two types of black men who lived in her home town: semiliterate roustabouts and respectable types who made the best of living in Maxwell despite the indignities they faced every day of their lives. The white man, too, rejected the hollow world of his friends and family and found fulfillment only with a black paramour who eventually got pregnant, but he was not strong enough to overcome his guilt over loving a person whom his upbringing told him was "merely a nigger-girl." Murdered by his lover's outraged brother, he symbolized a white South too weak to admit that white supremacy was as destructive to itself as to blacks.

In creating Maxwell, Smith tried to be as realistic as possible. She not only described the physical details and nuances of Southern life, but probed deeply into her many characters to show what they were feeling behind the facade of words they used to each other. Using her knowledge of psychology, she showed how frustrated and unhappy adults—especially whites—stifled the emotional growth of their children. She dealt candidly with such themes as the sexual needs of children, homosexuality, menopause, and abortion, because, along with miscegenation, these played a large role in the lives of her characters. During the course of the novel she twice used the word "fuckin." This got *Strange Fruit* outlawed in Massachusetts, helped the sale of the book immensely, and gave the public the misleading idea that Miss Smith had written a "dirty" book. Though her novel was intended to shock readers, *Strange Fruit*, even by 1944 standards, could hardly be considered pornographic.[27]

Controversy surrounded the book almost immediately after its release. Boston's suppression of the novel in April 1944 led to a landmark free speech case.[28] United States postal officials declared it obscene and refused to allow it through the mails; Eleanor Roosevelt, however, liked the book and spoke with her husband about its status. Shortly thereafter, a White House order lifted the Post Office's restriction. Not all of *Strange Fruit*'s many critics were Southern apologists, racists, or prudes. Since a Negro was burned to death by a mob of white mill workers, Communists attacked the novel as divisive to working class solidarity. Many blacks also took offense, claiming that black women—especially graduates of Spelman—did not carry on with white men the way Miss Smith's heroine had. For this reason Walter White disliked the novel and thought it harmful to the Negro's cause.[29] It must have been quite a shock to him when his own daughter, Jane White, played the heroine on Broadway in the 1946 stage adaptation of *Strange Fruit*.*

Because of this furor over the book, Smith found herself repeatedly explaining why she wrote it. Once on radio she insisted that the novel was not really about race prejudice and lynching but rather a fable of sons, mothers, brothers, and sisters searching for love. Though she recognized that her book dealt with racial segregation, she maintained that it was more concerned with segregation in a larger sense. This did not mean that she, like many Southern liberals, wanted to play down race in order to avoid facing Jim Crow, but rather that she considered caste so monstrous that its destructive tendencies went beyond the context of the American South. For her, segregation existed wherever people turned away from themselves and what they knew to be right and allowed fear to shut out richness from their lives. Still, *Strange Fruit* undoubtedly had its origin in the author's own childhood conflicts. "I knew, and have never forgotten," she said, "that segregation has something to do with white and black

* Produced and directed by José Ferrer and based on a script written by Lillian and her sister, Esther, the stage version failed to convey the lyrical drama of the novel. It also was a box office flop and ran on Broadway only from November 28, 1945 to January 19, 1946.

people—as everyone in America knows—but it also has to do with childhood, and with mothers and their children, and it has to do with the heart's deepest fears and the child's earliest dreams." In short, she meant the novel as an artistic expression of her moral outlook, which saw in segregation a symbol of modern man's alienation. She said that she accepted the teachings of Jesus Christ "with profound seriousness," but that, under segregation, it was "impossible to be a real Christian no matter how much one wants to." [30]

Though people such as Eugene Talmadge called the book a "literary corncob," *Strange Fruit,* quite to the astonishment of Lillian Smith, met with surprisingly little resistance in the South. No group in the South opposed the novel with the vehemence of the proper Bostonians; the book sold openly in Atlanta and Birmingham. According to Smith, the people of Clayton, Georgia accepted the book particularly well, and she even invited some of them to a party she gave for her New York editor. "They all wept a little, kissed me and embraced me, ate my chicken sandwiches and little cakes and went down the hill feeling that each of them had written at least one chapter of it," the obviously jubilant author informed Edwin Embree. "Bless them . . . as far as I know, things are going to be all right." [31]

Apart from her warm personal relationships with many segregationists, the fact that she came from a respected Southern family probably eliminated some pressures that she would otherwise have experienced. Her brother, Frank Adams Smith, was ordinary (executive manager) for Rabun County. When necessary, he used his influence to prevent people from harassing his sister. Also, Lillian Smith, like many Southern women reformers, had the ability to camouflage social radicalism with a ladylike image. Perhaps because they did not perceive her as a threat, many of her white neighbors apparently separated the "Miss Lil" whom they knew from the author of *Strange Fruit.* One Clayton woman explained to an inquiring reporter that Miss Smith was a "deeply religious woman" who would not have written all that "vulgar sexy stuff" had not her Northern publisher forced her to in order to sell books. Moreover, despite Lillian's earlier fears, Laurel Falls Camp continued to run smoothly until she herself decided to close it in 1948.[32] However, Smith did take one precaution. She wrote each of her wealthy camp patrons to offer a suggestion: their young daughters ought not to read her book.*

Prior to the publication of *Strange Fruit*, Lillian Smith, though vocal in her denunciation of racial injustice, had remained outside the major Southern liberal organizations. She attended meetings of SCHW and for a time headed an SCHW committee on creative arts. But, in general, she devoted most of her efforts to her magazine. An independent spirit, Smith was not one to work in a group. Her sudden fame, however, prompted leaders of the newly formed Southern Regional Council to invite her to join their organization. This proved to be a mistake. She not only refused to join the council but in *Common Ground* openly attacked the new group for its refusal to take a public stand against segregation.[33] Smith believed that the time had come for a hitherto Silent South to speak; she wrote to SRC director Guy Johnson:

> We must say why segregation is unendurable to the human spirit. We must somehow find the courage to say it aloud. For, however we rationalize our silence, it is fear that is holding our tongues today. A widespread denial of a belief in segregation will shake the pattern to its roots. Each of us, in our hearts, know this. To remain silent while the demagogues, the Negro haters, and the racists, loudly reaffirm their faith in segregation and the spiritual lynching which this way of life inflicts, is to be traitorous to everything that is good and creative and sane in human values. I believe that the time has come when we must take our stand.

Smith saw the Southern Regional Council indirectly sanctioning segregation by suggesting that it was the understandable product of Southern traditions, economic patterns, and poverty. In her eyes, segregation represented "cultural schizophrenia." [34] She also implied to Johnson that Howard Odum opposed her affiliation with the SRC and would consider it a liability.

Odum regarded Smith's letter, which included psychological as well as moral arguments against caste, as an indication that the

* Apparently some of her young campers thought that, since she was always telling them stories, Lillian Smith had written a book for them. A few even went so far as to request a copy from their schoolteachers.

woman was more interested in "Freudian promotion" than in helping blacks. He defined the proper position for white Southern liberals as twofold: 1) increase opportunities for Southern Negroes; 2) avert bloodshed. "We have no objection to people organizing for reconstruction of the white man and human nature and in helping all the world's needed ideologies," Odum explained to Guy Johnson. "The value of our organization is that it is specific, and that it is our business to work at our job and not on something else, and above all not to argue or debate." [35]

But Lillian Smith's war against caste, though waged only with words, did have an impact. Aubrey Williams, to whom Eleanor Roosevelt had sent a copy of *Strange Fruit,* told the First Lady that the people portrayed by Smith were "very live and real" and that he had known "hundreds" like them. Williams thought that the book's characterization of Southern whites was, if anything, too generous. "Their kindness to their niggers," he said, "resembled kindness to mules and dogs." J. Waties Waring, the South Carolina federal judge who had ruled against his state's effort to maintain the white primary, would refer to one of Smith's 1949 denunciations of racism as among the most penetrating analyses of the South that he had ever read. "If the people of this country and of the world can only see and understand the disease which has long lingered under a scab of romance wrapped in the Confederate flag," he confided to Williams, "they can and will find a way to restore to health our poor pitiful people whom you and I love and weep for." Even Virginius Dabney, who thought Lillian Smith "about as 'left-wing' as any white Southerner I know," admired her courage and ability.[36]

Not only did Smith strike a common chord for white Southern liberals of various persuasions, but she touched black sensibilities as well. She went to Morehouse College to deliver an address and stayed in the home of Benjamin Mays, who afterward recalled that she had shocked the black students. "When they heard her speak, many could not believe their ears," said Mays. "Such straight talk on race was hard to believe, especially coming from a Southern white woman." [37]

Between 1944 and 1947 she carried her campaign against segregation and cautious liberals into national magazines. In 1946, in a symbolic gesture, she joined the recently formed Congress of Racial Equality and became the most prominent white Southerner to associate with the Northern organization. She again criticized SCHW, this time for its promotion of former Georgia Governor Ellis Arnall as a great Southern liberal. Though he opposed Eugene Talmadge, Arnall, according to Smith, was a political opportunist who avoided the race issue like a plague. And silence, she declared, was a "poor weapon to use against a powerful club like white supremacy." She wrote in *Woman's Home Companion* that the earth belonged to children and that a segregated world turned them away from life and knowledge and toward death. "I know, with as much certainty as is the right of mortals to hold," she said, "that from this time on we live together on this earth as human beings with no barriers between us—or we die. I think it is as simple as that." [38]

This moralistic, evangelical tone was an essential part of Lillian Smith. From October 1948 to September 1949 she wrote a regular column for the *Chicago Defender*, "A Southerner Talking," that revealed her religious—almost mystical—outlook plus her passionate yearning for spiritual affirmation. She wrote of how the evil and misery in the world caused her to feel guilty, of her desire to help make the earth a safe place for children, of man's oneness with the universe, of spiritual love, and of her deep faith that human beings could, and would, resolve the gravest problems. She called for the establishment of a World Peace Center in Hiroshima and also suggested one for the study of children's growth where mothers from all over the globe could exchange information on child rearing. She wrote of her reaction to a Jim Crow sign in a Southern train station:

> It slapped this Southerner's mind hard, like an angry hand across the face. Once, I took those signs for granted. They were over doors when I was born and I accepted them without thinking, as I accepted heat and mosquitoes and sandspurs. Then one day my imagination woke. It was as if I felt those signs. If only all white Southerners could feel the meaning of them.[39]

In the *Defender* Lillian Smith also wrote about how she, by recognizing her rural origins, had achieved inner peace. She referred lovingly to her house in Clayton with its ample vegetable garden and considered her enjoyment of such simple pleasures a positive aspect of her smalltown Southern upbringing. Much of man's current turmoil, she felt, lay in his refusal to recognize that he was essentially a creature of the earth. Again she drew the analogy of segregation. "Always we split ourselves away from . . . plant and animal life," she said, "as if we could or would want to survive cut off from the dirt out of which we came, and to which we inevitably return." She said of New York City:

> Made by split, torn people it is a monument in commemoration of the most ambivalent culture that the world has ever seen. . . . I think only a schizoid culture could have dreamed up a skyscraper-subway city; only a people forever attempting to escape their roots and forever clinging to them, could have soared so high into the sky and burrowed so deep into the earth.[40]

Though Smith's columns for the *Defender* contained her usual indictment of racism, they were more significant for what they revealed about the Southern white woman who had written *Strange Fruit.* She maintained that her "world view" could best be understood by the words: "Life, growth, child, love, human being, whole man, whole earth, acceptance, knowledge, work with our hands, reverence." [41] All people had an urge to dream of freedom and dignity, she insisted, but only a few possessed the courage to realize their dreams.

In *Killers of the Dream,* published in 1949,[42] Lillian Smith offered her views on why this was particularly true of white Southerners. Written in prose as graceful as that of her novel, the book was an autobiographical, historical, and psychological examination of the triumph of white supremacy in the New South. It was a nonfictional sequel to *Strange Fruit,* and its author became more explicit about what it meant to be a white woman in the South.

The book examined Lillian's own childhood conflicts resulting from the South's biracial social structure and generalized them into an explanation of white racism. Guilt, fear, shame, defensiveness, hypocrisy, and violence, she suggested, resulted when white children were called upon to repress their true feelings toward blacks behind a mask of racial superiority. She referred to the "ghost relationships" between white men and black women, white fathers and mulatto children, white children and black nurses, and claimed that these haunted the South and shaped the lives and souls of white Southerners. Black children also suffered, but according to Smith, African ideas of child rearing, which still prevailed in some Southern Negro families, prevented many of them from becoming as emotionally disturbed as the whites. Particularly disturbed were white women who, like her own mother, jealously watched black women rear and win the affection of their own white children. For the white child, the conflicts within such a system were great.

> The mother who taught me tenderness and love and compassion taught me also the bleak ritual of keeping Negroes in their place. The father who rebuked me for an air of superiority toward schoolmates from the mill and rounded out his rebuke by reminding me that "all men are brothers," trained me in the steel-rigid decorums I must demand of every colored male. They who gravely taught me to split my body from my feelings and both from my "soul" taught me also to split my conscience from my acts and Christianity from southern tradition.[43]

As did Smith's other writing, *Killers of the Dream* mixed psychological explanations with moral judgments. But, as always, the latter predominated. Despite her familiarity with Freudian thought, Smith was not a scientific analyst of the South's problems. Most of her conclusions about racism were intuitive, and they were based on her own guilt and outrage. Her interest in psychology gave her another weapon with which to sermonize against caste.

Killers of the Dream enhanced Smith's reputation as the most outspoken white critic of segregation below the Mason-Dixon Line, and during the civil rights controversies of the 1950s and 1960s, she did not belie that reputation. Despite recurrent bouts with cancer from 1953 until her death from the disease in 1966, she wrote and spoke prolifically about the racial situation in the South. Always she maintained the highly personal and militantly antisegregationist tone of her earlier writing.[44] An admirer of Gandhi since the 1920s, Miss Smith was an active participant in as well as a chronicler of the civil rights movement. She greatly admired the nonviolent stance of Dr. Martin Luther King, Jr. Indeed, she thought that the "Movement," as led by Dr. King, was the essence of what religion ought to be: "love," "compassion," "grace," and "redemption." She was also a source of inspiration for civil rights activists. When in February 1960 reporters asked what prompted a group of black college students to undertake the first sit-in protest against segregation at a lunch counter in Greensboro, North Carolina, they replied they were influenced by the ideas of Gunnar Myrdal, Gandhi, and Lillian Smith. But on her deathbed in 1966 she resigned from CORE following that organization's abandonment of nonviolence for the principle of "black power." Opposed to segregation wherever she found it, Smith referred to black power advocates as "new killers of the dream." [45]

Lillian Smith, as she herself freely admitted, was a missionary whose evangelistic zeal caused her to focus on the "evil" of caste, the "guilt" of Southern whites, and the "redemption" of the South through integration. When she articulated these arguments during World War II, she won a reputation as the most outspoken white advocate of Negro rights in the South. For Lillian Smith, Jim Crow was not to be investigated, explained, and dealt with coldly in a scientific manner, or—even worse—defended. Whether to deny or affirm segregation was a moral choice between good and evil, life and death. In her mind the alternatives were clear and the answer was simple: segregation had to be eliminated, and the sooner the better. Lillian Smith thus fought segregation with the fervor of a fundamentalist preacher attacking sin. She believed that somewhere, deep inside the souls of white Southern Christians, there surely must have lurked the recognition that Jim Crow was a sin. This nonsegregated South of the spirit was the Silent South that Lillian Smith spoke for and appealed to.

CHAPTER TEN

Conclusion: They, Too, Had a Dream

White Southern liberalism during the Jim Crow era was an attempt to define some nonracist basis for Southern life. From George Washington Cable to Lillian Smith, Southern liberals not only sought to upgrade the status of the region's blacks but also attempted to liberate their fellow whites from what they saw as self-defeating prejudices. Indeed, on issues ranging from lynching, which all of them denounced, to segregation, which only a few did, a persistent theme of Southern liberalism was that race chauvinism harmed whites more than blacks.

In these years when anti-Negro discrimination appeared to be a permanent part of the Southern scene, a number of white Southerners asserted that racial justice was possible in their native region. These people, many of whom had grown up during the most intense years of racial reaction, inherited the enigma of a caste system. Most often they were newspaper editors, academics, or people with a religious motivation who took ideas about Christian brotherhood seriously. Though they differed in the degree of their commitment to the cause of blacks and disagreed over what constituted a proper basis for racial justice, they all acknowledged the discriminatory nature of

Southern race relations. To them Southern liberalism represented a hope that, if only white Southerners could appeal to other white Southerners in the proper manner, past wrongs could be righted and the quality of life improved for all.

Southern liberals, by promoting racial justice, also tried to alter the South's negative image. Although they recognized that brutalities occurred, they asserted that there was another side to the South, a liberal South, less obvious but nevertheless real. They offered evidence that many white Southerners did not accept the region's myths. Some, like Howard Odum, saw this liberal South as consisting of a majority of white Southerners who, though basically good people, had been misled into their burning hatreds. Others, such as Lillian Smith and Virginius Dabney, saw it in more elitist terms as educated or religiously motivated individuals who could combat racial injustices if only they spoke and acted more vigorously.

Racial liberals believed that, as white Southerners, they alone could effectively criticize the South without being written off as "outside agitators" or "uppity" Negroes. Though their own judgments often contributed to the South's negative reputation, they undertook such criticism because they thought it would induce positive change. Censure by outsiders, however, disturbed them. They believed that Northern critics sensationalized Southern injustices in an overly self-righteous manner and only compounded existing problems. This defensive attitude was shared by practically all Southern liberals—Lillian Smith and Aubrey Williams as well as Howard Odum and Virginius Dabney—though it was most pronounced among those who believed desegregation a mistake.

Their defensiveness had several causes. First, it revealed tensions resulting from a disparity between the concepts "Southern" and "liberalism." In espousing loyalty to the South, Southern liberals identified strongly with a region not noted for its liberalism, especially in regard to race. Similarly, identification with the idea of racial justice was somehow "un-Southern." To be both a Southerner and a racial liberal required emphasizing one's Southernness more than one's liberalism. One way to do this was to express hostility to outside critics. But another factor also was at work. During the Jim Crow era racism became increasingly identified as a peculiarly Southern problem, especially after segregation itself became the issue. Southern liberals, more than most white advocates of racial justice, quite correctly pointed out the national dimensions of racism. However, sometimes they used Northern "hypocrisy" to excuse Southern recalcitrance.

Southern liberals found themselves in a dilemma. They argued that the white South could not continue its unjust treatment of blacks, for as long as "nigger" remained "nigger," the region would suffer economic and political strangulation at the hands of ruthless exploiters and demagogues. Yet most Southern liberals did not go so far as to demand an immediate end to all racially discriminatory practices. They felt that advances had to be made slowly and cautiously.

Perhaps because of these tensions, and because they believed they could see the region's problems clearly, Southern liberals felt a strong need to explain the South to outsiders. They drew on their own experience as well as history, and much of their writing was autobiographical. In this "rage to explain," as some have called it, Southern liberals left an entire genre of interpretive works to which belong Odum's *An American Epoch*, Dabney's *Below the Potomac*, and Lillian Smith's *Killers of the Dream*.[1]

When examining their region's history, Southern liberals found a good deal that was discouraging. They believed that neither the abolitionist crusade prior to the Civil War nor the federal government's policies after the war had helped either blacks, whites, or Southern race relations. Although abolitionists and carpetbaggers had meant well, according to Southern liberals, their meddling in a complex situation retarded both material and racial progress in the South. During the age of Jim Crow the negative view of Reconstruction popularized by such historians as William A. Dunning and Claude Bowers prevailed. Southern liberals largely accepted this interpretation and pointed to the Reconstruction era's violence as the prime example of what would inevitably occur after any outside tampering with the South's racial situation. Rarely did white Southerners—Lillian Smith was an exception—explicitly question these assumptions.

But the liberals did not find the South's history uniformly bleak. There was, as C. Van Woodward showed in *Tom Watson* and *The Strange Career of Jim Crow*, paradox, irony, and hope. Despite the many brutalities, Southern liberals argued that blacks and whites understood one another better in the South than in the North and that there was love as well as hate between races. Most agreed that the South had inherited a Jeffersonian tradition of justice and democracy but that poisonous Negrophobia had triumphed over more liberal tenets. Although the latter never disappeared entirely, somehow the South had gotten off the track. Southern liberals, by continuously emphasizing the region's more positive elements, were in effect saying that freedom of thought, genuine democracy, and racial justice would one day hold their rightful place in the region.

The idea that Southern blacks and whites would ultimately "show the way" to overcoming the effects of years of racism was part of Southern liberalism's evangelistic Christian outlook. In this respect, Lillian Smith, one of the few Southern liberals to focus on segregation before World War II, was perhaps the quintessential figure.

Smith shared many values with other Southern liberals. Like them, she believed that silence abetted racial injustice and contributed to human misery. She, as did they, emphasized loyalty to the South and insisted that outsiders, especially "morally complacent" Northerners, could not easily understand the complexity of the Southern experience. And she certainly agreed that the South was not monolithic and that many white Southerners never wholly swallowed the regional mythology. What distinguished Smith was the evangelical zeal with which she denounced segregation. To her, a more liberal South was not something she could intellectualize but something she felt. It meant the difference between a reluctance to act and all-out commitment. Lillian Smith did not typify Southern liberalism, but she did represent the most important element in its tradition, evangelicism, which in softer tones was echoed by others.* This element seems to have become more important over time. As an antisegregationist position became increasingly vital to the credibility of Southern liberalism, those who viewed the race problem in

* Such as Will Alexander, Frank Graham, Howard Kester, Ralph McGill, Aubrey Williams. In contrast, Howard Odum and Virginius Dabney represent those Southern liberals who failed to see segregation as a moral problem. Odum's liberalism was based on his passion for scientific rationality; Dabney's on his mixture of Jeffersonian idealism and Menckenesque skepticism.

terms of Christian ethics were the ones who found the moral energy to make the leap from a separate-but-equal stance.

In looking at Southern liberals from George Washington Cable to Lillian Smith, one is struck by the continuity in who they were, how they thought, and what they did. Both Cable, the most militant racial liberal in the South as the Jim Crow era began, and Smith, who occupied a similar position toward its end, were literary figures. They were courageous, uncompromising, and aware that the racial status quo needed a full overhaul rather than tinkering. Each thought that many erstwhile silent white Southerners were outraged by the region's inequities, and if these people could only make known their desire for change, the South would overcome its misguided concern for white supremacy. Neither of them succeeded in getting an organization of Southern liberals to carry forward their ideas. Cable tried and failed. Smith, who criticized existing Southern liberal organizations, never even tried. Southern liberalism, at least in its insistence on the Silent South theme, was an act of faith. This helps to explain why a religious outlook was so pervasive among the most militant Southern liberals.

Despite the continuity of Southern liberalism, however, much happened to it between 1885, when *The Silent South* appeared, and 1949, the year *Killers of the Dream* was published. During that time, the entire focus of the racial situation in the South changed dramatically. The North no longer looked upon Jim Crow with approval or indifference. Scientific racism had lost its respectability and, because of Nazi Germany, became equated with fascism. Most important, Negroes themselves had advanced from their status as a minority group with little or no influence to an increasingly effective political bloc who, beginning with the New Deal, began to have an impact on national politics. Ironically for Southern liberals, these changes had little to do with their own activities in the South.

When George Washington Cable first called upon white Southerners to speak out against the denial of basic rights to their black fellow citizens, the response was hardly overwhelming. Occasionally, an individual would plead for more wisdom or decry some particularly nasty racial incident. But the overall impact of early Southern liberals was slight. The three decades following Cable's appeal were the nadir for Southern blacks, who continued to be intimidated, disfranchised, and segregated. Jim Crow ruled, and all classes of white Southerners either defended this arrangement or recognized it as a reality of the New South. No meaningful debate took place over other answers to the race question. That caste itself constituted a problem for the most part went unnoticed. Indeed, as the racism of such reformist groups as the Southern Populists and Progressives showed, Jim Crow often was seen as part of the solution to other regional ills.

But there were many flaws in this arrangement, the most important of which, was, for white Southern liberals, that it did not work. Removing the Negro from the electoral process did not make for more enlightened Southern politics. Legal segregation, introduced as a method of avoiding racial conflict, did not reduce tensions, which the Atlanta race riot of 1906 and the outbreak of lynching after World War I clearly demonstrated. Moreover, the South did not keep pace with other parts of the United States. It was the nation's "number 1 economic problem" well before New Dealers advertised the fact. In almost every indicator of social welfare—health, education, income, etc.—the former Confederate states were at or near the bottom.

White Southern liberals knew this situation. As early as 1912, with the organization of the Southern Sociological Congress, a reform-minded regional consciousness began to emerge. By 1920, with the founding of the Commission on Interracial Cooperation, a group of Southern liberals was contending that the supposedly resolved racial situation needed reexamination. From then until the end of the Jim Crow era, the primary question facing Southern liberals was how far they could, or would, go.

For the most part, they only tried to make "separate-but-equal" more humane. Southern liberals focused on the most blatant outrage the white supremacist movement had produced, lynching, and met some success in bringing about a reduction. At the same time, they sought to convince other whites to allow blacks a more dignified place in the region. This, the liberals argued, would be necessary if the South was to advance. They claimed that white self-interest and not black equality was their chief concern.

As long as segregation was not challenged, Southern liberals were able to make a contribution toward improved race relations. First, by averting violence and calling for fair play, they helped individual blacks and enlightened some whites. Second, they kept the race issue alive when most white Southerners would have preferred it buried. They did this through the press, work in universities and churches, and their own publications—such as *The Tragedy of Lynching,* which won wide acclaim in the South even though it portrayed a side of the region that whites did not like to discuss. Finally, association with the Interracial Commission led some Southern liberals to a greater commitment to Negro rights as events moved in that direction. The commission did not do nearly enough, as its own members knew, but in the South of the 1920s and early 1930s its approach was the best that could be hoped for.

The New Deal gave Southern liberals a new outlet for their efforts. For Will Alexander and Clark Foreman, the Interracial Commission proved a stepping-stone to newly created federal agencies. There they had authority and influence that they would not have had in the South. In Washington their perspectives broadened, and both men left the Roosevelt Administration with decidedly more radical outlooks on the race question than when they entered. Similarly, Aubrey Williams, who made the National Youth Administration highly responsive to blacks, continued his efforts on behalf of racial justice long after the New Deal.

The New Deal was also a spur to white liberals who remained in the South. For H. L. Mitchell and Howard Kester, the failure of AAA programs to help tenants and sharecroppers led to involvement with the Southern Tenant Farmers Union. But had it not been for the encouragement that the Roosevelt Administration gave to organized labor, it is unlikely that there would have been an STFU, or for that matter, CIO activity in the South. Little wonder so many Southern liberals looked upon the New Deal as their patron. People like Frank Graham, persuaded that the New Deal's support for the underdog was genuine, eagerly joined the Southern Conference for Human Welfare and worked to liberalize the South politically.

But the New Deal took Southern liberals only halfway. The incident over segregation during the 1938 Birmingham meeting of the

Southern Conference for Human Welfare demonstrated that Southern liberals, though opposed to the spirit of Jim Crow, were not ready to confront the issue directly. Southern blacks, in their view, stood to gain more from New Deal welfare legislation than from a concerted campaign for racial justice. Similarly, Southern liberal New Dealers deliberately played down black voting rights and concentrated on an issue, poll tax repeal, that they erroneously believed would not be confused with race.

Although Southern liberals did not attack Jim Crow, their actions during the New Deal had a great impact on their racial outlook. Those like Will Alexander, Virginia Durr, Frank Graham, Clark Foreman, and Aubrey Williams who were firm supporters of the New Deal were generally willing to take stronger stands against racism after World War II, when segregation could no longer be ignored. For one thing, they had found the Jim Crow system an obstacle to their larger reform aims; among Roosevelt's strongest opponents had been segregationist politicians like Eugene Talmadge who claimed that the New Deal would inevitably lead to "social equality" between the races. For another, having already identified with an activist national government, these Southern liberals were more likely to accept federal intervention in the area of civil rights. On the other hand, those like Howard Odum, Virginius Dabney, and Jessie Daniel Ames who were not as enthusiastic about Roosevelt's programs continued to point out the presumed "lessons" of Reconstruction and tended to be more critical of the growing civil rights movement. Some, particularly Dabney, would eventually side with the segregationists and thereby lose their credibility as liberals.

Beginning with World War II, Southern liberalism received a rude jolt. At best, liberals had ignored segregation; at worst, they had defended it. But now, whether they were committed to segregation or not, the issue was out in the open. To a nation fighting totalitarianism abroad, Jim Crow became an embarrassment. This defect in the country's moral armor carried over into the Cold War years as blacks and Northern liberals continued their offensive against caste. By 1948, these two groups, supported in the South only by the minority of Southern liberals belonging to the Southern Conference Educational Fund or by isolated figures such as Lillian Smith, had gotten the Truman Administration to advance a civil rights program. Together with Supreme Court decisions, this program, however limited it was, presaged the end of Jim Crow. The reluctance of so many white Southern liberals to abandon separate-but-equal during this period was Southern liberalism's most conspicuous failure.

The Southern Regional Council between 1944 and 1949 reflected the changing situation. The council had tried to sidestep segregation yet never seemed to get anywhere. Its Southern liberal members found forces outside their control—war, confrontation with Communist powers, black protest, the importance of the Negro vote—pushing them toward a showdown over segregation. After much soul searching, the council finally committed itself to an antisegregationist stance, but, as Virginius Dabney's resignation signified, it had narrowed its own base considerably.

Facing segregation proved difficult for Southern liberals. As long as Jim Crow was not threatened, it had been relatively easy for white Southerners to demonstrate their racial liberalism. Over the years Southern liberals spoke out in greater numbers. To be sure, they ran into opposition, but because other Southern whites did not perceive them as dangerous, they were tolerated. Thus Southern liberals living under Jim Crow often concluded that the South was becoming more liberal, or as so many of them put it, the makings of a racially just South existed amid the seemingly monolithic white racism. This belief in a Silent South, frequently expressed, undoubtedly motivated Southern liberals and gave them a visibility that they would lose during the civil rights struggles of the 1950s and 1960s.

But what difference did they make? Even as Southern liberals grew in numbers, blacks continued to be discriminated against, segregated, and dealt with capriciously by whites. The South's liberals possessed neither the power nor desire to force social change. If Southern blacks had followed only the Southern liberals' prescriptions for a gradual adjustment, it is doubtful whether the region's racial practices would have altered dramatically. White Southern liberals, though in other ways perceptive in their understanding of the South, simply erred in assuming that they represented the key to racial change. The depression, the New Deal, the war, and the civil rights movement, more than Southern liberals, contributed to the breakdown of Jim Crow.

Yet it would be wrong to argue that these liberals, by making Jim Crow more humane, hindered progress in race relations. For one thing, resistance to desegregation during the 1950s and 1960s was greatest in the Deep South, the area where Southern liberalism had had the least impact. In Atlanta, North Carolina, and, despite the state's official policy of "massive resistance," most of Virginia—places where Southern liberals had been more active—desegregation was less arduous. The long years of white liberals' attacking the Klan and admonishing against lynching had taken effect. Vigilantism became unacceptable to most white Southerners, who, unlike their forebears during Reconstruction, did not countenance violent resistance to civil rights measures. There were, to be sure, appalling incidents of murders and beatings, and clashes between segregationists and enforcers of civil rights laws, but these were not as widespread as the violence that had accompanied the establishment of Jim Crow. Once the last-ditch efforts to circumvent civil rights laws failed, the era of white "massive resistance" ended. Southern liberals, though most had warned outsiders to leave the race problem alone, had helped create a climate whereby a federally enforced revolution in the South was actually achieved.

The legacy of Southern liberals, then, is not the change they brought about. Rather it is their belief that the South would eventually resolve the race question in a manner that would surprise Americans outside the region. To Southern liberals, the South had always contained the seeds of racial justice. Their search for a Silent South was an effort to nurture these seeds so that the South would be a region, as James McBride Dabbs put it, "where the white and colored races can learn how to settle the frontier that now divides them." [2]

Was the liberals' search for a Silent South naive? Perhaps. Some of them clearly thought it had been. Sarah Patton Boyle, a white Virginian who fought against segregation in Charlottesville during the early 1950s, was bitterly disappointed when other whites failed to support her efforts. She later recalled: "If, when I first made it, a few others had endorsed my claim that many whites would welcome integration, I was sure that 'massive resistance' would not have become the battle cry of the demagogues. But, since the heart of my message was that others shared my views, when not one in my own community certified it, I was reduced from a spokesman to the South's prize fool, thus cutting the power of my voice, even as a lone one, to a minimum." [3] Keeping in mind that these words were written by a person who lived in the upper South, in a college town at that, they represent as fervent a denial of the Silent South as one could ever expect to find.

As elusive as the Silent South may have been, however, the vision that underlay the search never died. White Southern liberals continued to believe that the South, before the rest of the country, would discover interracial brotherhood, once white and black Southerners recognized that being Southern was more important to all of them than the fact that some were white and others black. This was the Southern liberals' dream, one which they shared with Negro civil rights leaders, such as Martin Luther King, who embodied the same Christian approach that had been the principal motivator of so many of them.

Directly related to their belief in the South's potential was the oft-expressed opinion of Southern liberals that their group, far more than white Northerners, truly understood race relations. This feeling was shared by all of them, the Williamses and Smiths as well as the Odums and Dabneys. Howard Kester, for one, was very blunt. "The only white man who comes close to understanding what racial justice really means is the Southerner," he said. "Once a white Southerner has made up his mind on this, you can bank on him, because he not only knows it intellectually—he feels it in his soul." Pat Watters, who during the 1960s was information director for the Southern Regional Council, wrote that Southern whites were much more likely to respond to the "deepest meanings" of the civil rights movement because what gave the movement its greatest strength—the mysticism and spirituality of the Southern Negro churches—was "not unlike the best ecstatic experiences in the fundamentalist churches of the white South." Aubrey Williams, in complimenting Hugo Black for his dedication to civil liberties, claimed Black was living proof that "when the South makes a good one, there are none better." Southern liberals, explained Virginia Durr, were "much better than Yankees in every way." In short, to other Southern liberals, a white Southerner, once he became a liberal, was the most unshakable liberal on earth. "Like the saints," Gerald Johnson once noted, "he is one who has come up through great tribulations and he is up to stay." [4]

One could easily dismiss this as self-puffery were it not for the fact that blacks, too, made the same point. The baseball player Jackie Robinson, reflecting upon his many years of involvement with racial issues, remarked: "Somehow it seems that those from below the Mason-Dixon line who come over to the liberal cause bring with them a firmness and sincerity that Northern liberals don't have." Benjamin Mays, who had often tried to push Southern liberals farther than they were willing to go, said, "The Southern white man is sometimes very determined and insistent when he is dead wrong," but "he often moves with equal determination when he is convinced that the cause is right and just." Another believer was Andrew Young, one of King's lieutenants in the Southern Christian Leadership Conference who later went on to become the first black congressman from Georgia since Reconstruction. "Blacks have always known," he said, "that our best allies are those Southern whites who have dared to live by their religious principles and who have been through the fires of persecution because of it." Vernon Jordan, the executive director of the National Urban League, was particularly emphatic: "I would rather do business with a converted Southerner than a Northern liberal. The Northern liberal is basically paternalistic. You feel he is always looking down on you. But the Southern white man who gets converted to the cause—why he would die for you." [5]

However, regardless of the enduring qualities that they saw in each other and that blacks saw in them, the Southern liberals, it must be admitted, failed to awaken a Silent South.

Yet there was something to what they said. Lillian Smith, in her mystical way, thought that believing in justice could make it happen.* In 1957, though isolated and ignored, she told a reporter that,

* Smith believed that a person's spiritual beliefs, like his physical activities, affected his relationship with the universe so that the "impossible becomes possible: the boat moves, the paraplegic walks, the sick mind gets well, the plane flies, the poem is written." Moreover, she strongly felt that idealists were never alone. Their ideals were always "shared, silently, by innumerable others in distant times and faraway places, or by the man next door. Somewhere in minds and hearts it is there: it may

contrary to what many Northerners perceived, there were "thousands of white Southerners who are working quietly day after day, who are speaking out in their small towns, their churches, their clubs." When she spoke, the white supremacists were riding high in Georgia as well as in other Southern states. This was well known and well publicized.[6]

Nonetheless, at around the same time that Smith was affirming her belief in the Silent South, a white peanut grower in the little Black Belt town of Plains, Georgia, Jimmy Carter, refused to join the local White Citizens Council and a few years later, as deacon, supported the integration of blacks into his Baptist church. As far as blacks or civil rights were concerned, little came from Carter's action. The Citizens Council functioned without him and his fellow church members outvoted him and his family on the question of admitting blacks. In all likelihood, his dissent, which caused him no great hardship, was unknown to Lillian Smith, let alone to observers in the North. Moreover, in the early 1960s, when the organized civil rights movement conducted one of its major campaigns in nearby Albany, Georgia, Carter did not march with them. One can only wonder what went through his mind during those years. Still, whatever it was, it led him, as the newly elected governor of Georgia, to proclaim in 1970 that "the time for racial discrimination is over." It was too bad that Lillian Smith was not alive to hear her governor say those words or, for that matter, to see him declare, while running for President of the United States six years later, that segregation "hung like a millstone around our necks" and that the Civil Rights Act was "the best thing that ever happened to the South." [7]

Carter's words took many Americans outside the South by surprise; but aside from the fact that a prominent white Southern politician had said them, they were not new. Indeed, there was a striking parallel between Carter's analysis of segregation and Lillian Smith's. According to Smith, segregation kept white Southerners apart from much more than blacks—from science, art, culture, the rest of the

---

be a dry seed that has not begun to germinate but it is there; it may be sprouting greenly but not yet ready to be brought forth in word and act, but it is there. And these people care. And there will come a time when all men will care." *The Journey* (Cleveland, 1954), pp. 52, 210.

nation, and meaningful relationships with their family and friends. "Break down the walls of segregation," she said, "and the other walls will tumble." [8] Carter spoke in nearly the same terms: "A new degree of freedom for both black and white Southerners evolved from the trauma of desegregation. Instead of constant preoccupation with the racial aspect of almost every question, public officials, black and white, are now at liberty to make objective decisions about education, health, employment, crime control, consumer protection, prison reform, and environmental quality." [9] Moreover, Carter's emphasis on his religion, which many found disturbing, becomes more understandable in the context of Southern liberalism.

Jimmy Carter's election to the presidency must be rewarding to all those who, like Lillian Smith, believed in a Silent South. The seed first planted by George Washington Cable back in 1885 took a long time to germinate and mature. It may just be beginning to produce its best fruit.

Preface

1. Ralph McGill, *The South and the Southerner* (Boston, 1963), p. 218.
2. Gunnar Myrdal, *An American Dilemma: The Negro Problem and Modern Democracy* (New York, 1944), vol. I, pp. 456, 466.
3. Ulrich B. Phillips, "The Central Theme of Southern History," *American Historical Review*, 24 (October 1928), 30–43. In his classic study *Southern Politics in State and Nation* (New York, 1949), the political scientist V. O. Key, Jr. endorsed Phillips's view with the contention that, in final analysis, regional political peculiarities derived mainly from the "impact of the black race" (p. 665). For a critique of Phillips's "central theme" see George B. Tindall, "The Central Theme Revisited" in Charles G. Sellers, ed., *The Southerner as American* (Chapel Hill, 1960), pp. 104–29.

CHAPTER ONE

The Silent South

1. C. Philip Butcher, *George W. Cable* (New York, 1962), pp. 19–30, 165–67. It should be noted that since Cable often portrayed them in an unfavorable light, New Orleans Creoles themselves took great exception to his stories and novels about them. Their criticism represented a counterpoint to the general praise Cable's fiction received.
2. George Washington Cable, *The Silent South* (New York, 1889), pp. 3–5, 16–17, 21, 45. Though the book originally appeared in 1885, all references here are to the 1889 edition.
3. The essay has been reprinted in Arlin Turner, ed., *The Negro Question: A Selection of Writings on Civil Rights in the South by George W. Cable* (New York, 1958), pp. 54–82 and in Charles W. Wynes, ed., *Forgotten Voices: Dissenting Southerners in an Age of Conformity* (Baton Rouge, 1967), pp. 13–26.
4. Arlin Turner, *George W. Cable: A Biography* (Baton Rouge, 1966), p. 197; *Atlanta Constitution*, January 12, 1885. Quoted in Paul M. Gaston, *The New South Creed: A Study in Southern Mythmaking* (New York, 1970), p. 140.
5. Turner, ed., *The Negro Question*, pp. 87–89 and *George W. Cable*, pp. 263–65; George M. Fredrickson, *The Black Image in the White Mind: The Debate on Afro-American Character and Destiny, 1817–1914* (New York, 1971), pp. 220–21.
6. Hill to Cable, June 6, 1886; August 10, 1886; October 2, 1887; December 7, 1888; January 7, 1889; April 8, 1889; and Hill to Moffatt, December 15, 1889 in the George Washington Cable Papers, Tulane University Library.
7. Dreher to Cable, November 4,1889 and Baskerville to Cable, January 8, 1890; October 18, 1891, Cable Papers.

8. Turner, ed., *Negro Question*, p. xix.
9. Turner, *George W. Cable*, p. 131; Du Bois to Cable, February 23, 1890. Quoted in Hugh C. Bailey, *Liberalism in the New South: Social Reformers and the Progressive Movement* (Coral Gables, 1969), p. 46; Arthur B. Lee to Cable, January 21, 1885. Quoted in *Wisconsin State Journal*, January 28, 1885.
10. Atticus G. Haygood, *Our Brother in Black* (Nashville, 1881); Harold W. Mann, *Atticus Greene Haygood: Methodist Bishop, Editor and Educator* (Athens, Ga., 1965).
11. For a full discussion of this point see Fredrickson, *Black Image in the White Mind*, pp. 228–82.
12. Mann, *Atticus Greene Haygood*, p. 183.
13. Lewis H. Blair, *The Prosperity of the South Dependent upon the Elevation of the Negro* (Richmond, 1889), pp. 9–11, 60, 138. C. Vann Woodward, on the other hand, maintains that Blair was primarily a moralist who tried to make his argument palatable to white Southerners. *American Counterpoint: Slavery and Racism in the North-South Dialogue* (Boston, 1971), p. 196.
14. C. Vann Woodward, *The Origins of the New South 1877–1913* (Baton Rouge, 1951), p. 257.
15. Ibid., p. 352.
16. Hugh C. Bailey, *Edgar Gardner Murphy: Gentle Progressive* (Coral Gables, 1968), p. 26. Bruce L. Clayton, "Southern Critics of the New South, 1890–1914" (Unpublished Ph.D. dissertation, Duke University, 1966), p. 80; William B. Hamilton, ed., *Fifty Years of the South Atlantic Quarterly* (Durham, N. C., 1952), p. 166; Gaston, *New South Creed*, p. 265*n*.
17. Carl Holliday, "The Young Southerner and the Negro," *South Atlantic Quarterly*, 8 (April 1909), 131.
18. Louis R. Harlan, "The Southern Education Board and the Race Issue in Public Education," *Journal of Southern History*, 23 (May 1957), 196, 198; Clayton, "Southern Critics," p. 14.
19. Edgar Gardner Murphy, "Backward or Forward," *South Atlantic Quarterly*, 8 (January 1909), 23; Clayton, "Southern Critics," pp. 153–55.
20. Andrew Sledd, "The Negro: Another View," *Atlantic Monthly*, 90 (July 1902), 65–73. Reprinted in Wynes, ed., *Forgotten Voices*, pp. 91–105. See also Henry Y. Warnock, "Andrew Sledd, Southern Methodists, and the Negro: A Case History," *Journal of Southern History*, 31 (August 1965), 251–71; John Spencer Bassett, "Stirring Up the Fires of Race Antipathy," *South Atlantic Quarterly*, 2 (October 1903), 297–305. Reprinted in Wynes, ed., *Forgotten Voices*, pp. 109–20; Charles Flint Kellogg, *NAACP: A History of the National Association for the Advancement of Colored People, 1909–1920* (Baltimore, 1967), p. 216.
21. Southern Society for the Promotion of the Study of Race Conditions and Problems in the South, *Race Problems in the South: Report of the Proceedings . . . at Montgomery, Alabama* (Richmond, 1900); Bailey, *Edgar Gardner Murphy*, pp. 29–38. Booker T. Washington, who was only a short distance from Montgomery at Tuskegee, was disappointed that he had not been asked to come.
22. John E. White, "The Need of a Southern Program on the Negro Problem" and John C. Kilgo, "The Silent South," *South Atlantic Quarterly*, 6 (April 1907), 177, 181, 186, 209–11.
23. For a particularly incisive discussion of the rural segregation movement see Jack

Temple Kirby, *Darkness at the Dawning: Race and Reform in the Progressive South* (Philadelphia, 1972), pp. 108–30.

24. Kellogg, *NAACP*, p. 217; W. D. Weatherford, *Negro Life in the South: Present Conditions and Needs* (New York, 1910), pp. 3–5, 7, 77–80 and *Present Forces in Negro Progress* (New York, 1912), passim.

25. James E. McCullach, ed., *The Call of the New South* (Nashville, 1912), *The South Mobilizing for Social Service* (Atlanta, 1913), and *Battling for Social Betterment* (Memphis, 1914).

26. Charles H. Brough, "Work of the Commission of Southern Universities on the Race Question," *Annals of the American Academy of Political and Social Science*, 49 (September 1913), 47–57.

27. E. Charles Chatfield, "The Southern Sociological Congress: Organization of Uplift," *Tennessee Historical Quarterly*, 19 (December 1960), 337–39, 346–47. See also the same author's "The Southern Sociological Congress: Rationale of Uplift" in ibid., 20 (March 1961), 51–64.

28. Brough, "Work . . . on the Race Question," pp. 55–56; McCullach, ed., *South Mobilizing for Social Service*, pp. 364, 347–60, 412–19; Lily H. Hammond, *In Black and White: An Interpretation of Southern Life* (New York, 1914), p. 89.

CHAPTER TWO

The Commission on Interracial Cooperation

1. W. D. Weatherford, "Race Relationships in the South," *Annals of the American Academy of Political and Social Science*, 49 (September 1913), 172.

2. Wilma Dykeman and James Stokely, *Seeds of Southern Change: The Life of Will Alexander* (Chicago, 1962), pp. 38–51, 54–55, 66; "The Reminiscences of Will W. Alexander" (Columbia Oral History Collection, 1952), p. 62. There were 72 Negroes lynched in 1919, the highest total since 1908. For a detailed account of the racial violence of 1919 see Arthur I. Waskow, *From Race Riot to Sit-In, 1919 and the 1960's: A Study in the Connections between Conflict and Violence* (Garden City, N. Y., 1966).

3. Dykeman and Stokely, *Seeds of Southern Change*, pp. 56–89; Edgar F. Burrows, "The Commission on Interracial Cooperation, 1919–1944: A Case Study in the History of the Interracial Movement in the South" (Unpublished Ph.D. dissertation, University of Wisconsin, 1955), pp. 46–47, passim; Gunnar Myrdal, *An American Dilemma* (New York, 1944), vol. II, p. 884. Italics added.

4. Samuel Chiles Mitchell, unpublished autobiography, p. 213 in the Samuel Chiles Mitchell Papers, Southern Historical Collection, University of North Carolina; R. W. Miles, "The Virginia Interracial Committee," *Journal of Social Forces*, 1 (January 1923), 153.

5. Burrows, "Commission on Interracial Cooperation," pp. 79, 80–82, 360.

6. Dykeman and Stokely, *Seeds of Southern Change*, pp. 15–16; H. H. Procter, "The Atlanta Plan of Interracial Cooperation," *Southern Workman*, 49 (January 1920), 10–11; Paul E. Baker, *Negro-White Adjustment: An Investigation and Analysis of Methods in the Interracial Movement in the United States* (Pittsfield, Mass.,

1934), p. 24; Bratton, Poteat, and Blackwell to Odum, August 5, 1920 in the Howard W. Odum Papers, Southern Historical Collection, University of North Carolina.
7. Alexander to Odum, September 1, 1920 and Woofter to Odum, September 29, 1920, Odum Papers.
8. C. Chilton Pearson, "Race Relations in North Carolina: A Field Study of Moderate Opinion," *South Atlantic Quarterly*, 23 (January 1924), 1–9.
9. Thomas J. Woofter, *The Basis of Racial Adjustment* (Boston, 1925), pp. 5–6, 13, 16–17, 23–25, 239–41.
10. Clement Eaton, *A History of the Old South* (2d rev. ed., New York, 1966), p. viii.
11. "Behind Birmingham," *Christian Century*, 43 (May 27, 1926), 672.
12. Author's interview with Arthur F. Raper, April 23, 1971; Will W. Alexander, "Better Race Relations," *Southern Workman*, 51 (August, 1922), 363–64 and "A Usable Piece of Community Machinery," *Journal of Social Forces*, 1 (November 1922), 42; "Minutes of the Anti-Lynching Conference of Southern White Women," Atlanta, November 1, 1930 in the Jessie Daniel Ames Papers, Southern Historical Collection, University of North Carolina.
13. "The Duties of Educated Southerners"; "Lectures to Institute on Race Relations, Swarthmore, Pennsylvania, July 12–13, 1933," Box 31 and "Address before Conference on Social and Economic Problems of the South, Chattanooga, Tennessee, October 27, 1935," Box 30, George Fort Milton Papers, Library of Congress.
14. M. Ashby Jones, "Counting the Cost," *Southern Workman*, 49 (January 1920), 12–13; "The Negro and the South," *Virginia Quarterly Review*, 3 (January 1927), 1–12; and "The Approach to the South's Race Question," *Journal of Social Forces*, 1 (November 1920), 41; George S. Mitchell to Samuel Chiles Mitchell, undated, c. 1930, Series F, 1914–48, Mitchell Papers.
15. Interview with Raper.
16. "The Memphis Meeting as Related to Miss Abigail Curlee by Dr. Will W. Alexander," October 8, 1920, Ames Papers; Ames to Johnson, January 31, 1924 and September 8, 1924, Ames Papers.
17. George M. Fredrickson, *The Black Image in the White Mind: The Debate on Afro-American Character and Destiny* (New York, 1971), pp. 273–75; John C. Kilgo, "An Inquiry Regarding Lynching," *South Atlantic Quarterly*, 1 (January 1902), 4–13; interview with Raper.
18. "Collegiate Move on Lynching," *Literary Digest*, 52 (January 22, 1916), 178; "The White South Protests against Lynching: A Press Symposium," *Southern Workman*, 48 (July 1919), 355, 358–59.
19. Dykeman and Stokely, *Seeds of Southern Change*, p. 134; Woofter, *Basis of Racial Adjustment*, pp. 136, 140–47; Baker, *Negro-White Adjustment*, p. 224.
20. "Impeaching Judge Lynch," Box 31 in the Milton Papers.
21. Arthur F. Raper, *The Tragedy of Lynching* (Chapel Hill, 1933), pp. 19, 48, 293, 305; White to Raper, May 9, 1933, Box C-311 in the National Association for the Advancement of Colored People Papers, Library of Congress.
22. Interview with Raper; author's interview with W. T. Couch, May 4, 1971.
23. Dykeman and Stokely, *Seeds of Southern Change*, p. 143; Minutes, November 1, 1930, Ames Papers; Willie Snow Ethridge, "Southern Women Attack Lynching," *Nation*, 131 (December 10, 1930), 650.
24. Interviews with Raper and Couch; Andrews to Mrs. A. W. Newell, December

14, 1931 and to Milton, November 15, 1931, Ames Papers; "Senator Tom Connally Opposes Bill Inspired by Eastern Politicians," *Sheriffs' Association of Texas Magazine*, 9 (April 1940), 15. Clipping in Box 126 of the Tom Connally Papers, Library of Congress.
25. Interview with Raper; Ames to Connally, December 29, 1939, Connally Papers; Ames to Mrs. A. W. Newell, September 1, 1938, Ames Papers; Jacquelyn Dowd Hall, "Revolt against Chivalry: Jessie Daniel Ames and the Women's Movement against Lynching" (Paper presented at the annual meeting of the Southern Historical Association, Dallas, 1974), pp. 9–10.
26. Dan T. Carter, *Scottsboro: A Tragedy of the American South* (Baton Rouge, 1969), pp. 115–16; "Progress Report, Association of Southern Women for the Prevention of Lynching," July 15, 1931, Ames Papers.
27. Carter, *Scottsboro*, pp. 83–84, 87, 114–18, 317.
28. Dykeman and Stokely, *Seeds of Southern Change*, p. 131; Burrows, "Commission on Interracial Cooperation," p. 320; Baker, *Negro-White Adjustment*, p. 18.
29. William O. Brown, "Interracial Cooperation: Some of Its Problems," *Opportunity*, 11 (September 1933), 272–73.
30. Reynolds to N. C. Newbold, August 19, 1933 and Newbold to James E. Shepard, March 17, 1933, Odum Papers.
31. On the changing nature of the race issue see Harvard Sitkoff, "The Emergence of Civil Rights as a National Issue: The New Deal Era" (Unpublished Ph.D. dissertation, Columbia University, 1975).

CHAPTER THREE

The Silent South of Howard Odum

1. Unless otherwise noted, all the biographical information about Odum in this chapter is from Rupert B. Vance and Katherine Jocher, "Howard W. Odum," *Social Forces*, 33 (March 1955), 203–17. A tribute from his colleagues, the article appeared as an obituary shortly after Odum's death in 1954 and included an extensive, extremely useful bibliography of his published writings. It was reprinted in Howard Odum, *Folk, Region, and Society: Selected Papers of Howard W. Odum*, ed. by Katherine Jocher, et al. (Chapel Hill, 1967).
2. Odum to Josephus Daniels, February 12, 1925, Howard Washington Odum Papers, Southern Historical Collection, University of North Carolina.
3. Thomas Pearce Bailey, *Race Orthodoxy in the South and Other Aspects of the Negro Question* (New York, 1914), pp. 331–49, passim., and Bailey's appendix to Howard Odum, *Social and Mental Traits of the Negro: Research into the Conditions of the Negro Race in Southern Towns, A Study in Race Traits, Tendencies and Prospects*, Columbia University Studies in History, Economics and Public Law, vol. 37, no. 3 (New York, 1910), p. 302. The University of Mississippi, succumbing to the pervasive racism of the times, ultimately forced Bailey to drop his program of racial studies.
4. Howard Odum, "Religious Folk-Songs of the Southern Negroes," *American Journal of Religious Psychology and Education*, 3 (July 1909), 265–365 and "Folk-Song

and Folk-Poetry as Found in the Secular Songs of Southern Negroes," *Journal of American Folk-Lore*, 24 (July–September 1911), 255–94 and (October–December 1911), 251–396; Odum, *Folk, Region, and Society*, p. 7; "Folk-Song . . . of Southern Negroes," pp. 284, 357.
5. Odum, *Social and Mental Traits*, pp. 13, 264–66, 270–74, 286, passim.
6. Odum to Edwin L. Clarke, March 21, 1922 and Odum to V. E. Daniel, April 7, 1936, Odum Papers.
7. Howard Odum, "Effective Democracy," *Journal of Social Forces*, 1 (January 1923), 178, 181–82.
8. Howard Odum, "The Journal of Social Forces," ibid. (November 1922), 59.
9. Odum to Julia Collier Harris, January 31, 1926, Odum Papers.
10. Ray Ginger, *Six Days or Forever? Tennessee v. John Thomas Scopes* (Chicago, 1969), pp. 45, 129; Mencken to Odum, September 10, 1923, Odum Papers.
11. Odum to Mencken, September 12, 1923 and to Daniels, February 12, 1925, Odum Papers; Howard Odum, "The Discovery of the People," *Journal of Social Forces*, 4 (December 1925), 416 and "The Duel to the Death," ibid. (September 1925), 189–92.
12. Howard Odum, ed., *Southern Pioneers in Social Interpretation* (Chapel Hill, 1925), pp. 3–27.
13. Ibid., pp. 10, 12, 15–17, 20–24.
14. Odum to Leonard Outhwaite, June 26, 1925, Odum Papers.
15. Howard Odum and Guy Johnson, *The Negro and His Songs: A Study of Typical Negro Songs of the South* (Chapel Hill, 1925); *Negro Workaday Songs* (Chapel Hill, 1926).
16. Odum to A. C. Barnes Foundation, November 18, 1926, Odum Papers.
17. Howard Odum, *Rainbow Round My Shoulder: The Blue Trail of Black Ulysses* (Indianapolis, 1928). The other two novels in the series were *Wings on My Feet: Black Ulysses at the Wars* (Indianapolis, 1929) and *Cold Blue Moon: Black Ulysses Afar Off* (Indianapolis, 1931).
18. Odum, *Rainbow Round My Shoulder*, pp. 9, 17–18.
19. Odum to D. L. Chambers, February 23, 1927 and November 7, 1930; Odum to Cecile Phillips, January 9, 1928; Odum to Gerald Johnson, January 4, 1928, Odum Papers.
20. Odum to White, May 17, 1927; September 10, 1930; September 18, 1930; Odum to Worth M. Tippy, October 30, 1929; Odum to Ogburn, October 28, 1929, ibid.
21. Gerald Johnson to Odum, July 16, 1931; Odum to Gerald Johnson, July 18, 1931, ibid.
22. Howard Odum, "A Tragedy of Race Conflict," *Yale Review*, 25 (September 1935), 215–16.
23. Howard Odum, "Lynchings, Fears, and Folkways," *Nation*, 133 (December 30, 1931), 720.
24. Odum to Cash, November 27, 1929, Odum Papers.
25. Howard Odum, *An American Epoch: Southern Portraiture in the National Picture* (New York, 1930), pp. 53, 59–65, 136, 266–67, 270, 275–76.
26. George B. Tindall, *The Emergence of the New South 1913–1945* (Baton Rouge, 1967), pp. 584–88; Harvey A. Kantor, "Howard W. Odum: The Implications of Folk, Planning, and Regionalism," *American Journal of Sociology*, 79 (September

1973), 278–95; Benjamin B. Kendrick and Alex M. Arnett, *The South Looks at Its Past* (Chapel Hill, 1935), p. 3; John Gunther, *Inside U.S.A.* (New York, 1947), p. 654.
27. Tindall, *The Emergence of the New South*, p. 588.
28. Howard Odum, *Southern Regions of the United States* (Chapel Hill, 1936), pp. 57, 59, passim.

CHAPTER FOUR

Southern Liberals and the New Deal

1. Erskine Caldwell and Margaret Bourke-White, *You Have Seen Their Faces* (New York, 1937), p. 2. Other prominent examples of the depression genre of writing and photography about the South include Gerald Johnson, *The Wasted Land* (Chapel Hill, 1937); H. Clarence Nixon, *Forty Acres and Steel Mules* (Chapel Hill, 1938); James Agee and Walker Evans, *Let Us Now Praise Famous Men* (Boston, 1941); Richard Wright and Edward Rossham, *12 Million Black Voices: A Folk History of the Negro in the United States* (New York, 1941). In addition to *Tobacco Road* (New York, 1932), which was produced as a play on the stage and made into a motion picture, a study that grew out of the Federal Writers Project, W. T. Couch, ed., *These Are Our Lives* (Chapel Hill, 1939) also contributed to the image of a downtrodden region. For an analysis of the photographers who made this image vivid see F. Jack Hurley, *Portrait of a Decade: Roy Stryker and the Development of Documentary Photography in the Thirties* (Baton Rouge, 1972).
2. Joseph P. Lash, *Eleanor and Franklin: The Story of Their Relationship, Based on Eleanor Roosevelt's Private Papers* (New York, 1971), pp. 396–97; Frank Freidel, *F.D.R. and the South* (Baton Rouge, 1965), p. 2.
3. Milton to Robert T. Crane, April 26, 1933; Milton to Odum, May 2, 1933; Milton, Odum, Woofter, and Lewis C. Gray to Morgan, June 15, 1933, Box 13, and Odum to Milton, July 29, 1933, Box 14, George Fort Milton Papers, Library of Congress.
4. "Reminiscences of Will Alexander" (Columbia Oral History Collection, 1952), pp. 367–68, 454; Charles S. Johnson, Edwin R. Embree, and Will W. Alexander, *The Collapse of Cotton Tenancy: A Summary of Field Studies and Statistical Surveys, 1933–1935* (Chapel Hill, 1935); Sidney Baldwin, *Poverty and Politics: The Rise and Decline of the Farm Security Administration* (Chapel Hill, 1968), pp. 145–60.
5. Sitkoff, "The Emergence of Civil Rights as a National Issue: The New Deal Era" (Unpublished Ph.D. dissertation, Columbia University, 1975), chapter 3; Brooks Hays, *A Southern Moderate Speaks* (Chapel Hill, 1959), p. 19; Baldwin, *Poverty and Politics*, pp. 279–80; Donald Holley, "The Negro and the New Deal Resettlement Program," *Agricultural History*, 45 (July 1971), 179–93.
6. Mary Bragiotti, "Southern Progressive," *New York Post*, March 3, 1945, clipping, Box 43 in the Carl and Anne Braden Papers, State Historical Society of Wisconsin; Raymond Wolters, *Negroes and the Great Depression: The Problem of Economic Recovery* (Westport, Conn., 1970), pp. 107, 136, 142–43. Early in 1942, Foreman was removed from his position in the Federal Works Agency at the behest of Southern

congressmen who demanded his ouster in return for their voting appropriations for defense housing.

7. Author's interview with Mrs. George S. Mitchell, April 20, 1971.

8. The biographical data on Williams are based on scattered materials in the Aubrey Williams Papers, Franklin D. Roosevelt Library. These include Williams's unpublished and incomplete 1958 autobiography, "A Southern Rebel," Box 44; "Personal History," an undated vita, Box 36; Undated and Untitled Personal Statement, Box 37; clippings from the *New York Post*, February 3, 1945 and Madison, Wisconsin *Capital-Times*, September 30, 1934, Box 37.

9. Arthur J. Altmeyer, "The Wisconsin Idea and Social Security," *Wisconsin Magazine of History*, 42 (Autumn 1958), 19–25; Madison, Wisconsin *Capital-Times*, September 30, 1934.

10. Williams, "A Southern Rebel," pp. 11–31, 37–39 and Personal Statement, Williams Papers.

11. Aubrey Williams, "Twelve Million Unemployed: What Can Be Done," *New York Times Magazine*, March 27, 1938; "The Job Ahead," Speech before the Young Democrats of North Carolina, Winston-Salem, September 11, 1937, Box 19 in the Charles Taussig Papers, Franklin D. Roosevelt Library; *Memphis Commercial Appeal*, October 17, 1943.

12. Williams, "The Job Ahead"; "A Southern Rebel," p. 73; Eleanor Roosevelt, *This I Remember* (New York, 1949), p. 173.

13. Sitkoff, "Emergence of Civil Rights as a National Issue," chapter 3; "National Youth Administration Activities with Special Reference to Negro Youth," February 12, 1936 in the Eleanor Roosevelt Papers, Franklin D. Roosevelt Library; Irwin Klibaner, "The Southern Conference Educational Fund: A History" (Unpublished Ph.D. dissertation, University of Wisconsin, 1971), p. 14; George P. Rawick, "The New Deal and Youth: The Civilian Conservation Corps, the National Youth Administration and the American Youth Congress" (Unpublished Ph.D. dissertation, University of Wisconsin, 1957), pp. 231–50.

14. Williams to Mrs. Roosevelt, January 1, 1940, Eleanor Roosevelt Papers; Lash, *Eleanor and Franklin*, pp. 668–97.

15. Wolters, *Negroes and the Great Depression*, pp. 3–55, 83–215; John B. Kirby, "The Roosevelt Administration and Blacks: An Ambivalent Legacy" in Barton J. Bernstein and Allen J. Matusow, eds., *Twentieth Century America: Recent Interpretations* (2d ed., New York, 1972), pp. 265–88; Leslie H. Fishel, Jr., "The Negro in the New Deal Era," *Wisconsin Magazine of History*, 48 (Winter 1964), 111–26.

16. Michael S. Holmes, *The New Deal in Georgia: An Administrative History* (New York, 1975), pp. 12–13, 106, 132, 146, 148, 317–18.

17. Alexander to Howard Odum, October 13, 1934, Howard Washington Odum Papers, Southern Historical Collection, University of North Carolina.

18. Sterling D. Spero and Abram L. Harris, *The Black Worker: The Negro and the Labor Movement* (New York, 1931), pp. 272–74, 373.

19. Ibid., pp. 352–62; Horace R. Cayton and George S. Mitchell, *Black Workers and the New Unions* (Chapel Hill, 1939), pp. 316–20.

20. George B. Tindall, *The Emergence of the New South: 1913–1945* (Baton Rouge, 1967), p. 531; Katherine Du Pre Lumpkin, *The South in Progress* (New York, 1940) and *The Making of a Southerner* (New York, 1947).

21. Cayton and Mitchell, *Black Workers and the New Unions*, pp. 344–47.

22. The ordeal of one black participant in this movement in Alabama, who in 1932

was arrested for his efforts, is compellingly related in Theodore Rosengarten, ed., *All God's Dangers: The Life of Nate Shaw* (New York, 1974), pp. 296 ff.
23. H. L. Mitchell, "The Founding and Early History of the Southern Tenant Farmers Union," *Arkansas Historical Quarterly*, 32 (Autumn 1973), 342–69. See also Donald H. Grubbs, *Cry from the Cotton: The Southern Tenant Farmers Union and the New Deal* (Chapel Hill, 1971).
24. Kester, *Revolt among the Sharecroppers*, pp. 55–59.
25. Mitchell, "Founding and Early History of the Southern Tenant Farmers Union," pp. 351–52, 355–57. The indifferent attitude of Secretary Wallace and AAA leaders to the plight of the Arkansas sharecroppers outraged Department of Agriculture liberals, such as Rexford Tugwell and Jerome Frank, and it contributed to their resigning from the agency in 1935. See Baldwin, *Poverty and Politics*.
26. Howard Kester, Unpublished autobiography, c. 1939, in the Southern Tenant Farmers Union Papers, Southern Historical Collection, University of North Carolina; "November–December, 1934," Box C-207, NAACP Papers, Library of Congress; author's interview with H. L. Mitchell, May 25, 1971. Unidentified flyer, c. December 1939, Box 1 in the Fellowship of Southern Churchmen Papers, Southern Historical Collection, University of North Carolina; John Egerton, *A Mind to Stay Here: Profiles from the South* (New York, 1970), pp. 84–86; Grubbs, *Cry from the Cotton*, p. 76.
27. Butler to McKinney, February 18, 1937; Mitchell to Evelyn Smith, December 27, 1936; Mitchell to Franklin, December 27, 1936, STFU Papers.
28. Jonathan Daniels, *A Southerner Discovers the South* (New York, 1938), pp. 50–51.
29. "National Executive Council Meeting," October 4, 1936, STFU Papers.
30. Author's interview with Frank P. Graham, May 22, 1971; Alexander to Howard Odum, June 19, 1930, and Johnson to Odum, June 15, 1936, Odum Papers; Daniels to Couch, November 2, 1936, Jonathan Daniels Papers, Southern Historical Collection, University of North Carolina; Interview with Graham; Graham to Josephus Daniels, undated, 1936, Folder 494 in the Frank P. Graham Presidential Papers, Southern Historical Collection, University of North Carolina.
31. Josephus Daniels to Ickes, September 29, 1938, Box 84 in the Josephus Daniels Papers, Library of Congress; Foreman to Jonathan Daniels, April 24, 1940, Jonathan Daniels Papers.
32. Josephus Daniels to Franklin Roosevelt, May 13, 1936, Box 96, Josephus Daniels Papers; Odum, Unsigned memorandum, February, 1942, Odum Papers; Jonathan Daniels, *Tar Heels: A Portrait of North Carolina* (New York, 1941), p. 270.
33. *Missouri Ex Rel. Gaines* v. *Canada*, 305 U.S. 337 (1938); Graham to Murray, February 2, 1939 and Murray to Graham, February 6, 1939, Folder 821, Graham Presidential Papers.

CHAPTER FIVE

The Southern Conference for Human Welfare

1. Samuel I. Rosenman, ed., *The Public Papers and Addresses of Franklin D. Roosevelt* (New York, 1938), vol. VII, p. 469; Williams to Roosevelt, March 24, 1938, Box 4, Aubrey Williams Papers, Franklin D. Roosevelt Library.

2. National Emergency Council, *Report on the Economic Conditions of the South* (Washington, 1938); George B. Tindall, *The Emergence of the New South 1913–1945* (Baton Rouge, 1967), p. 627.
3. Nixon to Howard Odum, April 3, 1937, Howard Washington Odum Papers, Southern Historical Collection, University of North Carolina.
4. Thomas A. Krueger, *And Promises to Keep: The Southern Conference for Human Welfare, 1938–1948* (Nashville, 1968), pp. 3–19; Jerold S. Auerbach, *Labor and Liberty: The La Follette Committee and the New Deal* (Indianapolis, 1966), pp. 94–96; Author's interview with W. T. Couch, May 4, 1971; Nixon to Howard Odum, October 5, 1938, Odum Papers.
5. "Southern Conference for Human Welfare, November 20–23 in Birmingham, Alabama," Box 95 in the Julius Rosenwald Fund Papers, Amistad Research Center, Dillard University.
6. President's Research Committee on Recent Social Trends, *Recent Social Trends in the United States* (New York, 1933). See also Harvey A. Kantor, "Howard W. Odum: The Implications of Folk, Planning, and Regionalism," *American Journal of Sociology*, 79 (September 1973), 283; Williams to Albert E. Barnett, November 14, 1952, Box 39, Williams Papers; *New York Post*, March 3, 1945.
7. Odum to Emily H. Clay, August 15, 1938, Odum Papers; George B. Tindall, "The Significance of Howard W. Odum to Southern History: A Preliminary Estimate," *Journal of Southern History*, 24 (August 1958), 300–1.
8. Ames to Mrs. W. A. Newell, September 13, 1938 and undated, Jessie Daniel Ames Papers, Southern Historical Collection, University of North Carolina.
9. Krueger, *And Promises to Keep*, pp. 21–23.
10. Charles S. Johnson to Howard Odum, September 6, 1938, Odum Papers; H. Clarence Nixon, *Forty Acres and Steel Mules* (Chapel Hill, 1938), p. 96.
11. W. T. Couch, ed., *Culture in the South* (Chapel Hill, 1934), pp. 432–77, 437.
12. Nixon to Miller, October 19, 1938. Quoted in Krueger, *And Promises to Keep*, p. 25.
13. Interviews with Mitchell and Raper.
14. Clark Foreman, "The Decade of Hope," in Bernard Sternsher, ed., *The Negro in Depression and War: Prelude to Revolution, 1930–1945* (Chicago, 1969), pp. 155–56. Foreman's article originally appeared in *Phylon*, 12 (Second Quarter, 1951), 137–50.
15. W. T. Couch, "Southerners Inspect the South," *New Republic*, 97 (December 14, 1938), 168–69.
16. Tindall, *Emergence of the New South*, p. 637; *Report of the Proceedings of the Southern Conference for Human Welfare* (Birmingham, 1938), pp. 14–15; Krueger, *And Promises to Keep*, pp. 26–27.
17. *Proceedings* (1938), 14–15.
18. *Chicago Defender*, November 27, 1938; Charles S. Johnson, "More Southerners Discover the South," *Crisis*, 46 (January 1939), 14–15; Sterling A. Brown, "South on the Move," *Opportunity*, 16 (December 1938), 366–68.
19. Graham to Dr. L. A. Crowell, Jr., December 22, 1938; Ethridge to Graham, November 30, 1938; and Mason to Graham, December 6, 1938 in the Frank P. Graham Papers, Southern Historical Collection, University of North Carolina.
20. Miller to Graham, December 6, 1938, ibid.
21. Interview with Graham; Graham to Mrs. Robert A. McWhorter, December 1, 1939, Graham Papers.

22. Krueger, *And Promises to Keep*, pp. 42–43. V. O. Key estimated that poll tax repeal would have increased Southern voter turnout from between 5 to 10 percent. *Southern Politics in State and Nation* (New York, 1949), pp. 599–618. See also Steven F. Lawson, *Black Ballots: Voting Rights in the South, 1944–1969* (New York, 1976).
23. *Alabama Journal* (Montgomery), May 10 and 11, 1954.
24. Krueger, *And Promises to Keep*, pp. 44–46; Katherine Du Pre Lumpkin, *The South in Progress* (New York, 1940), pp. 221–22; Richard B. Henderson, *Maury Maverick: A Political Biography* (Austin, 1970), pp. 223–24.
25. "The Poll Tax," SCHW Publications, Box 43 and "Minutes," Southern Conference for Human Welfare Executive Board Meeting, Chattanooga, March 21, 1940, Box 42, Carl and Anne Braden Papers, State Historical Society of Wisconsin, Madison.
26. "The Poll Tax," SCHW Publications, Box 43, Braden Papers; U.S. Congress, Senate, Committee on Judiciary, *Hearings on S. 1280: A Bill Concerning the Qualifications of Voters or Electors . . . Making Unlawful the Requirement for the Payment of a Poll Tax as a Prerequisite to Voting in a Primary or General Election for National Office*, 77 Cong. 2 sess., pt. 1 (1942), p. 76.
27. *Hearings*, 77 Cong. 2 sess., pt. 2 (1942), p. 531; *Atlanta Constitution*, December 21, 1944; U.S. Congress, Senate, Committee on Rules and Administration, *Hearings on H. R. 29: An Act Making Unlawful the Requirement for the Payment of a Poll Tax as a Prerequisite to Voting in a Primary or Other Election for National Offices*, 80 Cong. 2 sess. (1948), p. 221.
28. Harvard Sitkoff, "The Emergence of Civil Rights as a National Issue: The New Deal Era" (Unpublished Ph.D. dissertation, Columbia University, 1975), chapter 5.
29. Krueger, *And Promises to Keep*, pp. 46–47; Virginia Durr to Barry Bingham, January 6, 1941, Graham Papers; *Poll Tax Repealer*, 2 (February 1943), 2. Copy in Series 1943, Folder 93, Graham Papers; *Hearings*, 77 Cong. 2 sess., pt. 1 (1942), p. 71; "Citizen in Name Only," Southern Electoral Reform League Pamphlet, Series 1942, Graham Papers; Jennings Perry, *Democracy Begins at Home: The Tennessee Fight on the Poll Tax* (Philadelphia, 1944); "Report of January 23–24, 1944 Executive Board Meeting of the Southern Conference for Human Welfare," Series 1944, Graham Papers.
30. *Southern Frontier*, 1 (July 1940), 33.
31. *Breedlove* v. *Suttles*, 302 U.S. 277, 283 (1938).
32. *Smith* v. *Allwright*, 321 U.S. 649 (1944).
33. *Elmore* v. *Rice*, 72 F. Supp. 516 (1947). On Waring see "The Reminiscences of J. Waties Waring" (Columbia Oral History Collection, 1955–57) and Key, *Southern Politics*, pp. 628–32.
34. See Lawson, *Black Ballots*.
35. *Hearings*, 80 Cong. 2 sess. (1948), p. 105.

CHAPTER SIX

Jim Crow and the War

1. Alexander to Embree, December 13, 1941, Box 94, Julius Rosenwald Fund Papers, Amistad Research Center, Dillard University, New Orleans.

2. E. P. M. to Frank Graham, January 5, 1945, Series 1945, Frank Porter Graham Papers (Personal and Presidential), Southern Historical Collection, University of North Carolina, Chapel Hill; Harvard Sitkoff, "The Emergence of Civil Rights as a National Issue: The New Deal Era" (Unpublished Ph.D. dissertation, Columbia University, 1975), chapter 12; Richard M. Dalfiume, "The Forgotten Years of the Negro Revolution," in Bernard Sternsher, ed., *The Negro in Depression and War: Prelude to Revolution, 1930–1945* (Chicago, 1969), p. 306. Reprinted from *Journal of American History*, 55 (June 1968), 90–106. See also Harvard Sitkoff, "Racial Militancy and Interracial Violence in the Second World War," *Journal of American History*, 58 (December 1971), 661–81 and Richard Dalfiume, *Fighting on Two Fronts: Desegregation of the Armed Forces, 1939–1953* (Columbia, Mo., 1969).
3. George B. Tindall, *The Emergence of the New South 1913–1945* (Baton Rouge, 1967), pp. 717–18; David L. Cohn, "How the South Feels," *Atlantic Monthly*, 173 (January 1944), 49; *PM* (New York), September 9, 1942.
4. Frank Daniels to Jonathan Daniels, August 25, 1942 and Jonathan Daniels to Odum, August 24, 1942, Jonathan Daniels Papers; Ethridge to Jessie Daniel Ames, May 27, 1942, Jessie Daniel Ames Papers, Southern Historical Collection, University of North Carolina.
5. Jonathan Daniels, *White House Witness 1942–1945* (Garden City, N.Y., 1975), pp. 204–5; Jessie Daniel Ames to Virginius Dabney, July 26, 1943 and Jonathan Daniels to Dabney, July 29, 1943, Series 7690, Box 5 in the Virginius Dabney Papers, Alderman Library, University of Virginia.
6. Herbert Agar, *A Time for Greatness* (Boston, 1942), pp. 140, 147; Harris to Dabney, August 28, 1942, Series 7690, Box 5, Dabney Papers.
7. Tindall, *Emergence of the New South*, p. 714; Walter White, "Southern Liberals," *Negro Digest*, 1 (January 1943), 43; Ethridge to Dabney, August 8, 1942, Series 7690, Box 5, Dabney Papers.
8. *Southern Frontier*, 4 (October 1943), 1; "Call for a Southern Win-the-War Mass Meeting," Raleigh, North Carolina, July 14, 1942, Southern Conference for Human Welfare Publications and "Southern Editors Defend Negro GI's," SCHW Scrapbook, Box 43, Carl and Anne Braden Papers, State Historical Society of Wisconsin, Madison; Graham to Frederick D. Patterson, June 24, 1942, Graham Papers.
9. Roy P. Basler, "As One Southerner to Another: Concerning Lincoln and the Declaration of Independence," *South Atlantic Quarterly*, 42 (January 1943), 50; *Southern Frontier*, 4 (July 1943), 1; Thomas Sancton, "Trouble in Dixie: Race Fear Sweeps the South," *New Republic*, 118 (January 18, 1943), 81–82.
10. Eleazer to Harvey Wickham, April 16, 1930. Quoted in Edward F. Burrows, "The Commission on Interracial Cooperation: A Case Study on the History of the Interracial Movement in the South" (Unpublished Ph.D. dissertation, University of Wisconsin, 1955), p. 175.
11. Author's interview with Arthur F. Raper, April 23, 1971; author's interview with Virginius Dabney, May 1, 1971; Couch to Jonathan Daniels, October 31, 1936 and Jonathan Daniels to Couch, November 2, 1936, Jonathan Daniels Papers; Couch, publisher's introduction to Rayford Logan, ed., *What the Negro Wants* (Chapel Hill, 1945), p. xx; Cohn, "How the South Feels," p. 50.
12. Odum to Jonathan Daniels, August 21, 1942, Howard Washington Odum Papers, Southern Historical Collection, University of North Carolina.
13. Odum to Charles Johnson, November 28, 1938, Odum Papers; Jonathan Dan-

iels, *Tar Heels: A Portait of North Carolina* (New York, 1941), p. 274; Odum to Virginius Dabney, December 12, 1944, Series 7690, Box 8, Dabney Papers.
14. Odum to F. W. Bradley, June 19, 1944, Odum Papers; Howard Odum, *Race and Rumors of Race: Challenge to American Crisis* (Chapel Hill, 1943), pp. 18–19, 77, 143.
15. Odum to Gerald Johnson, April 12, 1944, Odum Papers; Odum to Virginius Dabney, June 21, 1943, Series 7690, Box 8, Dabney Papers.
16. Odum to Gerald Johnson, January 28, 1944, Odum Papers.
17. David W. Southern, "*An American Dilemma* Revisited: Myrdalism and White Southern Liberals," *South Atlantic Quarterly*, 75 (Spring 1976), 182–97.
18. Tindall, *Emergence of the New South*, p. 568; Gunnar Myrdal, *An American Dilemma: The Negro Problem and Modern Democracy* (New York, 1944), vol. II, p. 848; Odum to Davis, March 3, 1938; Odum to Frank Graham, July 2, 1938; Odum to Will Alexander, August 14, 1939, Odum Papers; W. E. B. Du Bois, "The Position of the Negro in the American Social Order: Where Do We Go from Here?" *Journal of Negro Education*, 8 (July 1939), 559.
19. Clay to Howard Odum, October 12–13, 1939, and Jones to Odum, June 13, 1940, Odum Papers.
20. Burrows, "The Commission on Interracial Cooperation," pp. 273–74, 329; Tindall, *Emergence of the New South*, pp. 718–19; Odum to Cole, June 25, 1943, Odum Papers; Ames to Dabney, July 12, 1943, Series 7690, Box 5, Dabney Papers; Ames to P. B. Young, July 12, 1943, Ames Papers.
21. Ames to Hancock, April 7, 1942 and Memorandum, March 22, 1950, Ames Papers; Hancock to Ames, May 20, 1942 and Ames to Hancock, July 24, 1942, Series 7690, Box 4, Dabney Papers; [Ames,] "The South Has a 'Bottleneck,' " *Southern Frontier*, 2 (February 1941), 2–3.
22. Charles Johnson, et al., *To Stem This Tide: A Survey of Racial Tension Areas in the United States* (Boston, 1943), pp. 131–39, 138.
23. Thomas Sancton, "The Negro Press," *New Republic*, 108 (April 26, 1943), 560; Chappell to Ames, January 7, 1943, Ames Papers; Charles Johnson, et al., *To Stem This Tide*, pp. 140–42; Dabney to Young, April 17, 1943, Series 7690, Box 4, Dabney Papers.
24. Interview with Dabney; Odum to Gerald Johnson, April 13, 1944 and Odum to Jonathan Daniels, September 15, 1943, Odum Papers; Odum to Virginius Dabney, June 21, 1943, Series 7690, Box 8, Dabney Papers; Alexander to Edwin Embree, May 24, 1943, Box 94, Rosenwald Fund Papers; *Southern Frontier*, 4 (August 1943), 3.
25. Henry Paul Houser, "The Southern Regional Council" (Unpublished M.A. thesis, University of North Carolina, 1950), pp. 38–41; Odum to Virginius Dabney, July 9, 1943, Series 7690, Box 8, Dabney Papers; Alexander to Odum, January 13, 1944, Odum Papers.

CHAPTER SEVEN

Virginius Dabney: Publicist for a Liberal South

1. William Henry Dabney, *Sketch of the Dabneys of Virginia: With Some of Their Family Records* (Chicago, 1888), pp. 23–47, 74–82, passim; "Richard Heath Dab-

ney," *American Historical Review*, 52 (July 1947), 834–35; *Current Biography*, 1948, pp. 127–29. Virginius Dabney's namesake grandfather was the author of *The Story of Don Miff* (1886), a novel that in its day achieved both popular and critical acclaim, and a less successful effort, *Gold That Did Not Glitter* (1889).
2. Susan Dabney Smedes, *Memorials of a Southern Planter*, ed. by Fletcher M. Green (New York, 1965), pp. ix–xlvi.
3. *Current Biography*, 1948, pp. 127–29.
4. Interview with Dabney, May 2, 1971. Mr. Dabney stated that while he had come to realize that legalized segregation was an unjust system that ultimately had to be eliminated, he remained opposed to miscegenation.
5. Dabney to Walter White, March 19, 1938, Box C-266, NAACP Papers, Library of Congress.
6. Interview with Dabney; Virginius Dabney, *Dry Messiah: The Life of Bishop Cannon* (New York, 1949), pp. viii, 190.
7. Virginius Dabney, *Liberalism in the South* (Chapel Hill, 1932), pp. 165–70, 254–55, 264, 427–28.
8. Raper to W. T. Couch, January 14, 1933, Howard Washington Odum Papers, Southern Historical Collection, University of North Carolina; Clarence Cason, *90° in the Shade* (Chapel Hill, 1935), p. 172.
9. Virginius Dabney, "If the South Had Won the War," *American Mercury*, 39 (October 1936), 199, 204. Dabney was critical of the Vanderbilt agrarians for wishing that the South had held off Union armies just a little bit longer.
10. Charles H. Martin, *The Angelo Herndon Case and Southern Justice* (Baton Rouge, 1976), p. 74; Francis Pickens Miller, *Man from the Valley: Memoirs of a 20th Century Virginian* (Chapel Hill, 1971), p. 84; V. O. Key, *Southern Politics in State and Nation* (New York, 1949), p. 19.
11. "For a Federal Antilynching Bill," *Richmond Times-Dispatch*, February 2, 1937; Virginius Dabney, "Dixie Rejects Lynching," *Nation*, 145 (November 27, 1937), 579–80.
12. White to Dabney, February 12, 1937, April 9, 1937, May 12, 1937; White to Ackerman, April 26, 1937, March 8, 1938; Dabney to White, May 13, 1937, Box C-266, NAACP Papers.
13. Dabney to Frank P. Graham, November 7, 1938, Series 1938, Folder 77, Frank Porter Graham Papers (Personal and Presidential), Southern Historical Collection, University of North Carolina; Interview with Dabney; Virginius Dabney, "Shall the Poll Tax Go?" *New York Times Magazine*, February 12, 1939, p. 9.
14. P. B. Young to Walter White, July 26, 1939 and White to Young, August 9, 1939, Box C-266, NAACP Papers; T. Burton Dunn, Jr. to Dabney, February 8, 1941, Series 7690, Box 4, Virginius Dabney Papers, Alderman Library, University of Virginia; Interview with Dabney.
15. Virginius Dabney, *Below the Potomac: A Book about the New South* (New York, 1942), pp. 4–6, 63, 178, 183, 202, 205–36, 224, passim. For Percy's views see William Alexander Percy, *Lanterns on the Levee: Recollections of a Planter's Son* (New York, 1941).
16. Dabney, *Below the Potomac*, pp. 300–4, 315–16.
17. Dabney to Ethridge, August 3, 1942, Series 7690, Box 5; Dabney to Graves, June 13, 1942, Series 7690, Box 7; Dabney to Alfred S. Dasheill, August 4, 1942, Series 7690, Box 5, Dabney Papers.

18. Virginius Dabney, "Nearer and Nearer the Precipice," *Atlantic Monthly*, 171 (January 1943), 94, 96, 98, 100.
19. "Here to Yonder," *Chicago Defender*, January 5, 1943; Young to Dabney, January 12, 1943 and January 20, 1943, Series 7690, Box 4, Dabney Papers.
20. Cy W. Record, "What's Happened to the 'Southern Liberals'?" *New Leader*, July 10, 1943, p. 5.
21. Dabney to R. Beverly Herbert, July 19, 1943, Series 7690, Box 5, Dabney Papers.
22. Dabney, "The Dynamic New South," *New York Times Magazine*, October 17, 1943, p. 17; "The South Marches On," *Survey Graphic*, 32 (November 1943), 442–44, 462.
23. "To Lessen Race Friction" and "The Conservative Course in Race Relations," *Richmond Times-Dispatch*, November 13 and 21, 1943.
24. "Sanity in the South," *Pittsburgh Courier*, December 4, 1943; Prattis to Dabney, December 2, 1943; Wilkins to Dabney, December 1, 1943 and December 15, 1943; *Progressive*, December 27, 1943, clipping all in Series 7690, Box 6, Dabney Papers.
25. Interview with Dabney; Dabney to Mrs. S. F. Hart, December 4, 1943, Series 7690, Box 4, Dabney Papers.
26. Jaffe to Dabney, November 15, 1943 and Dabney to Jaffe, November 16, 1943, Series 7690, Box 4, Dabney Papers.
27. Interview with Dabney; Dabney to Golightly, January 8, 1944, Series 7690a, Box 3, ibid.; "Dabney and the Doukhobors," *Time*, 44 (December 4, 1944), 72.
28. Major Osmond T. ("Mutt") Jamerson to Dabney, August 2, 1942 and Dabney to Jamerson, August 4, 1942, Series 7690, Box 5, Dabney Papers.
29. Dabney to Mrs. Oscar de Wolf Randolph, September 28, 1942; Dabney to Mrs. W. S. Copeland, February 5, 1943; Dabney to P. B. Young, June 19, 1943; Dabney to Ethridge, January 11, 1943, ibid.
30. Sancton to Dabney, August 20, 1942 and Dabney to Sancton, December 10, 1942, ibid.
31. Sancton to Dabney, December 30, 1942, ibid.
32. Dabney to Sancton, January 4, 1943, ibid.

CHAPTER EIGHT

Liberals amid Dixiecrats

1. Foreman to Edwin Embree, May 7, 1940, Box 348, Julius Rosenwald Fund Papers, Amistad Research Center, Dillard University, New Orleans; Odum to Virginius Dabney, August 13, 1943, Series 7690, Box 8, Virginius Dabney Papers, Alderman Library, University of Virginia; Odum to Gerald Johnson, April 12, 1944, Howard Washington Odum Papers, Southern Historical Collection, University of North Carolina; "All the Bad—Some of the Good," Mailing Flyer for *Southern Frontier*, c. 1942, Series 7690, Box 5, Dabney Papers; Thomas A. Krueger, *And Promises to Keep: The Southern Conference for Human Welfare, 1938–1948* (Nashville, 1968), pp. 119–22.

2. Kenneth Douty, "The Southern Conference for Human Welfare: A Report," Unpublished manuscript, c. 1955, pp. 63–66 in the Frank McCallister Papers, Southern Historical Collection, University of North Carolina; Foreman to Graham, March 20, 1940, Frank Porter Graham Papers (Personal and Presidential), Southern Historical Collection, University of North Carolina; "Resolutions Adopted, Second Meeting—Southern Conference for Human Welfare," Chattanooga, April 14–16, 1940, Box 42, Carl and Anne Braden Papers, State Historical Society of Wisconsin, Madison.
3. Graham to Howard Kester, December 1, 1939; Bingham to John B. Thompson, April 12, 1941; Graham to Joseph Lieb, April 19, 1941; Charlton to Graham, July 28, 1941, Graham Papers; Douty, "Southern Conference for Human Welfare," pp. 93–96.
4. Durr to Bingham, January 6, 1941, Series 1941, Folder 27, Graham Papers.
5. Krueger, *And Promises to Keep*, pp. 88–89, 105–6; George B. Tindall, *The Emergence of the New South, 1913–1945* (Baton Rouge, 1967), p. 633; Hild W. Smith to Graham, February 4, 1942, Series 1942, Folder 112, Graham Papers.
6. Frank Graham, "The Negro and the War," *Motive: Magazine of the Methodist Student Movement*, 5 (January 1945), 28.
7. Krueger, *And Promises to Keep*, pp. 96–108, 108.
8. Ibid., p. 115; "Report of January 23–24, 1944 Executive Board Meeeting of the Southern Conference for Human Welfare," January 24, 1944, Graham Papers; Mason to Embree, November 10, 1945, Box 95, Rosenwald Fund Papers.
9. Foreman to Potential Supporters of the Southern Conference for Human Welfare, undated (1945) memo, Series 1945, Folder 34, Graham Papers; James A. Dombrowski, "The New South on the March," *Nation*, 160 (March 3, 1945), 244–45; "Thomas Jefferson Award Presentation to Justice Hugo L. Black," April 3, 1945, Southern Conference for Human Welfare Publications, Box 42, Braden Papers.
10. Foreman to James Dombrowski, February 10, 1947; Clement to Foreman, February 14, 1947; Foreman to Aubrey Williams, April 1947, Clark Foreman Correspondence, Box 43, Braden Papers; V. O. Key, *Southern Politics in State and Nation* (New York, 1949), pp. 106–29. The Georgia Supreme Court finally ruled Thompson the legitimate governor. However, in 1948 Herman Talmadge received a measure of vindication by decisively defeating Thompson in the Democratic gubernatorial primary. See Robert Sherrill, *Gothic Politics in the Deep South: Stars of the New Confederacy* (New York, 1968), pp. 37–51.
11. Krueger, *And Promises to Keep*, pp. 152–55, 159–62; Mary Bragiotti, "Southern Progressive," *New York Post*, March 3, 1945, clipping, Box 43, Braden Papers.
12. Walter Gellhorn, "Report on a Report of the House Committee on Un-American Activities," *Harvard Law Review*, 60 (October 1947), 1233.
13. "South Prospers When All Get Fair Chance, SCHW Tells Senate," unidentified clipping, March 13, 1945, Box 95, Rosenwald Fund Papers; Bilbo to Dombrowski, November 5, 1942. Quoted in Douty, "Southern Conference for Human Welfare," pp. 142–43; Krueger, *And Promises to Keep*, pp. 136, 146, 150, 153.
14. Krueger, *And Promises to Keep*, pp. 152–54; "Proceedings of the Fourth Biennial Southern Conference for Human Welfare Convention," New Orleans, November 28–30, 1946 and F. Palmer Weber to Dombrowski, December, 1946, James Dombrowski Correspondence with Board, Box 42, Braden Papers.

15. Lucy R. Mason, "Memorandum to the Board of Directors of the Southern Conference for Human Welfare," April 19, 1947, Box 42, Braden Papers.
16. Krueger, *And Promises to Keep*, pp. 155–57; Irwin Klibaner, "The Southern Conference Educational Fund: A History" (Unpublished Ph.D. dissertation, University of Wisconsin, 1971), pp. 55–56, 79–80; Dombrowski to Foreman, October 20, 1947, Clark Foreman Correspondence, Box 43, Braden Papers; *New York Times*, December 3, 1948; "Presenting the Southern Conference for Human Welfare," undated flyer, Box 35, Aubrey Williams Papers, Franklin D. Roosevelt Library.
17. *St. Louis Post-Dispatch*, March 3, 1945; John A. Salmond, "Postscript to the New Deal: The Defeat of the Nomination of Aubrey W. Williams as Rural Electrification Administrator in 1945," *Journal of American History*, 61 (September 1974), 417–36.
18. Williams to Gould Beach, April 5, 1948, Box 34, Williams Papers; Klibaner, "Southern Conference Educational Fund," pp. 164–67. In 1948, after he had become aware of how difficult it was for blacks to obtain real estate mortgages, Williams also helped start a group, American Family Homes, that built homes for blacks in the Birmingham area.
19. *To Secure These Rights: The Report of the President's Committee on Civil Rights* (New York, 1947).
20. Klibaner, "Southern Conference Educational Fund," pp. 66–75, 87–88; Williams to Fielding Wright, February 24, 1948 and undated draft, Box 35, Williams Papers; *New York Times*, November 21, 1948.
21. Richard M. Dalfiume, *Fighting on Two Fronts: Desegregation of the Armed Forces 1939–1953* (Columbia, Mo., 1969), pp. 132–38.
22. *To Secure These Rights*, passim; William C. Berman, *The Politics of Civil Rights in the Truman Administration* (Columbus, 1970), pp. 70–71; Alonzo L. Hamby, *Beyond the New Deal: Harry S. Truman and American Liberalism* (New York, 1973), p. 189; Gilbert Osofsky, ed., *The Burden of Race: A Documentary History of Negro-White Relations in America* (New York, 1967), p. 428.
23. William Ernest Juhnke, Jr., "Creating a New Charter of Freedom: The Organization and Operation of the President's Committee on Civil Rights, 1946–1948" (Unpublished Ph.D. dissertation, University of Kansas, 1974), pp. 141–68.
24. Ibid., pp. 164–66.
25. Dabney to Dr. James E. Paullin, July 19, 1943, Series 7690, Box 5, Dabney Papers.
26. Stetson Kennedy, "Design for Racial Democracy," Box 95, Rosenwald Fund Papers.
27. J. Saunders Redding, "Southern Defensive—I" and Lillian Smith, "Southern Defensive—II" in *Common Ground*, 4 (Spring 1944), 36–42, 43–45; Tindall, *Emergence of the New South*, pp. 719–20; Johnson to Howard Odum, February 1, 1944, Odum Papers; Guy B. Johnson, "Southern Offensive," *Common Ground*, 4 (Summer 1944), 87–93; Johnson to Dabney, June 19, 1944, Series 7690a, Box 4, Dabney Papers.
28. Alexander to Odum, March 27, 1935, Odum Papers; Alexander to Drew Pearson, January 4, 1945, Box 96, Rosenwald Fund Papers; Clipping from *Atlanta Daily World*, February 18, 1944, Box 94, Rosenwald Fund Papers; Memorandum for Marvin McIntyre, January 1, 1942, Jonathan Daniels Papers.
29. Will W. Alexander, "Our Conflicting Racial Policies," *Harper's*, 190 (January

1945), 173–74, 177–78; Guy Johnson to Virginius Dabney, May 8, 1945, Series 7690a, Box 4, Dabney Papers.

30. Dabney to George Watts Hill, May 3, 1945, Series 7690a, Box 4, Dabney Papers; Odum to John Temple Graves, August 4, 1944, Odum Papers; George B. Tindall, "The Significance of Howard W. Odum to Southern History: A Preliminary Estimate," *Journal of Southern History*, 24 (August 1958), 287; Interview with Dabney.

31. Johnson to Odum, January 9, 1945, Odum Papers; Johnson to Virginius Dabney, Series 7690a, Box 4, Dabney Papers.

32. Odum to Johnson, January 13, 1945, Odum Papers.

33. Odum to Lt. Col. P. S. Finn, Jr., June 28, 1946, ibid.

34. Howard Odum, "Social Change in the South," *Journal of Politics*, 10 (May 1948), 250; Work Memo, "The Unchanged South," April 12, 1948, Odum Papers.

35. Odum, "Social Change in the South," p. 248.

36. Interview with Dabney; Dabney to Francis R. Bridges, January 4, 1945; Dabney to Johnson, January 6, 1945; and Dabney to Jessie Daniel Ames, July 12, 1945, Series 7690a, Box 4, Dabney Papers.

37. "The Dangers of a Permanent FEPC," *Richmond Times-Dispatch*, June 11, 1945; Dabney to J. K. M. Newton, August 2, 1945, Series 7690a, Box 3, Dabney Papers.

38. Virginius Dabney, "Is the South That Bad?" *Saturday Review of Literature*, 29 (April 13, 1946), 9–10, 86–88.

39. William C. Allred, Jr., "The Southern Regional Council, 1943–1961" (Unpublished M.A. thesis, Emory University, 1966), pp. 79, 98; Southern Regional Council, *It Seems Queer . . . : The Southern Veteran Speaks* (Atlanta, 1945). Reprinted from *Fort Worth Star Telegram*, August 14, 1945; Tindall, *Emergence of the New South*, p. 721.

40. "SRC Annual Meeting Charts Course for 1947," *New South* 1 (December 1946), 1–2; Johnson to Alexander, February 13, 1947, Box 7 in the Guy B. Johnson Papers, Southern Historical Collection, University of North Carolina; "Civil Rights in the South," *New South*, 2 (August 1947), 1–5.

41. Benjamin E. Mays, *Born to Rebel* (New York, 1971), pp. 252–53; "Reminiscences of Will W. Alexander" (Columbia Oral History Collection, 1952), pp. 710–11; Clay to Johnson, April 13, 1947, Johnson Papers.

42. Interview with Mrs. George S. Mitchell.

43. Charles Johnson, "The Will and the Way," *New South*, 2 (May 1947), 1; "Fourth Annual Meeting Plans 1948 Program," *New South*, 2–3 (December–January 1947–48), 1; "SRC Executive Committee Minutes," February 25, 1948, Box 7, Guy Johnson Papers.

44. Paul Williams, "SRC President's Address to Membership Meeting," *New South*, 2–3 (December–January 1947–48), 21, 11.

45. "An Honest Answer in the Civil Rights Controversy," *New South*, 3 (September 1948), 1–6.

46. "The Supreme Court Considers Segregation," *New South*, 4 (November–December 1949), 4–6.

47. Paul Williams, "The Task Ahead," *New South*, 5 (November 1950), 3–8.

48. Walter White, *A Man Called White: The Autobiography of Walter White* (New York, 1948), pp. 347–48; Dalfiume, *Fighting on Two Fronts*, pp. 138–39.

49. On the growth of civil rights as an issue during the Truman years see Berman, *Politics of Civil Rights in the Truman Administration;* Dalfiume, *Fighting on Two Fronts;* Hamby, *Beyond the New Deal;* Monroe Billington, "Civil Rights, President Truman and the South," *Journal of Negro History,* 58 (April 1973), 127–39; Harvard Sitkoff, "Harry S. Truman and the Election of 1948: The Coming of Age of Civil Rights in American Politics," *Journal of Southern History,* 37 (November 1971), 597–616; Barton J. Bernstein, "The Ambiguous Legacy: The Truman Administration and Civil Rights," in Bernstein, ed., *Politics and Policies of the Truman Administration* (Chicago, 1970), pp. 269–314.
50. Sherrill, *Gothic Politics,* pp. 138–52; Numan V. Bartley, *The Rise of Massive Resistance: Race and Politics in the South During the 1950's* (Baton Rouge, 1969), pp. 39–40; Samuel Lubell, *The Future of American Politics* (3d rev. ed., New York, 1965), pp. 106–13.
51. Allred, "Southern Regional Council," pp. 59–60, 64.
52. Odum to George S. Mitchell, May 31, 1954; Odum to Dr. Charles F. Carroll, June 5, 1954; Odum to Johnson, October 13, 1954, Odum Papers.
53. Virginius Dabney, "What We Think of Senator Byrd's Machine," *Saturday Evening Post,* 222 (January 7, 1950), 92–94; Key, *Southern Politics,* p. 19.
54. Virginius Dabney, "Southern Crisis: The Segregation Decision," *Saturday Evening Post,* 225 (November 8, 1952), 41; Interview with Dabney; Virginius Dabney, "Race Relations Now 'Definitely Worse,' " *U.S. News & World Report,* 40 (February 24, 1956), 144, and "School Crisis in Dixie!" *American Magazine,* 162 (August 1956), 26. See also Dabney's chapter "The Era of 'Massive Resistance' " in his *Virginia: The New Dominion* (Garden City, N.Y., 1971), pp. 528–47.
55. Virginius Dabney, "A Frank Talk to North and South about Integration," *U.S. News & World Report,* 42 (March 15, 1957), 112 ff. and "Virginia's 'Peaceable, Honorable Stand,' " *Life,* 45 (September 22, 1958), 51 ff.; Byrd to Dabney, September 23, 1958. Quoted in James W. Ely, Jr., *The Crisis of Conservative Virginia: The Byrd Organization and the Politics of Massive Resistance* (Knoxville, 1976), p. 15.
56. Aubrey Williams, "The Failure of Gradualism," speech before Alpha Phi Alpha, Atlanta, December 28, 1949; Williams to John E. Ivey, Jr., March 6, 1950, Box 39, Williams Papers; Klibaner, "Southern Conference Educational Fund," p. 139.
57. Klibaner, "Southern Conference Educational Fund," pp. 176–82, 228; *Firing Line,* 4 (May 1, 1955 and July 1, 1955), clippings in Box 34, Williams Papers.
58. Aubrey Williams, "A Southern Rebel," pp. 64–66, Williams Papers, and "What's Happening in the South Today," *Lawyers Guild Review,* 16 (Spring 1956), 21–23. This contrasts significantly with Williams's earlier optimism about the South becoming more liberal. See "Liberal Renaissance from the South?" *New South,* 2 (May 1947), 2 and "There Is a Break," *Nation,* 169 (August 6, 1949), 128–30.
59. "Reminiscences of Will Alexander," 724–25; Alexander to Odum, June 20, 1951, Odum Papers; Charles P. Roland, *The Improbable Era: The South Since World War II* (Lexington, Ky., 1975), p. 39.
60. Durr to Black January 25, 1954 and July 15, 1959, Box 8, Hugo L. Black Papers, Library of Congress.
61. Samuel Lubell, *Revolt of the Moderates* (New York, 1956), p. 198; Harry S. Ashmore, *An Epitaph for Dixie* (New York, 1958), p. 159.

Southern liberals wrote frequently about their lonely struggles during the Eisenhower and Kennedy years. See Anne Braden, *The Wall Between* (New York, 1958); P. D. East, *The Magnolia Jungle* (New York, 1960); James McBride Dabbs, *The Southern Heritage* (New York, 1958); Sarah Patton Boyle, *The Desegregated Heart: A Virginian's Stand in Time of Transition* (New York, 1962); James W. Silver, *Mississippi: The Closed Society* (New York, 1964); Frank Smith, *Congressman from Mississippi* (New York, 1964).

CHAPTER NINE

Lillian Smith: The Southern Liberal as Evangelist

1. Alexander to Odum, June 20, 1951, Howard Washington Odum Papers, Southern Historical Collection, University of North Carolina; "Summary by Frank P. Graham of His Written and Spoken Statements on the Case of the Chapel Hill Presbyterian Church," January 24, 1953, Frank Porter Graham Papers (Personal and Presidential), Southern Historical Collection, University of North Carolina; *New York Times*, August 20, 1972; John Egerton, *A Mind to Stay Here: Profiles from the South* (New York, 1970), p. 84; James McBride Dabbs, *Haunted by God: The Cultural and Religious Experience of the South* (Richmond, 1972).
2. Alexander to Robert B. Eleazer, March 8, 1945, Box 95, Julius Rosenwald Fund Papers, Amistad Research Center, Dillard University, New Orleans.
3. Dorothy C. Kinsella, "Southern Apologists: A Liberal Image" (Unpublished Ph.D. dissertation, St. Louis University, 1971), pp. 52–53; Harold Martin, *Ralph McGill, Reporter* (Boston, 1973), p. 194.
4. Louise Blackwell and Frances Clay, *Lillian Smith* (New York, 1971), pp. 11–23. Unless otherwise noted, all biographical information about Lillian Smith contained in this chapter is from this source. Other biographical information may be found in *Current Biography*, 1944, pp. 635–38; Lillian Smith, *Memory of a Large Christmas* (New York, 1961) and *Killers of the Dream* (New York, 1949); Carolyn Jennings, "A Bio-Bibliography of Lillian Eugenia Smith (1897–1966)" (Unpublished M.A. thesis, Catholic University, 1968), p. 4.
5. Smith, *Killers of the Dream*, pp. 24–28.
6. Redding S. Sugg, Jr., "Lillian Smith and the Condition of Woman," *South Atlantic Quarterly*, 71 (Spring 1972), 156–57.
7. *Chicago Defender*, August 20, 1949; Lillian Smith, "He That Is Without Sin," *North Georgia Review*, 1 (Winter 1937–38), 31–32.
8. Sugg, "Lillian Smith and the Condition of Woman," p. 157; "Personal History of 'Strange Fruit': Statement of Purposes and Intentions," *Saturday Review of Literature*, 27 (February 17, 1945), 9–10. Miss Smith once mused over the prospect of women from the Pacific Islands asking Western mothers why they feared to have their children engage in masturbation. "The Americans' answer," she concluded, "would be worth a trip around the globe to hear." *Chicago Defender*, March 19, 1949. For her views on homosexuality, see Smith's portrayal of a relationship between two women in her novel *One Hour* (New York, 1959), pp. 352–55. "It is the quality of a relationship that counts," another woman reassuringly tells one of the

guilt-ridden lovers. "Easy to paste a good label on something spurious and cheap, easy to paste a bad one on something fine and delicate." Upon hearing these words, Smith's heroine commented: "When she said this simple, obvious thing it burst on me like a revelation" (p. 355). See also *Strange Fruit* (New York, 1944), pp. 54–64 for Lillian Smith's depiction of the ill effects of sexual repression.

9. Lillian Smith, "Dope with Lime," *North Georgia Review*, 2 (Spring 1937), 23.

10. Helen White and Redding S. Sugg., Jr., eds., *From the Mountain: An Anthology of the Magazine Successively Titled Pseudopodia, the North Georgia Review, and South Today* (Memphis, 1972), pp. 11, 31–37, 66.

11. Ibid., p. 70.

12. Lillian Smith, "On More Sigh for the Good Old South," *Pseudopodia*, 1 (Fall 1936), 6, 15.

13. Lillian Smith, "Wisdom Crieth in the Streets . . . ," *North Georgia Review*, 2 (Fall 1937), 4, 18.

14. See Carl N. Degler, *Neither Black nor White: Slavery and Race Relations in Brazil and the United States* (New York, 1971).

15. Du Bois to Edwin R. Embree, December 10, 1938 and Harper to George R. Reynolds, March 22, 1939, Box F, Rosenwald Fund Papers.

16. Embree to Smith, June 21, 1939, ibid. Embree had collaborated with Charles S. Johnson and Will Alexander in the "sociological treatise" *The Collapse of Cotton Tenancy: Summary of Field Studies and Statistical Surveys, 1933–1935* (Chapel Hill, 1935).

17. Smith to Embree, July 7, 1939; Smith to George Reynolds, August 7, 1939; and Smith to Embree, December 12, 1939, Box F. Rosenwald Fund Papers; Blackwell and Clay, *Lillian Smith*, p. 30; Smith to Embree, December 12, 1939, Box F, Rosenwald Fund Papers.

18. Embree to Howard Odum, February 1, 1942, and Smith to William C. Haygood, August 15, 1941, Box F, Rosenwald Fund Papers.

19. Smith, "Dope with Lime" and "Southern Conference," *North Georgia Review*, 5 (Spring 1940), 4, 23.

20. Lillian Smith, "Are We Not All Confused?" *South Today*, 7 (Spring 1942), 30–34.

21. Smith to Dabney, August 3, 1942, Series 7690, Box 5, Virginius Dabney Papers, Alderman Library, University of Virginia.

22. Lillian Smith, "Buying a New World with Old Confederate Bills," *South Today*, 7 (Autumn–Winter, 1942–43), 22.

23. Lillian Smith, "Addressed to Intelligent White Southerners: 'There Are Things to Do'," ibid., pp. 41–43 and "Putting Away Childish Things," *South Today*, 8 (Spring–Summer, 1944), 63.

24. Smith to William C. Haygood, February 10, 1943, Box 348, Rosenwald Fund Papers.

25. "Feverish Fascination," *Time*, 43 (March 20, 1944), 99–100, 102.

26. "Herald of the Dream," ibid., 88 (October 7, 1966), 36–37; "Slain on 'Strange Fruit' Date," *Chicago Defender*, October 23, 1948.

27. The most complete discussion of *Strange Fruit* is in Blackwell and Clay, *Lillian Smith*, pp. 37–60. See also Sugg, "Lillian Smith and the Condition of Woman," pp. 160–61; and Neil Thorborn, " 'Strange Fruit' and Southern Tradition," *Midwest Quarterly*, 12 (Winter 1971), 157–71. For contemporary reviews see Joseph Mc-

Sorley, "*Strange Fruit*," *Catholic World*, 159 (May 1944), 182; Diana Trilling, "Fiction in Review," *Nation*, 157 (March 19, 1944), 342; Edwin Weeks, "Strange Fruit," *Atlantic Monthly*, 173 (May 1944), 127; Malcolm Cowley, "Southways," *New Republic*, 110 (March 6, 1944), 320–22; Struthers Burt, "The Making of a New South," *Saturday Review of Literature*, 27 (March 11, 1944), 10.

28. *Commonwealth* v. *Isenstadt*, Supreme Judicial Court of Massachusetts (1945). Bernard De Voto, who helped initiate a test case on the banning of *Strange Fruit*, reviewed the incidents of the case in "Decision in the Strange Fruit Case: The Obscenity Statute in Massachusetts," *New England Quarterly*, 30 (June 1946), 147–83. See also Edward De Grazia, ed., *Censorship Landmarks* (New York, 1969), pp. 125–30. The Supreme Court of Massachusetts upheld the banning of the book, but the case's notoriety helped to bring about the eventual downfall of Boston's obscenity law.

29. Blackwell and Clay, *Lillian Smith*, pp. 56–60; Walter White, *A Man Called White: The Autobiography of Walter White* (New York, 1948), pp. 338–39.

30. "Of Men and Books," 3 (March 4, 1944), Transcript of Northwestern University Radio Broadcast, Box 345, Rosenwald Fund Papers; "Lillian Smith Answers Some Questions about *Strange Fruit*," typed manuscript in Box 348, Rosenwald Fund Papers; Smith, "Personal History of 'Strange Fruit,' " p. 10.

31. Bernard De Voto, "The Easy Chair," *Harper's*, 188 (May 1944), 527; Smith to Embree, February 24, 1944, Box 348, Rosenwald Fund Papers.

32. Sam Grafton, "We're Mighty Fond of Our Miss Lill," *Colliers*, 125 (January 28, 1950), 29; Smith to Edwin Embree, February 24, 1944, Box 348, Rosenwald Fund Papers.

33. Lillian Smith and Paula Snelling, "Crossing Over Jordan into Democracy," *South Today*, 7 (Spring 1942), 47–50; Lillian Smith, "Southern Defensive—II," *Common Ground*, 4 (Spring 1944), 43–45.

34. Smith to Johnson, June 12, 1944, Box 348, Rosenwald Fund Papers.

35. Odum to Johnson, June 20 and June 22, 1944, Howard Washington Odum Papers, Southern Historical Collection, University of North Carolina.

36. Williams to Eleanor Roosevelt, February 22, 1944, Eleanor Roosevelt Papers, Franklin D. Roosevelt Library; Waring to Williams, July 21, 1949, Box 39, Aubrey Williams Papers, Franklin D. Roosevelt Library; Dabney to P. L. Prattis, December 4, 1943, Series 7690, Box 5, Dabney Papers.

37. Benjamin E. Mays, *Born to Rebel* (New York, 1971), p. 130.

38. Smith to Members of the Board of the Southern Conference for Human Welfare, May 18, 1945, Box 95, Rosenwald Fund Papers; Lillian Smith, "Pay Day in Georgia," *Nation*, 164 (February 1, 1947), 119 and "The Right to Grow," *Woman's Home Companion*, 70 (October 1946), 25. See also Smith's "Address to White Liberals," *New Republic*, 111 (September 18, 1944), 331–33 and "How to Work for Racial Equality," *New Republic*, 113 (July 2, 1945), 23–24.

39. *Chicago Defender*, November 6, 1948; December 4, 1948; January 22, 1949; February 19, 1949; March 12, 1949; March 19, 1949; April 30, 1949.

40. Ibid., November 20, 1948 and June 15, 1949.

41. Ibid., February 26 and March 5, 1949.

42. In 1963 a revised and enlarged paperback edition of the book appeared that contained a lengthy letter to the publisher written by Miss Smith. See Lillian Smith, *Killers of the Dream*, Anchor Books edition (New York, 1963).

43. Smith, *Killers of the Dream* (1963 ed.), pp. 17–18, 131.
44. Among Lillian Smith's later books, two, *Now is the Time* (New York, 1955) and *Our Faces, Our Words* (New York, 1964), were directly concerned with the racial situation in the South. Both nonfiction works, they once again revealed Miss Smith's symbolic view of segregation and her passionate identification with those committed to breaking down racial barriers. *The Journey* (Cleveland, 1954), a volume of personal reminiscences, was a testimony to the dignity of the human spirit that only tangentially touched upon the race issue. Her only other novel, *One Hour* (New York, 1959), dealt with the themes of sin, guilt, and false accusation in a nonracial setting.

During the 1950s and 1960s Lillian Smith contributed many articles on the civil rights movement to national magazines. These included "No Easy Way Now," *New Republic*, 127 (December 16, 1957), 12–16; "And Suddenly Something Happened," *Saturday Review*, 41 (September 20, 1958), 21; "Ordeal of Southern Women," *Redbook*, 119 (August 1962), 44–45; "Now the Lonely Decision for Right or Wrong," *Life*, 53 (October 12, 1962), 44; "A Strange Kind of Love," *Saturday Review*, 45 (October 20, 1962), 18–20, 94.
45. Smith, "A Strange Kind of Love," p. 20; Pat Watters, *Down to Now: Reflections on the Southern Civil Rights Movement* (New York, 1971), p. 73; George B. Leonard, "Not Black Power, but Human Power: An Interview with Lillian Smith," *Look*, 30 (September 6, 1966), 40, 42–43. See also "Miss Smith on SNCC," *New South*, 21 (Winter 1966), 64–66.

CHAPTER TEN

Conclusion: They, Too, Had a Dream

1. Others in this tradition include Ellis Arnall, *The Shore Dimly Seen* (Philadelphia, 1946); Harry Ashmore, *An Epitaph for Dixie* (New York, 1958); Sarah Patton Boyle, *The Desegrated Heart* (New York, 1962); Erskine Caldwell, *In Search of Bisco* (New York, 1965); Robert Canzoneri, "*I Do So Politely*" (Boston, 1965); Hodding Carter, *Southern Legacy* (Baton Rouge, 1950); W. J. Cash, *The Mind of the South* (New York, 1941); Clarence Cason, *90° in the Shade* (Chapel Hill, 1935); James McBride Dabbs, *The Southern Heritage* (New York, 1958); Jonathan Daniels, *A Southerner Discovers the South* (New York, 1938); P. D. East, *The Magnolia Jungle* (New York, 1960); John Egerton, *The Americanization of Dixie* (New York, 1974); John Temple Graves, *The Fighting South* (New York, 1943); Lily Hammond, *In Black and White* (New York, 1914); Brooks Hays, *A Southern Moderate Speaks* (Chapel Hill, 1959); Stetson Kennedy, *Southern Exposure* (New York, 1946); Katherine Du Pre Lumpkin, *The Making of a Southerner* (New York, 1947); Ralph McGill, *The South and the Southerner* (Boston, 1963); Francis Pickens Miller, *Man from the Valley* (Chapel Hill, 1971); Edwin Mims, *The Advancing South* (Garden City, N.Y., 1926); Willie Morris, *North toward Home* (Boston, 1967); John Rice, *I Came out of the Eighteenth Century* (New York, 1942); James Silver, *Mississippi: The Closed Society* (New York, 1964); Frank Smith, *Congressman from Mississippi* (New York, 1964); Pat Watters, *The South and the Nation* (New York, 1969); Charles Weltner, *South-*

erner (Philadelphia, 1966); Thomas Woofter, *Southern Race Progress* (Washington, 1957).

2. Dabbs, *The Southern Heritage*, pp. 215–16.

3. Boyle, *The Desegregated Heart*, p. 270.

4. John Egerton, *A Mind to Stay Here: Profiles from the South* (New York, 1970), p. 91; Pat Watters, *Down to Now: Reflections on the Southern Civil Rights Movement* (New York, 1971), pp. 412–13; Williams to Black, March 15, 1961, Box 55 and Durr to Black, May 3, 1957, Box 8, Hugo L. Black Papers, Library of Congress; Gerald Johnson, "Why the South Is Different," *New Republic*, 132 (April 25, 1955), 16.

5. Jackie Robinson, *I Never Had It Made* (New York, 1972), p. 212; Benjamin E. Mays, *Born to Rebel* (New York, 1971), p. 299; Andrew Young, "Why I Support Jimmy Carter," *Nation*, 222 (April 3, 1976), 397; "Away from Hate," *Time*, 108 (September 27, 1976), 48.

6. Homer A. Jack, "Lillian Smith of Clayton, Georgia," *Christian Century*, 74 (October 2, 1957), 1166–67.

7. Jimmy Carter, *Why Not the Best?* (New York, 1976—paperback edition), pp. 40, 72–78, 124–25; *Washington Post*, July 5, 1976.

8. Lillian Smith, "Mind and Soul of the South," *Look*, 29 (November 16, 1965), 142.

9. Carter, *Why Not the Best?*, p. 124.

BIBLIOGRAPHY

Like most students of recent American history, I found that an abundance rather than a lack of material presents the greatest problem to the researcher. It has proven quite impossible to visit every pertinent manuscript collection, contact all surviving participants, or read every appropriate book and article. What follows, then, is by necessity an incomplete list of the sources dealing with Southern liberalism. Nevertheless, it is representative of the kinds of materials that are available and upon which I have relied most heavily.

The best general bibliography for the South during this period is the one in George B. Tindall, *The Emergence of the New South 1913–1945* (Baton Rouge: Louisiana State University Press, 1967). It is a model of organization, thoroughness, and general helpfulness.

There are excellent published bibliographies of the extensive writings of Lillian Smith and Howard Odum, and, consequently, no attempt is made here to cite all of their works that were used in this study. These are in Louise Blackwell and Frances Clay, *Lillian Smith*, Twayne's United States Authors Series (New York: Twayne Publishers, 1971) and in Rupert B. Vance and Katherine Jocher, "Howard W. Odum," *Social Forces*, 33 (March 1955), 203–17. The Odum bibliography was reprinted in *Folk, Region, and Society: Selected Papers of Howard W. Odum*, edited by Katherine Jocher, et al. (Chapel Hill: University of North Carolina Press, 1964).

MANUSCRIPT COLLECTIONS

Alderman Library, University of Virginia, Charlottesville
Virginius Dabney Papers
James Hardy Dillard Papers
Amistad Research Center, Dillard University, New Orleans
Charles S. Johnson Papers
Julius Rosenwald Fund Papers
Franklin D. Roosevelt Library, Hyde Park
Lowell Mellett Papers
Franklin D. Roosevelt Papers
Eleanor Roosevelt Papers
Charles Taussig Papers
Aubrey Williams Papers

Howard-Tilton Memorial Library, Tulane University, New Orleans
George Washington Cable Papers
Library of Congress
Hugo L. Black Papers
Tom Connally Papers
Josephus Daniels Papers
George Fort Milton Papers
National Association for the Advancement of Colored People Papers
Arthur F. Raper Papers, Custody of Mr. Raper, Oakton, Virginia
Southern Historical Collection, University of North Carolina, Chapel Hill
Jessie Daniel Ames Papers
Jonathan Daniels Papers
Fellowship of Southern Churchmen Papers
Frank Porter Graham Papers (Personal and Presidential)
Guy B. Johnson Papers
Frank McCallister Papers
Samuel Chiles Mitchell Papers
Howard Washington Odum Papers
Southern Tenant Farmers Union Papers
State Historical Society of Wisconsin, Madison
Carl and Anne Braden Papers

PERSONAL INTERVIEWS

W. T. Couch, May 4, 1971.
Virginius Dabney, May 2, 1971.
Frank P. Graham, May 22, 1971.
Mrs. George S. Mitchell, April 20, 1971.
H. L. Mitchell, May 19 and 25, 1971.
Arthur F. Raper, April 23, 1971.

COLUMBIA ORAL HISTORY COLLECTION

Will W. Alexander
H. L. Mitchell
J. Waties Waring

OTHER UNPUBLISHED MATERIAL

Allred, William C., Jr. "The Southern Regional Council, 1943–1961." M.A. thesis, Emory University, 1966.

Belles, A. Gilbert. "The Julius Rosenwald Fund: Efforts in Race Relations 1928–1948." Ph.D. dissertation, Vanderbilt University, 1972.

Burns, Augustus M. "North Carolina and the Negro Dilemma 1930–1950." Ph. D. dissertation, University of North Carolina, 1969.

Burrows, Edward F. "The Commission on Interracial Cooperation, 1919–1944: A Case Study in the History of the Interracial Movement in the South." Ph.D. dissertation, University of Wisconsin, 1955.

Clayton, Bruce Lynn. "Southern Critics of the New South, 1890–1914." Ph.D. dissertation, Duke University, 1966.
Crites, Laura Hardy. "A History of the Association of Southern Women for the Prevention of Lynching." M.A. thesis, American University, 1965.
Douty, Kenneth. "The Southern Conference for Human Welfare: A Report." Frank McCallister Papers.
Hall, Jacquelyn Dowd. "Revolt against Chivalry: Jessie Daniel Ames and the Women's Campaign against Lynching." Paper delivered at the 1974 annual convention of the Southern Historical Association.
Holmes, Michael S. "The New Deal in Georgia: An Administrative History." Ph.D. dissertation, University of Wisconsin, 1969.
Houser, Henry Paul. "The Southern Regional Council." M.A. thesis, University of North Carolina, 1950.
Jennings, Carolyn. "A Bio-Bibliography of Lillian Eugenia Smith (1897–1966)." M.A. thesis, Catholic University, 1968.
Juhnke, William Ernest, Jr. "Creating a New Charter of Freedom: The Organization and Operation of the President's Committee on Civil Rights, 1946–1948." Ph.D. dissertation, University of Kansas, 1974.
Kester, Howard. Autobiography. Southern Tenant Farmers Union Papers.
Kifer, Allen F. "The Negro under the New Deal, 1933–1941." Ph.D. dissertation, University of Wisconsin, 1961.
Kinsella, Dorothy C. "Southern Apologists: A Liberal Image." Ph.D. dissertation, St. Louis University, 1971.
Klibaner, Irwin. "The Southern Conference Educational Fund: A History." Ph.D. dissertation, University of Wisconsin, 1971.
Mitchell, Samuel Chiles. Autobiography. Samuel Chiles Mitchell Papers.
Rawick, George P. "The New Deal and Youth: The Civilian Conservation Corps, the National Youth Administration and the American Youth Congress." Ph.D. dissertation, University of Wisconsin, 1957.
Sitkoff, Harvard. "The Emergence of Civil Rights as a National Issue: The New Deal Era." Ph.D. dissertation, Columbia University, 1975.
Williams, Aubrey. "A Southern Rebel." Aubrey Williams Papers, 1958.

FILMS AND RECORDINGS

The Face of the South. Board of Christian Education of the American Presbyterian Church in Cooperation with the Southern Regional Council. Directed by Frank Willard and Narrated by George S. Mitchell, c. 1958.
Lillian Smith Reads Strange Fruit. New York: Spoken Arts Recording 964, 1966.

Lillian Smith Reads Our Faces, Our Words. New York: Spoken Arts Recording 916, 1966.

NEWSPAPERS AND PERIODICALS

Atlanta Constitution
Atlantic Monthly
Chicago Defender
Common Ground
Crisis
Harper's
Journal of Politics
Journal of Social Forces (Social Forces)
Nation
New Republic
New York Times
Pittsburgh Courier
Pseudopodia (North Georgia Review and *South Today)*
Richmond Times-Dispatch
Saturday Review of Literature (Saturday Review)
South Atlantic Quarterly
Southern Frontier (New South)
Southern Patriot
Virginia Quarterly Review

GOVERNMENTAL AND ORGANIZATIONAL PUBLICATIONS

Hammond, Lily H. *Southern Women and Racial Adjustment.* Occasional Papers, no. 19. Lynchburg, Va.: John F. Slater Fund, 1915.

Hearings on H.R. 29: An Act Making Unlawful the Requirement for the Payment of a Poll Tax as a Prerequisite to Voting in a Primary or Other Election for National Offices. Washington: Senate Rules and Administration Committee, 1948.

Hearings on the Nomination of Aubrey W. Williams to Be Administrator, Rural Electrification Administration. Washington: Senate Agriculture and Forestry Committee, 1945.

Hearings on S. 1280: A Bill Concerning the Qualifications of Voters or Electors . . . Making Unlawful the Requirement for the Payment of a Poll Tax as a Prerequisite to Voting in a Primary or General Election for National Office. Washington: Senate Judiciary Committee, 1942.

It Seems Queer . . . : The Southern Veteran Speaks. Atlanta: Southern Regional Council, 1945.

McCulloch, James E., ed. *The Call of the New South.* Nashville: Southern Sociological Congress, 1912.

—— ed. *The South Mobilizing for Social Service.* Nashville: Southern Sociological Congress, 1913.

Public Papers of the Presidents: Harry S. Truman, 1947. Washington, 1963.
Report of the Proceedings of the Southern Conference for Human Welfare. Birmingham: Southern Conference for Human Welfare, 1938.
Report on the Economic Conditions of the South. Washington: National Emergency Council, 1938.
Rosenman, Samuel I., ed. *The Public Papers and Addresses of Franklin D. Roosevelt, 1938*. New York: Macmillan, 1941.
A Statement from Governor Hugh M. Dorsey as to the Negro in Georgia. Atlanta, 1921.
To Secure These Rights: The Report of the President's Committee on Civil Rights. New York: Simon and Schuster, 1947.
Vance, Rupert B. *Wanted: The South's Future for the Nation*. Atlanta: Southern Regional Council, 1946.
Winton, Rev. G. B. *Sketch of Bishop Atticus G. Haygood*. Occasional Papers, no. 16. Lynchburg, Va.: John F. Slater Fund, 1915.

BOOKS

Abshire, David M. *The South Rejects a Prophet: The Life of Senator D. M. Key*. New York: F. A. Praeger, 1967.
Agar, Herbert. *A Time for Greatness*. Boston: Little Brown, 1942.
Agee, James, and Walker Evans. *Let Us Now Praise Famous Men*. Boston: Houghton Mifflin, 1941.
Arnall, Ellis Gibbs. *The Shore Dimly Seen*. Philadelphia: J. B. Lippincott, 1946.
—— *What the People Want*. Philadelphia: J. B. Lippincott, 1948.
Ashmore, Harry S. *An Epitaph for Dixie*. New York: W. W. Norton, 1958.
Auerbach, Jerold S. *Labor and Liberty: The La Follette Committee and the New Deal*. Indianapolis: Bobbs Merrill, 1966.
Bailey, Hugh C. *Edgar Gardner Murphy: Gentle Progressive*. Coral Gables: University of Miami Press, 1968.
—— *Liberalism in the New South: Social Reformers and the Progressive Movement*. Coral Gables: University of Miami Press, 1969.
Bailey, Kenneth K. *Southern White Protestantism in the Twentieth Century*. New York: Harper and Row, 1964.
Bailey, Thomas Pearce. *Race Orthodoxy in the South and Other Aspects of the Negro Question*. New York: Neale Publishing Co., 1914.
Baker, Paul E. *Negro-White Adjustment: An Investigation and Analysis of Methods in the Interracial Movement in the United States*. Pittsfield, Mass.: Sun Printing Co., 1934.

Baldwin, Sidney. *Poverty and Politics: The Rise and Decline of the Farm Security Administration.* Chapel Hill: University of North Carolina Press, 1968.

Bartley, Numan V. *The Rise of Massive Resistance: Race and Politics in the South During the 1950's.* Baton Rouge: Louisiana State University Press, 1969.

Bartley, Numan V., and Hugh D. Graham. *Southern Politics and the Second Reconstruction.* Baltimore: Johns Hopkins University Press, 1975.

Berman, William C. *The Politics of Civil Rights in the Truman Administration.* Columbus: Ohio State University Press, 1970.

Bernstein, Barton J. *Politics and Policies of The Truman Administration.* Chicago: Quadrangle Books, 1970.

Bernstein, Barton J., and Allen J. Matusow, eds. *Twentieth Century America: Recent Interpretations.* New York: Harcourt Brace Jovanovich, 1972.

Blackwell, Louise, and Frances Clay. *Lillian Smith.* United States Authors series. New York: Twayne Publishers, 1971.

Blair, Lewis H. *The Prosperity of the South Dependent upon the Elevation of the Negro.* Richmond, 1889.

Boyle, Sarah Patton. *The Desegregated Heart: A Virginian's Stand in Time of Transition.* New York: William Morrow, 1962.

Braden, Anne. *The Wall Between.* New York: Monthly Review Press, 1958.

Brown, William Garrott. *The Lower South in American History.* New York: Macmillan, 1903.

Butcher, C. Philip. *George W. Cable.* United States Authors series. New York: Twayne Publishers, 1962.

—— *George W. Cable: The Northampton Years.* New York: Columbia University Press, 1959.

Cable, George Washington. *The Silent South.* New York: Charles Scribner's Sons, 1889.

Caldwell, Erskine. *In Search of Bisco.* New York: Farrar, Straus and Giroux, 1965.

Caldwell, Erskine, and Margaret Bourke-White. *You Have Seen Their Faces.* New York: Modern Age Books, 1937.

Canzoneri, Robert. *"I Do So Politely": A Voice from the South.* Boston: Houghton Mifflin, 1965.

Carter, Dan T. *Scottsboro: A Tragedy of the American South.* Baton Rouge: Louisiana State University Press, 1969.

Carter, Hodding. *Southern Legacy.* Baton Rouge: Louisiana State University Press, 1950.

—— *The Winds of Fear.* New York: Farrar and Rinehart, 1944.

Carter, Jimmy. *Why Not the Best?* New York: Bantam Books, 1976.

Cash, W. J. *The Mind of the South.* New York: Alfred A. Knopf, 1941.

Cason, Clarence. *90° in the Shade.* Chapel Hill: University of North Carolina Press, 1935.

Cayton, Horace R., and George S. Mitchell. *Black Workers and the New Unions.* Chapel Hill: University of North Carolina Press, 1939.

Clayton, Bruce, *The Savage Ideal: Intolerance and Intellectual Leadership in the South, 1890–1914.* Baltimore: Johns Hopkins University Press, 1972.

Coles, Robert. *Farewell to the South.* Boston: Atlantic–Little Brown, 1972.

Conrad, David. *The Forgotten Farmers: The Story of the Sharecroppers in the New Deal.* Urbana: University of Illinois Press, 1965.

Couch, W. T., ed. *Culture in the South.* Chapel Hill: University of North Carolina Press, 1934.

—— ed. *These Are Our Lives: As Told by the People and Written by Members of the Federal Writers Project of the Works Progress Administration in North Carolina, Tennessee, and Georgia.* Chapel Hill: University of North Carolina Press, 1939.

Dabbs, James McBride. *Haunted by God: The Cultural and Religious Experience of the South.* Richmond: John Knox Press, 1972.

—— *The Southern Heritage.* New York: Alfred A. Knopf, 1958.

—— *Who Speaks for the South?* New York: Funk and Wagnalls, 1964.

Dabney, Virginius. *Below the Potomac: A Book about the New South.* New York: D. Appleton Century, 1942.

—— *Dry Messiah: The Life of Bishop Cannon.* New York: Alfred A. Knopf, 1949.

—— *Liberalism in the South.* Chapel Hill: University of North Carolina Press, 1932.

—— *Virginia: The New Dominion.* Garden City, N.Y.: Doubleday, 1971.

Dalfiume, Richard M. *Fighting on Two Fronts: Desegregation of the Armed Forces, 1939–1953.* Columbia: University of Missouri Press, 1969.

Daniel, Pete. *The Shadow of Slavery: Peonage in the South.* Urbana: University of Illinois Press, 1972.

Daniels, Jonathan. *A Southerner Discovers the South.* New York: Macmillan, 1938.

—— *Tar Heels: A Portrait of North Carolina.* New York: Dodd Meade, 1941.

—— *White House Witness 1942–1945.* Garden City, N.Y.: Doubleday, 1975.

Degler, Carl N. *The Other South: Southern Dissenters in the Nineteenth Century*. New York: Harper and Row, 1974.

Dombrowski, James A. *The Early Days of Christian Socialism in America*. New York: Columbia University Press, 1936.

Dykeman, Wilma. *Prophet of Plenty: The First Ninety Years of W. D. Weatherford*. Knoxville: University of Tennessee Press, 1966.

Dykeman, Wilma, and James Stokley. *Seeds of Southern Change: The Life of Will Alexander*. Chicago: University of Chicago Press, 1962.

East, P. D. *The Magnolia Jungle: The Life, Times and Education of a Southern Editor*. New York: Simon and Schuster, 1960.

Egerton, John. *The Americanization of Dixie: The Southernization of America*. New York: Harper's Magazine Press, 1974.

—— *A Mind to Stay Here: Profiles from the South*. New York: Macmillan, 1970.

Ely, James W., Jr. *The Crisis of Conservative Virginia: The Byrd Organization and the Politics of Massive Resistance*. Knoxville: University of Tennessee Press, 1976.

Embree, Edwin R. *Brown America: The Story of a New Race*. New York: Viking Press, 1931.

Embree, Edwin R., and Julia Waxman. *Investment in People: The Story of the Julius Rosenwald Fund*. New York, 1949.

Fredrickson, George M. *The Black Image in the White Mind: The Debate on Afro-American Character and Destiny, 1817–1914*. New York: Harper and Row, 1971.

Freidel, Frank. *F.D.R. and the South*. Baton Rouge: Louisiana State University Press, 1965.

Friedman, Lawrence J. *The White Savage: Racial Fantasies in the Postbellum South*. Englewood Cliffs, N. J.: Prentice-Hall, 1970.

Gaston, Paul M. *The New South Creed: A Study in Southern Mythmaking*. New York: Alfred A. Knopf, 1970.

Ginger, Ray. *Six Days or Forever? Tennessee v. John Thomas Scopes*. 1958. Reprint, Chicago: Quadrangle Books, 1969.

Goodwyn, Lawrence. *Democratic Promise: The Populist Moment in America*. New York: Oxford University Press, 1976.

Grantham, Dewey W., Jr., ed. *The South and the Sectional Image: The Sectional Theme Since Reconstruction*. New York: Harper and Row, 1968.

Graves, John Temple. *The Fighting South*. New York: G. P. Putnam's Sons, 1943.

Green, A. Wigfall. *The Man Bilbo*. Baton Rouge: Louisiana State University Press, 1963.

Grubbs, Donald H. *Cry from the Cotton: The Southern Tenant Farmers Union and the New Deal.* Chapel Hill: University of North Carolina Press, 1971.

Gunther, John. *Inside U.S.A.* New York: Harper Brothers, 1947.

Hackney, Sheldon. *Populism to Progressivism in Alabama.* Princeton: Princeton University Press, 1969.

Hamby, Alonzo L. *Beyond the New Deal: Harry S. Truman and American Liberalism.* New York: Columbia University Press, 1973.

Hamilton, William B., ed. *Fifty Years of the South Atlantic Quarterly.* Durham: Duke University Press, 1952.

Hammond, Lily H. *In Black and White: An Interpretation of Southern Life.* New York: Fleming H. Revell, 1914.

Harlan, Louis R. *Separate and Unequal: Public School Campaigns and Racism in the Southern Seaboard States, 1901–1915.* Chapel Hill: University of North Carolina Press, 1958.

Havard, William C., ed. *The Changing Politics of the South.* Baton Rouge: Louisiana State University Press, 1972.

Haygood, Atticus G. *Our Brother in Black: His Freedom and His Future.* Nashville: Southern Methodist Publishing House, 1881.

Hays, Brooks. *A Southern Moderate Speaks.* Chapel Hill: University of North Carolina Press, 1959.

Henderson, Richard B. *Maury Maverick: A Political Biography.* Austin: University of Texas Press, 1970.

Holmes, Michael. *The New Deal in Georgia: An Administrative History.* Westport, Conn.: Greenwood Press, 1975.

Holmes, William F. *The White Chief: James Kimble Vardaman.* Baton Rouge: Louisiana State University Press, 1970.

Holt, Rackham. *Mary McLeod Bethune: A Biography.* Garden City, N. Y.: Doubleday, 1964.

Hurley, F. Jack. *Portrait of a Decade: Roy Stryker and the Development of Documentary Photography in the Thirties.* Baton Rouge: Louisiana State University Press, 1972.

Johnson, Charles S., et al. *To Stem This Tide: A Survey of Racial Tension Areas in the United States.* Boston: The Pilgrim Press, 1943.

Johnson, Charles S., Edwin R. Embree, and Will W. Alexander. *The Collapse of Cotton Tenancy: Summary of Field Studies and Statistical Surveys, 1933–1935.* Chapel Hill: University of North Carolina Press, 1935.

Johnson, Gerald J. *The Wasted Land.* Chapel Hill: University of North Carolina Press, 1937.

Kellogg, Charles Flint. *NAACP: A History of the National Association for the Advancement of Colored People*, vol. I, *1909–1920*. Baltimore: Johns Hopkins University Press, 1967.

Kendrick, Benjamin B., and Alex M. Arnett. *The South Looks at Its Past*. Chapel Hill: University of North Carolina Press, 1935.

Kennedy, Stetson. *Southern Exposure*. New York: Doubleday, 1946.

Kester, Howard. *Revolt among the Sharecroppers*. New York: Arno Press, 1969.

Key, V. O., Jr. *Southern Politics in State and Nation*. New York: Alfred A. Knopf, 1949.

Killian, Lewis M. *White Southerners*. New York: Random House, 1970.

Kirby, Jack Temple. *Darkness at the Dawning: Race and Reform in the Progressive South*. Philadelphia: J. B. Lippincott, 1972.

Krueger, Thomas A. *And Promises to Keep: The Southern Conference for Human Welfare, 1938–1948*. Nashville: Vanderbilt University Press, 1968.

Lash, Joseph P. *Eleanor and Franklin: The Story of Their Relationship, Based on Eleanor Roosevelt's Private Papers*. New York: W. W. Norton, 1971.

Lawson, Stephen F. *Black Ballots: Voting Rights in the South*. New York: Columbia University Press, 1976.

Logan, Rayford, ed. *What the Negro Wants*. Chapel Hill: University of North Carolina Press, 1945.

Lumpkin, Katherine Du Pre. *The Making of a Southerner*. New York: Alfred A. Knopf, 1947.

—— *The South in Progress*. New York: International Publishers, 1940.

McGill, Ralph. *The South and the Southerner*. Boston: Little, Brown, 1963.

McLaurin, Melton Alonza. *Paternalism and Protest: Southern Cotton Mill Workers and Organized Labor, 1875–1905*. Westport, Conn.: Greenwood, 1971.

Mann, Harold W. *Atticus Greene Haygood: Methodist Bishop, Editor, and Educator*. Athens: University of Georgia Press, 1965.

Martin, Charles H. *The Angelo Herndon Case and Southern Justice*. Baton Rouge: Louisiana State University Press, 1976.

Martin, Harold. *Ralph McGill, Reporter*. Boston: Little Brown, 1973.

Mays, Benjamin E. *Born to Rebel*. New York: Charles Scribner's Sons, 1971.

Mecklin, John M. *Democracy and Race Friction: A Study in Social Ethics*. New York: Macmillan, 1921.

—— *My Quest for Freedom*. New York: Charles Scribner's Sons, 1945.

Meier, August, and Elliott Rudwick. *CORE: A Study in the Civil Rights Movement, 1942–1968*. New York: Oxford University Press, 1973.

Michie, Allan A., and Frank Ryhlick. *Dixie Demagogues.* New York: Vanguard Press, 1939.
Miller, Francis Pickens. *Man from the Valley: Memoirs of a 20th Century Virginian.* Chapel Hill: University of North Carolina Press, 1971.
Mims, Edwin. *The Advancing South: Stories of Progress and Reaction.* Garden City, N. Y.: Doubleday, Page and Co., 1926.
Morris, Willie. *North toward Home.* Boston: Houghton Mifflin, 1967.
Morrison, Joseph L. *W. J. Cash: Southern Prophet.* New York: Alfred A. Knopf, 1967.
Murray, Albert. *South to a Very Old Place.* New York: McGraw-Hill, 1971.
Muse, Benjamin. *Virginia's Massive Resistance.* Bloomington: Indiana University Press, 1961.
Myrdal, Gunnar. *An American Dilemma: The Negro Problem and Modern Democracy.* 2 vols. New York: Harper Brothers, 1944.
Newby, I. A. *Jim Crow's Defense: Anti-Negro Thought in America, 1900–1930.* Baton Rouge: Louisiana State University Press, 1965.
Nixon, H. Clarence. *Forty Acres and Steel Mules.* Chapel Hill: University of North Carolina Press, 1938.
Odum, Howard W. *An American Epoch: Southern Portraiture in the National Picture.* New York: Henry H. Holt, 1930.
—— *Folk, Region and Society: Selected Papers of Howard W. Odum.* Edited by Katherine Jocher, et al. Chapel Hill: University of North Carolina Press, 1964.
—— *Race and Rumors of Race: Challenge to American Crisis.* Chapel Hill, University of North Carolina Press, 1943.
—— *Rainbow Round My Shoulder: The Blue Trail of Black Ulysses.* Indianapolis: Bobbs-Merrill, 1928.
—— *Social and Mental Traits of the Negro: Research into the Conditions of the Negro Race in Southern Towns, A Study in Race Traits, Tendencies and Prospects.* Columbia University Studies in History, Economics, and Public Law, vol. 37, no. 3. New York: Longmans, Green and Co., 1910.
—— ed. *Southern Pioneers in Social Interpretation.* Chapel Hill: University of North Carolina Press, 1925.
—— *Southern Regions of the United States.* Chapel Hill: University of North Carolina Press, 1936.
—— *The Way of the South: Toward the Regional Balance of America.* New York: Macmillan, 1947.
Osofsky, Gilbert, ed. *The Burden of Race: A Documentary History of Negro-White Relations in America.* New York: Harper and Row, 1967.
Percy, William Alexander. *Lanterns on the Levee: Recollections of a Planter's Son.* New York: Alfred A. Knopf, 1941.

Perry, Jennings. *Democracy Begins at Home: The Tennessee Fight on the Poll Tax.* Philadelphia: J. B. Lippincott, 1944.

Polenberg, Richard. *War and Society: The United States, 1941–1945.* Philadelphia: J. B. Lippincott, 1972.

Pope, Liston. *Millhands and Preachers: A Study of Gastonia.* New Haven: Yale University Press, 1942.

Potter, David M. *The South and the Sectional Conflict.* Baton Rouge: Louisiana State University Press, 1968.

Raper, Arthur, F. *Preface to Peasantry.* Chapel Hill: University of North Carolina Press, 1936.

—— *The Tragedy of Lynching.* Chapel Hill: University of North Carolina Press, 1933.

Rice, John A. *I Came Out of the Eighteenth Century.* New York: Harper Brothers, 1942.

Robinson, Jackie. *I Never Had It Made.* New York: Putnam, 1972.

Roland, Charles P. *The Improbable Era: The South since World War II.* Lexington: University Press of Kentucky, 1975.

Roosevelt, Eleanor. *This I Remember.* New York: Harper Brothers, 1949.

Rosengarten, Theodore, ed. *All God's Dangers: The Life of Nate Shaw.* New York: Alfred A. Knopf, 1974.

Rubin, Louis D. *George W. Cable: The Life and Times of a Southern Heretic.* New York: Pegasus, 1969.

Rubin, Louis D., and James Kilpatrick. *The Lasting South: Fourteen Southerners Look at Their Home.* Chicago: Henry Regnery, 1957.

Savage, Henry J. *Seeds of Time: The Background of Southern Thinking.* New York: Henry H. Holt, 1959.

Scott, Anne Firor. *The Southern Lady: From Pedestal to Politics, 1830–1930.* Chicago: University of Chicago Press, 1970.

Seligman, Lester G., and Elmer E. Cornwell, Jr., eds. *New Deal Mosaic: Roosevelt Confers with His National Emergency Council 1933–1936.* Eugene: University of Oregon Press, 1965.

Sellers, Charles G., ed. *The Southerner as American.* Chapel Hill: University of North Carolina Press, 1960.

Sherrill, Robert. *Gothic Politics in the Deep South: Stars of the New Confederacy.* New York: Grossman, 1968.

Shriver, Donald W., Jr., ed. *The Unsilent South: Prophetic Preaching in Racial Crisis.* Richmond: John Knox Press, 1965.

Silver, James W. *Mississippi: The Closed Society.* New York: Harcourt, Brace and World, 1964.

Skaggs, William H. *The Southern Oligarchy: An Appeal in Behalf of the*

Silent Masses of Our Country against the Despotic Rule of the Few. New York: Devin-Adair, 1924.

Smedes, Susan Dabney. *Memorials of a Southern Planter.* Edited by Fletcher M. Green. New York: Alfred A. Knopf, 1965.

Smith, Frank E. *Congressman from Mississippi.* New York: Pantheon Books, 1964.

—— *Look Away from Dixie.* Baton Rouge: Louisiana State University Press, 1965.

Smith, Lillian. *The Journey.* Cleveland: World Publishing Co., 1954.

—— *Killers of the Dream.* New York: W. W. Norton, 1949.

—— *Memory of a Large Christmas.* New York: W. W. Norton, 1961.

—— *Now is the Time.* New York: Viking Press, 1955.

—— *One Hour.* New York: Harcourt, Brace and Company, 1959.

—— *Our Faces, Our Words.* New York: W. W. Norton, 1964.

—— *Strange Fruit.* New York: Reynal and Hitchcock, 1944.

Spero, Sterling D., and Abram L. Harris. *The Black Worker: The Negro and the Labor Movement.* New York: Columbia University Press, 1931.

Sternsher, Bernard, ed. *The Negro in Depression and War: Prelude to Revolution, 1930–1945.* Chicago: Quadrangle Books, 1969.

Tannenbaum, Frank. *Darker Phases of the South.* New York: G. P. Putnam's Sons, 1924.

Tindall, George B. *The Emergence of the New South 1913–1945.* Baton Rouge: Louisiana State University Press, 1967.

Turner, Arlin. *George W. Cable: A Biography.* Baton Rouge: Louisiana State University Press, 1966.

—— ed. *The Negro Question: A Selection of Writings on Civil Rights in the South by George W. Cable.* New York: Doubleday, 1958.

Twelve Southerners. *I'll Take My Stand: The South and the Agrarian Tradition.* New York: Harper Brothers, 1930.

Vance, Rupert B. *Human Geography of the South: A Study in Regional Resources and Human Adequacy.* Chapel Hill: University of North Carolina Press, 1932.

Watters, Pat. *Down to Now: Reflections on the Southern Civil Rights Movement.* New York: Pantheon Books, 1971.

—— *The South and the Nation.* New York: Pantheon Books, 1969.

Weatherford, W. D. *Negro Life in the South: Present Conditions and Needs.* New York: Young Men's Christian Association Press, 1910.

—— *Present Forces in Negro Progress.* New York: Association Press, 1912.

Weltner, Charles Longstreet. *Southerner.* Philadelphia: J. B. Lippincott, 1966.

White, Helen, and Redding S. Sugg, Jr., eds. *From the Mountain: An Anthology of the Magazine Successively Titled Pseudopodia, the North Georgia Review, and South Today.* Memphis: Memphis State University Press, 1972.
White, Walter. *A Man Called White: The Autobiography of Walter White.* New York: Viking Press, 1948.
Williams, Aubrey W. *Work, Wages, and Education.* Cambridge, Mass.: Harvard University Press, 1940.
Williams, T. Harry. *Huey Long.* New York: Alfred A. Knopf, 1969.
Wolters, Raymond. *Negroes and the Great Depression: The Problem of Economic Recovery.* Westport, Conn.: Greenwood, 1970.
Woodward, C. Vann. *American Counterpoint: Slavery and Racism in the North-South Dialogue.* Boston: Little Brown, 1971.
—— *The Burden of Southern History.* Rev. ed. New York: Mentor Books, 1968.
—— *The Origins of the New South 1877–1913.* Baton Rouge: Louisiana State University Press, 1951.
—— *The Strange Career of Jim Crow.* 2d ed., rev. New York: Oxford University Press, 1966.
—— *Tom Watson: Agrarian Rebel.* New York: Macmillan, 1938.
Woofter, Thomas J. *The Basis of Racial Adjustment.* Boston: Ginn and Co., 1925.
—— *Southern Race Progress: The Wavering Color Line.* Washington: Public Affairs Press, 1957.
Wright, Richard. *12 Million Black Voices: A Folk History of the Negro in the United States.* New York: Viking Press, 1941.
Wynes, Charles E., ed. *Forgotten Voices: Dissenting Southerners in an Age of Conformity.* Baton Rouge: Louisiana State University Press, 1967.
Zinn, Howard. *The Southern Mystique.* New York: Alfred A. Knopf, 1964.

ARTICLES

Ader, Emile B. "Why the Dixiecrats Failed." *Journal of Politics*, 15 (August 1953), 356–69.
Alexander, Will W. "Better Race Relations." *Southern Workman*, 51 (August 1922), 362–64.
—— "Our Conflicting Racial Policies." *Harper's*, 190 (January 1945), 172–79.
—— "Southern White Schools Study Race Questions." *Journal of Negro Education*, 2 (April 1933), 139–46.

—— "A Usable Piece of Community Machinery." *Journal of Social Forces*, 1 (November 1922), 41–42.

Allen, Ivan, Jr. "Growing Up Liberal in Atlanta." *New York Times Magazine*, December 27, 1970, pp. 4 ff.

Ames, Jessie Daniel. "Reminiscences of Jessie Daniel Ames: 'I Really Do Like a Good Fight'." *New South*, 27 (Spring 1972), 31–41.

Arnall, Ellis G. "Revolution Down South." *Colliers*, 166 (July 28, 1945), 17 ff.

Basler, Roy P. "As One Southerner to Another: Concerning Lincoln and the Declaration of Independence." *South Atlantic Quarterly*, 42 (January 1943), 45–53.

Bassett, John Spencer. "The Reign of Passion." *South Atlantic Quarterly*, 1 (October 1902), 301–9.

—— "Stirring Up the Fires of Race Antipathy." *South Atlantic Quarterly*, 2 (October 1903), 297–305.

"Behind Birmingham." *Christian Century*, 43 (May 27, 1926), 672–73.

Bernstein, Victor. "How *damnyankees* Foster Race Hate in the South." *New York PM*, September 9, 1942.

Billington, Monroe. "Civil Rights, President Truman and the South." *Journal of Negro History*, 58 (April 1973), 127–39.

Boyd, Thomas. "Defying the Klan." *Forum*, 67 (July 1926), 48–56.

Brough, Charles H. "Work of the Commission of Southern Universities on the Race Question." *Annals of the American Academy of Political and Social Science*, 49 (September 1913), 47–57.

Brooks, Robert P. "Georgia Goes Marching On." *Forum*, 76 (November 1926), 748–55.

—— "A Southern Professor on Lynching." *Nation*, 103 (October 5, 1916), 321–22.

Brown, William O. "Interracial Cooperation: Some of Its Problems." *Opportunity*, 11 (September 1933), 272–73 ff.

Burt, Struthers. "The Making of a New South." *Saturday Review of Literature*, 27 (March 11, 1944), 10.

Butcher, C. Philip. "George W. Cable and Booker T. Washington." *Journal of Negro Education*, 17 (Fall 1948), 462–68.

—— "George W. Cable and George W. Williams: An Abortive Collaboration." *Journal of Negro History*, 53 (October 1968), 334–44.

Carleton, William G. "The Conservative South—A Political Myth." *Virginia Quarterly Review*, 22 (Spring 1946), 179–92.

—— "The Southern Politician—1900 and 1950." *Journal of Politics*, 13 (May 1951), 215–31.

Carter, Hodding. "New Rebel Yell in Dixie." *Colliers*, 124 (July 9, 1949), 13–15 ff.

Chamberlain, John. "Arnall of Georgia." *Life*, 19 (August 6, 1945), 68–76.

Chatfield, E. Charles. "The Southern Sociological Congress: Organization of Uplift." *Tennessee Historical Quarterly*, 19 (December 1960), 328–47.

—— "The Southern Sociological Congress: Rationale of Uplift." *Tennessee Historical Quarterly*, 20 (March 1961), 51–64.

Clark, Thomas D. "The Country Newspaper: A Factor in Southern Opinion, 1865–1930." *Journal of Southern History*, 14 (February 1948), 3–33.

Clayton, Bruce L. "An Intellectual on Politics: William Garrott Brown and the Ideal of a Two-Party South." *North Carolina Historical Review*, 42 (Summer 1965), 319–34.

Cohn, David L. "How the South Feels." *Atlantic Monthly*, 173 (January 1944), 47–51.

"Collegiate Move on Lynching." *Literary Digest*, 52 (January 22, 1916), 178.

Couch, W. T. "Southerners Inspect the South." *New Republic*, 97 (December 14, 1938), 168–69.

—— "A University Press in the South." *Southwest Review*, 19 (Winter 1934), 196–204.

Crowe, Charles. "Tom Watson, Populists, and Blacks Reconsidered." *Journal of Negro History*, 55 (April 1970), 99–116.

Dabney, Virginius. "Dixie Rejects Lynching." *Nation*, 145 (November 27, 1937), 579–80.

—— "The Dynamic New South." *New York Times Magazine*, October 17, 1943, pp. 17 ff.

—— "A Frank Talk to North and South about Integration." *U.S. News & World Report*, 42 (March 15, 1957), 112–14 ff.

—— "The Good Southern Universities." *Harper's*, 230 (March 1965), 86–88 ff.

—— "If the South Had Won the War." *American Mercury*, 39 (October 1936), 199–205.

—— "Is the South That Bad?" *Saturday Review of Literature*, 29 (April 13, 1946), 9–10 ff.

—— "Nearer and Nearer the Precipice." *Atlantic Monthly*, 171 (January 1943), 94–100.

—— "Next in the South's Schools: 'Limited Integration.' " *U. S. News & World Report*, 48 (January 18, 1960), 92–94.

—— "The Pace Is Important." *Virginia Quarterly Review*, 41 (Spring 1965), 176–91.

—— "Race Relations Now Definitely Worse." *U. S. News & World Report*, 40 (February 24, 1956), 144.

—— "Richmond's Quiet Revolution." *Saturday Review*, 47 (February 29, 1964), 18–19 ff.

—— "School Crisis in Dixie!" *American Magazine*, 162 (August 1956), 26–30 ff.

—— "Shall the South's Poll Tax Go?" *New York Times Magazine*, February 12, 1939, pp. 9 ff.

—— "The South Marches On." *Survey Graphic*, 32 (November 1943), 441–43 ff.

—— "Southern Crisis: The Segregation Decision." *Saturday Evening Post*, 225 (November 8, 1952), 40–41 ff.

—— "Virginia's 'Peaceable, Honorable Stand.' " *Life*, 45 (September 22, 1958), 51–52 ff.

—— "What the GOP is Doing in the South." *Harper's*, 226 (May 1963), 86–88 ff.

—— "What We Think of Senator Byrd's Machine." *Saturday Evening Post*, 222 (January 7, 1950), 30–31 ff.

—— "With All Possible Speed." *Saturday Review*, 45 (August 18, 1962), 43–44.

"Dabney and the Doukhobors." *Time*, 44 (December 4, 1944), 72–73.

"Dabney vs. Dabbs on Integration." *Life*, 45 (September 22, 1958), 34.

Dalfiume, Richard M. "The 'Forgotten Years' of the Negro Revolution." *Journal of American History*, 55 (June 1968), 90–106.

Dauer, Manning J. "Recent Southern Political Thought." *Journal of Politics*, 10 (May 1948), 327–53.

Davidson, Donald. "Dilemma of the Southern Liberals." *American Mercury*, 31 (February 1934), 222–35.

—— "Sociologist in Eden: A. F. Raper in Macon County." *American Review*, 8 (December 1936), 177–204.

Davis, Lambert. "North Carolina and Its University Press." *North Carolina Historical Review*, 43 (April 1966), 149–56.

De Voto, Bernard. "Decision in the *Strange Fruit* Case: The Obscenity Statute in Massachusetts." *New England Quarterly*, 19 (June 1946), 147–83.

Dillard, James H. "Fourteen Years of the Jeannes Fund." *South Atlantic Quarterly*, 22 (July 1923), 193–201.

—— "Liberalism." *South Atlantic Quarterly*, 16 (January 1917), 21–29.

Doherty, Herbert J., Jr. "Voices of Protest from the New South, 1875–1910." *Mississippi Valley Historical Review*, 42 (June 1955), 45–66.

Dombrowski, James A. "The New South on the March." *Nation*, 160 (March 3, 1945), 244–45.

—— "The Southern Conference for Human Welfare." *Common Ground*, 6 (Summer 1946), 14–25.

Du Bois, W. E. B. "The Position of the Negro in the American Social Order: Where Do We Go from Here?" *Journal of Negro Education*, 8 (July 1939), 551–70.

Dyson, Lowell K. "The Southern Tenant Farmers Union and Depression Politics." *Political Science Quarterly*, 88 (June 1973), 230–52.

Eaton, Clement. "Edwin A. Alderman—Liberal of the New South." *North Carolina Historical Review*, 23 (April 1946), 206–21.

Ethridge, Mark. "About Will Alexander." *New Republic*, 105 (September 22, 1941), 366–67.

—— "The South's New Industrialism and the Press." *Annals of the American Academy of Political and Social Science*, 153 (January 1931), 251–56.

Ethridge, Willie S. "Liberalism Stirs Southern Churches." *Christian Century*, 49 (March 9, 1932), 317–19.

—— "Southern Women Attack Lynching." *Nation*, 131 (December 10, 1930), 647–50.

Evitts, William J. "The Savage South: H. L. Mencken and the Roots of a Persistent Image." *Virginia Quarterly Review*, 49 (Autumn 1973), 596–611.

Fish, John O. "Southern Methodism and Accommodation of the Negro, 1902–1915." *Journal of Negro History*, 55 (July 1970), 200–14.

Fishel, Leslie H., Jr. "The Negro in the New Deal Era." *Wisconsin Magazine of History*, 48 (Winter 1964), 111–26.

Fisher, Isaac. "Christian Justice and the Negro." *Southern Workman*, 48 (September 1919), 448–55.

Foreman, Clark. "The Decade of Hope." *Phylon*, 12 (Second Quarter, 1951), 137–50.

Garner, James W. "Recent Agitation of the Negro Question in the South." *South Atlantic Quarterly*, 7 (January 1908), 11–22.

Gavins, Raymond. "Gordon Hancock: An Appraisal." *New South*, 25 (Fall 1970), 36–43.

Gellhorn, Walter. "Report on a Report of the House Committee on Un-American Activities." *Harvard Law Review* 60 (October 1947), 1195–1234.

"Georgia's Body-Blow at Mob Murder." *Literary Digest*, 91 (December 4, 1926), 10.

Golightly, Cornelius L. "Southern Liberals Speak Only for Whites." *Time*, 65 (March 21, 1955), 37.

Goodwyn, Lawrence C. "Populist Dreams and Negro Rights: East Texas as a Case Study." *American Historical Review*, 76 (December 1971), 1435–56.

Grafton, Sam. "We're Mighty Fond of Our Miss Lill." *Colliers*, 125 (January 28, 1950), 29 ff.

Graham, Frank P. "The Meaning of the Civil War." *Virginia Quarterly Review*, 38 (Winter 1962), 36–70.

—— "The Need for Wisdom: Two Suggestions for Carrying Out the Supreme Court's Decision against Segregation." *Virginia Quarterly Review*, 31 (Spring 1955), 192–212.

Grantham, Dewey W., Jr. "The Regional Imagination: Social Scientists and the American South." *Journal of Southern History*, 34 (February 1968), 3–32.

Graves, John Temple. "The Southern Negro and the War Crisis." *Virginia Quarterly Review*, 18 (Autumn 1942), 500–17.

Green, James R. "The Brotherhood of Timber Workers 1910–1913: A Radical Response to Industrial Capitalism in the Southern U.S.A." *Past and Present*, 60 (August 1973), 161–200.

Hackney, Sheldon. "The South as a Counterculture." *American Scholar*, 42 (Spring 1973), 283–93.

Hammond, L. H. "The White Man's Debt to the Negro." *Annals of the American Academy of Political and Social Science*, 49 (September 1913), 67–73.

Harlan, Louis R. "The Southern Education Board and the Race Issue in Public Education." *Journal of Southern History*, 23 (May 1957), 189–202.

Holley, Donald. "The Negro and the New Deal Resettlement Program." *Agricultural History*, 45 (July 1971), 179–93.

Holliday, Carl. "The Young Southerner and the Negro." *South Atlantic Quarterly*, 8 (April 1909), 117–31.

Holmes, Michael S. "The New Deal and Georgia's Black Youth." *Journal of Southern History*, 38 (August 1972), 443–60.

Irish, Marion D. "The Proletarian South." *Journal of Politics*, 2 (August 1940), 231–58.

Jack, Homer A. "Lillian Smith of Clayton, Georgia." *Christian Century*, 74 (October 2, 1957), 1166–68.

Jaffe, Louis I. "The Democracy and Al Smith." *Virginia Quarterly Review*, 3 (July 1927), 321–41.

Johnson, Charles S. "More Southerners Discover the South." *Crisis*, 46 (January 1939), 14–15.

—— "The Will and the Way." *New South*, 2 (May 1947), 1–5 ff.

Johnson, Gerald W. "Graham of Carolina: Portrait of a Citizen-at-Large." *Survey Graphic*, 31 (April 1942), 188–91.
—— "The Horrible South." *Virginia Quarterly Review*, 11 (April, 1935), 201–17.
—— "Journalism Below the Potomac." *American Mercury*, 9 (September 1926), 77–82.
—— "North Carolina in a New Phase." *Current History*, 27 (March 1928), 843–48.
—— "Southern Image-Breakers." *Virginia Quarterly Review*, 4 (October 1928), 508–19.
Johnson, Guy B. "Southern Offensive." *Common Ground*, 4 (Summer 1944), 87–93.
Jones, C. B. "Down South in Georgia." *American Mercury*, 27 (September 1932), 92–97.
—— "The Georgia Plan (Politics)." *American Mercury*, 23 (July 1931), 311–20.
Jones, M. Ashby. "The Approach to the South's Race Question." *Journal of Social Forces*, 1 (November 1922), 40–41.
—— "Counting the Cost." *Southern Workman*, 49 (January 1920), 12–14.
—— "The Interracial Commission: An Experiment in Racial Relations." *Southern Frontier*, 5 (January 1944), 1.
—— "The Negro and the South." *Virginia Quarterly Review*, 3 (January 1927), 1–12.
Kantor, Harvey A. "Howard W. Odum: The Implications of Folk, Planning, and Regionalism." *American Journal of Sociology*, 79 (September 1973), 278–95.
Kennedy, Stetson. "Total Equality and How to Get It." *Common Ground*, 6 (Winter 1946), 61–69.
Kilgo, John C. "An Inquiry Regarding Lynching." *South Atlantic Quarterly*, 1 (January 1902), 4–13.
—— "The Silent South." *South Atlantic Quarterly*, 6 (April 1907), 200–11.
Kousser, J. Morgan. "Post-Reconstruction Suffrage Restrictions in Tennessee: A New Look at the V. O. Key Thesis." *Political Science Quarterly*, 88 (December 1973), 655–83.
Leonard, George B. "Not Black Power, but Human Power: An Interview with Lillian Smith." *Look*, 30 (September 6, 1966), 40 ff.
Long, Margaret. "Lillian Smith: A Match for Old Screamer." *Progressive*, 29 (February 1965), 35–38.
McGill, Ralph. "Civil Rights for the Negro." *Atlantic Monthly*, 184 (November 1949), 65–66.

McPherson, James M. "White Liberals and Black Power in Negro Education, 1865–1915." *American Historical Review*, 75 (June 1970), 1357–86.
Maund, Alfred. "Aubrey Williams: Symbol of a New South." *Nation*, 177 (October 10, 1953), 289–90.
Mecklin, John M. "Contessio Nominis non Examinatio Criminis." *Nation*, 104 (February 15, 1917), 186–87.
Mencken, H. L. "The South Astir." *Virginia Quarterly Review*, 11 (January 1935), 47–60.
Mezerik, A. G. "Dixie in Black and White." *Nation*, 164 (March 22, 1947), 324–27 (March 29, 1947), 360–63 (April 19, 1947), 448–51 (May 3, 1947), 509–12 (May 31, 1947), 655–57 (June 21, 1947), 740–41.
Milton, George F. "Compulsory Education in the South." *Annals of the American Academy of Political and Social Science*, 32 (July 1908), 57–66.
—— "The Impeachment of Judge Lynch." *Virginia Quarterly Review*, 8 (April 1932), 247–56.
Mitchell, H. L. "The Founding and Early History of the Southern Tenant Farmers Union." *Arkansas Historical Quarterly*, 32 (Autumn 1973), 342–69.
Morse, Josiah. "The University Commission on Southern Race Questions." *South Atlantic Quarterly*, 19 (October 1920), 302–10.
Murphy, Edgar Gardner. "Backward or Forward." *South Atlantic Quarterly*, 8 (January 1909), 19–38.
—— "Lynching and the Franchise Rights of the Negro." *Annals of the American Academy of Political and Social Science*, 15 (May 1900), 493–97.
Nixon, H. C. "The Changing Political Philosophy of the South." *Annals of the American Academy of Political and Social Science*, 153 (January 1931), 246–50.
—— "Politics of the Hills." *Journal of Politics*, 8 (May 1946), 123–33.
—— "The South after the War." *Virginia Quarterly Review*, 20 (Summer 1944), 321–34.
—— "The Southern Governors' Conference as a Pressure Group." *Journal of Politics*, 6 (August 1944), 338–45.
O'Brien, Michael. "C. Vann Woodward and the Burden of Southern Liberalism." *American Historical Review*, 78 (June 1973), 589–604.
Odum, Howard W. "The Discovery of the People." *Journal of Social Forces*, 4 (December 1925), 414–17.
—— "Fundamental Principles Underlying Inter-Racial Co-Operation." *Journal of Social Forces*, 1 (March 1923), 282–85.
—— "Lynchings, Fears and Folkways." *Nation*, 133 (December 30, 1931), 719–20.

—— "The Position of the Negro in the American Social Order of 1950." *Journal of Negro Education*, 8 (July 1939), 587–94.

—— "Social Change in the South." *Journal of Politics*, 10 (May 1948), 242–58.

—— "A Tragedy of Race Conflict." *Yale Review*, 25 (September 1935), 214–16.

Owsley, Frank L. "Scottsboro the Third Crusade: The Sequel to Abolitionism and Reconstruction." *American Review*, 1 (June 1933), 257–82.

Pearson, C. Chilton. "Race Relations in North Carolina: A Field Study of Moderate Opinion." *South Atlantic Quarterly*, 23 (January 1924), 1–9.

Phillips, Ulrich B. "The Central Theme of Southern History." *American Historical Review*, 24 (October 1928), 30–43.

Preece, Harold. "The South Stirs." *Crisis*, 48 (October 1941), 317–18 (November 1941), 350–51 (December 1941), 388–89.

Price, Hugh R. "The Negro and Florida Politics, 1944–1954." *Journal of Politics*, 17 (May 1955), 198–220.

Procter, H. H. "The Atlanta Plan of Interracial Cooperation." *Southern Workman*, 49 (January 1920), 9–12.

Rainey, Glenn W. "What Happened in Georgia." *Nation*, 167 (October 2, 1948), 371–72.

Record, Cy W. "What's Happened to the 'Southern Liberals'?" *New Leader*, July 10, 1943, p. 5.

Redding, J. Saunders. "Southern Defensive—I." *Common Ground*, 4 (Spring, 1944), 36–42.

Salmond, John A. "Postscript to the New Deal: The Defeat of the Nomination of Aubrey W. Williams as Rural Electrification Administrator in 1945." *Journal of American History*, 61 (September 1974), 417–36.

Sancton, Thomas. "The Negro Press." *New Republic*, 108 (April 26, 1943), 557–60.

—— "The South Needs Help." *Common Ground*, 3 (Winter 1943), 12–16.

—— "Southern Train." *Common Ground*, 9 (Winter 1949), 61–67.

—— "Southern Yankees." *South Today*, 7 (Spring 1943), 15–20.

—— "Trouble in Dixie: Race Fear Sweeps the South." *New Republic*, 118 (January 4, 1943), 11–14 (January 11, 1943), 50–51 (January 18, 1943), 81–83.

Saunders, Robert. "Southern Populists and the Negro 1893–1895." *Journal of Negro History*, 54 (July 1969), 240–61.

Sellers, Charles G., Jr. "Walter Hines Page and the Spirit of the New South." *North Carolina Historical Review*, 29 (October 1952), 481–99.

Shannon, Jasper B. "Presidential Politics in the South." *Journal of Politics*, 10 (August 1948), 464–89.

—— "Presidential Politics in the South: 1938." *Journal of Politics*, 1 (May 1939), 146–70 (August 1939), 278–300.

Shriver, Donald W., Jr. "James McBride Dabbs: 'He Made You Feel Like Somebody.' " *New South*, 25 (Summer 1970), 2–6.

Sitkoff, Harvard. "Harry Truman and the Election of 1948: The Coming of Age of Civil Rights in American Politics." *Journal of Southern History*, 37 (November 1971), 597–616.

—— "Racial Militancy and Interracial Violence in the Second World War." *Journal of American History*, 58 (December 1971), 661–81.

Smith, Frank E. "The Changing South." *Virginia Quarterly Review*, 31 (Spring 1955), 161–79.

Smith, Lillian. "Declaration of Faith in America." *New York Times Magazine*, September 21, 1952, pp. 13 ff.

—— "Democracy Was Not a Candidate." *Common Ground*, 3 (Winter 1943), 7–10.

—— "Mind and Soul of the South." *Look*, 29 (November 16, 1965), 140–42.

—— "Novelists Need a Commitment." *Saturday Review*, 43 (December 24, 1960), 18–19.

—— "Personal History of 'Strange Fruit': Statement of Purposes and Intentions." *Saturday Review of Literature*, 27 (February 17, 1945), 9–10.

—— "The Right Way Is Not a Moderate Way." *Phylon*, 18 (December 1956), 335–41.

—— "Southern Defensive—II." *Common Ground*, 4 (Spring, 1944), 43–45.

—— "A Strange Kind of Love." *Saturday Review*, 45 (October 20, 1962), 18–20 ff.

—— "Ten Years from Today." *Vital Speeches*, 17 (August 15, 1951), 669–72.

—— "The Walls of Segregation Are Crumbling." *New York Times Magazine*, July 15, 1951, pp. 9 ff.

—— "The Winner Names the Age." *Phylon*, (October, 1957), 203–12.

Somers, Dale A. "Black and White in New Orleans: A Study in Urban Race Relations 1865–1900." *Journal of Southern History*, 40 (February 1974), 19–42.

Sosna, Morton. "The South in the Saddle: Racial Politics during the Wilson Years." *Wisconsin Magazine of History*, 54 (Autumn 1970), 30–49.

—— "The South Old and New: A Review Essay." *Wisconsin Magazine of History*, 55 (Spring 1972), 231–35.

"South Split over the Scottsboro Verdict." *Literary Digest*, 115 (April 22, 1933), 3–4.

Southern, David W. "*An American Dilemma* Revisited: Myrdalism and White Southern Liberals." *South Atlantic Quarterly*, 75 (Spring 1976), 182–87.

Stephenson, Gilbert T. "The Segregation of the White and Negro Races in Rural Communities in North Carolina." *South Atlantic Quarterly*, 8 (April 1914), 107–17.

Stevenson, Elizabeth. "Southern Manners." *South Atlantic Quarterly*, 48 (October 1949), 507–28.

Stewart, Herbert L. "The Casuistry of Lynch Law." *Nation*, 103 (August 24, 1916), 173–74.

—— "The Southern Views of Lynching." *Nation*, 104 (January 25, 1917), 102–3.

Sugg, Redding S., Jr. "Lillian Smith and the Condition of Woman." *South Atlantic Quarterly*, 71 (Spring 1972), 155–64.

Thomas, David. "Open Letter to Ex-Governor Dorsey of Georgia." *Southern Workman*, 50 (August 1921), 371–72.

Thorborn, Neil. " 'Strange Fruit' and Southern Tradition." *Midwest Quarterly*, 12 (Winter 1971), 157–71.

Tindall, George B. "The Benighted South: Origins of a Modern Image." *Virginia Quarterly Review*, 40 (Spring 1964), 281–94.

—— "Beyond the Mainstream: The Ethnic Southerners." *Journal of Southern History*, 40 (February 1974), 3–18.

—— "The Significance of Howard W. Odum to Southern History : A Preliminary Estimate." *Journal of Southern History*, 24 (August 1958), 285–307.

Vance, Rupert B., and Katherine Jocher. "Howard W. Odum." *Social Forces*, 33 (March 1955), 203–17.

Warnock, Henry Y. "Andrew Sledd, Southern Methodists, and the Negro: A Case History." *Journal of Southern History*, 31 (August 1965), 251–71.

Weatherford, W. D. "Changing Attitudes of Southern Students." *Journal of Negro Education*, 2 (April 1933), 147–50.

—— "Race Relationships in the South." *Annals of the American Academy of Political and Social Science*, 49 (September 1913), 164–72.

White, Rev. John E. "The Need of a Southern Program on the Negro Problem." *South Atlantic Quarterly*, 6 (April 1907), 177–88.

White, Walter. "Southern Liberals." *Negro Digest*, 1 (January 1943), 43–46.

"The White South's Protest against Lynching: A Press Symposium." *Southern Workman*, 48 (July 1919), 350–61.

Williams, Aubrey. "Liberal Renaissance from the South?" *New South*, 2 (May 1947), 2.

—— "There Is a Break." *Nation*, 169 (August 6, 1949), 128–30.

Williams, T. Harry. "Huey, Lyndon, and Southern Radicalism." *Journal of American History*, 60 (September 1973), 267–93.

Wilson, Walter. "Georgia Suppresses Insurrection." *Nation*, 139 (August 1, 1934), 127–28.

Winn, William. "Conversations with Erskine Caldwell." *New South*, 25 (Summer 1970), 33–38.

Winston, Robert Watson. "An Uncolored Answer to the Negro Question." *South Atlantic Quarterly*, 1 (July 1902), 265–68.

Wright, R. Charlton. "The Southern White Man and the Negro." *Virginia Quarterly Review*, 9 (April 1933), 175–94.

Wye, Christopher G. "The New Deal and the Negro Community: Toward a Broader Conceptualization." *Journal of American History*, 59 (December 1972), 621–39.

Wynn, Dudley. "A Liberal Looks at Tradition." *Virginia Quarterly Review*, 7 (January 1936), 57–79.

Young, Andrew. "Why I Support Jimmy Carter." *Nation*, 222 (April 3, 1976), 397–98.

INDEX

ABBREVIATIONS

Interracial Commission—Commission on Interracial Cooperation
NAACP—National Association for the Advancement of Colored People
SCEF—Southern Conference Educational Fund
SCHW—Southern Conference for Human Welfare
SRC—Southern Regional Council